MW01672674

Roy Cheville

The Patriarch Years

A Biography by
Malcolm L. Ritchie
1997

Roy Cheville
The Patriarch Years

A Biography by
Malcolm L. Ritchie
1997

Center for Christian Leadership
Graceland College
Lamoni, Iowa 50140

Dedication

This book is dedicated with grateful thanks to Roberta (Bobbie) Ann Gossadge Ritchie, who has been my companion and my counsel since we were married by Roy Cheville in the Graceland College chapel May 30, 1947.

All rights reserved. Except for brief quotations in critical articles or reviews, no part of this book may be reproduced in any manner without prior written permission from the Graceland College Center for Christian Leadership.

Copyright © 1997
Malcolm L. Ritchie
Dayton, Ohio

Printed in the United States of America

Library of Congress Cataloging-in-Publication Data
Ritchie, Malcolm

Roy Cheville: The Patriarch Years
Malcolm L. Ritchie
ISBN

Published by
Center for Christian Leadership
Graceland College
Lamoni, Iowa 50140

Table of Contents

Appendices

List of Photographs

Preface

In this second volume of the biography of Roy Cheville, Dr. Ritchie continues his carefully researched and deeply thoughtful analysis of a remarkable life. Volume, I, Roy Cheville: the Graceland College Years, describes Cheville's developmental years and his outstanding career as teacher and theologian at Graceland College. The present volume deals with the more difficult period of Cheville's career—as church leader. Taken together, the two volumes reveal a complex and gifted personality. One cannot imagine a more definitive study of Cheville, given the care Dr. Ritchie has taken with public sources and the treasure of primary materials in his possession. His years of work have produced an important resource for those whose lives were influenced by Dr. Cheville and for those who wish to contemplate the theological development of the RLDS Church.

The story told here is the always fascinating account of the complex relationship between an able individual and the institution he serves, as well as a description of the full flower and fading of a brilliant career.

This account has further value in the questions of "what might have been," which it raises. Cheville obviously had tremendous influence on patriarchal ministry within the church. What might have happened had he been able to adapt more successfully to a collegial relationship? What might have happened had he been able to put aside the professor-student mode in which he had functioned so successfully at Graceland? What might have happened had senior church leaders welcomed him as a full member of their councils?

Cheville's experience raises a host of basic questions. How does a small institution accommodate the diverse gifts of strong, creative people? How do newcomers into full-time church leadership become full partners? How do individuals who have been extremely successful in one career learn to adapt the skills and habits which have made them so successful to another and quite different environment? And finally, the question always raised by the experiences of the very gifted and very successful—how do individuals learn to keep in check the ego which has been the engine of their success but can also become their greatest handicap?

The story of Roy Cheville raises important questions for the RLDS Church. The most important may well be a consideration of what we can learn from Cheville's experience that will inform the continuing development of an appropriate theology for the RLDS Church. It seems tragic to this reader that the church's theological journey during the past 25 years has ignored Cheville's thought. In his best moments he would certainly have been the first to acknowledge that he did not have all the answers. However, many of his ideas, largely ignored now, justify revisiting. His attempt, however imperfect it may have been, to build a theology on the foundation of Joseph Smith's founding grove experience is valid. Whatever the all-too-human reasons for it, the failure of Cheville and other church leaders who were influenced by Protestant seminary study to engage in a productive theological dialogue has had far reaching negative consequences. Many church leaders felt that he was unwilling to participate in a dialogue of equal participants, and he felt that he was ignored. Cheville believed so strongly in the importance of human effort in responding to God that he could not talk about grace. On the other hand, the traditional absence of a concept of grace within the Restoration needed long-overdue corrective. How unfortunate that the discussion did not occur during Cheville's lifetime. The church has yet to develop a theology which describes the relation between God and humankind more fully than either the extremes of grace on the one hand or human initiative on the other. Such a theology might mitigate the temptation of human passivity which sometimes accompanies the doctrine of grace and the tendency toward arrogance which sometimes accompanies the doctrine of human effort. Such a theology might well take its inspiration from that moment in a grove of trees when a human mind and the Holy Spirit connected uniquely and powerfully.

As current leadership reminds the church of its unique origins, perhaps that dialogue can still take place. It would be Roy Cheville's most appropriate memorial and his most important legacy.

Barbara Higdon, Director
Center for Christian Leadership
Graceland College

Foreword

This book describes the career and activities of Roy A. Cheville after he completed his tenure on the faculty at Graceland College and moved to the headquarters of the RLDS Church in Independence, Missouri as presiding patriarch. The transition began in October 1958 and was complete in June of 1960. He was ordained Presiding Patriarch in 1958 and named Presiding Patriarch Emeritus in 1974, a position he held until his death in 1986.

I described Roy Cheville's thought and activities prior to 1958 in *Roy Cheville: The Graceland College Years,* published in 1995 by the Center for Christian Leadership at Graceland College. Repeated from that book are the lists of Cheville's publications. The following brief narrative summarizes the facts of his life up to 1958:

> Roy Cheville was born on a farm near Maxwell, Iowa October 2, 1897. At age 16 he was baptized a member of the RLDS Church in Rhodes, Iowa. He attended Drake University for one year, then taught school in a one-room school in rural Iowa for two years. He became a full-time minister for the Church and went to Graceland College for ministerial training. He was graduated in 1921 with an A.A. in liberal arts and religious education. He attended the University of Chicago from 1921 until 1923, earning a baccalaureate and a Masters degree and completing a Bachelor of Divinity in 1925 and a Ph.D. in 1942. He joined the Graceland faculty in 1923.

He married Nelle Weldon in 1929 and they had two children. Richard Arthur was born in 1931 and Charlotte Estelle in 1937.

Roy spent 35 years as a master teacher and minister at Graceland, ending his career there with the development of a four year religion major. He was ordained Presiding Patriarch of the RLDS Church in 1958 and named Presiding Patriarch Emeritus in 1974. This book, volume two of his biography, tells his story from 1958 until his death in 1986.

For years I have been encouraged in this project by Bill and Barbara Higdon, Dick and Lila Cheville, Bob and Charlotte (Cheville) Farrand, Ed and Charlene Gleazer, and Wayne and Ruth Zion. The personnel of the libraries and archives of Graceland College and the RLDS Church, particularly Church Archivists Ron Romig and Barbara Bernauer, have been helpful, interested, and enthusiastic. Henry Inouye, Jr. has been a supportive colleague and consultant, having written his own book, *Roy A. Cheville: Explorer of Spiritual Frontier*, published by the Herald House in 1995. Henry did a tremendous service in organizing the Roy Cheville collection in the RLDS Archives. Roberta Ritchie, my companion and an archivist, has put in long hours of constructive help, and has given steady understanding support. Our three children, Karen Ritchie, Jennie Bowen, and Bill Ritchie have provided warm support and challenging interest. Karen has focussed my attention on personal issues in societal contexts, Jennie on the ubiquitous nature of spiritual experience, and Bill on the issues of Roy Cheville's relation to the politics of large organizations. Everett Graffeo has guided me to much useful material. He and Phillip Caswell have helped me identify locations and people in several photographs. My brother Wilson has served as a consultant and able guide to the details of grammar and punctuation. Ed McGuire of the Herald Publishing House has been very helpful in translating the type material into quality printed form.

I am especially indebted to Barbara Higdon for her superb technical skills as an editor, for the range of her knowledge and insights about the church and its people, and for her commitment to getting the story of Roy Cheville available as accurately and as well-written as possible.

Much of the reference material for this book is to be found in the Library and Archives of the Reorganized Church of Jesus Christ of Latter Day Saints, located in the Temple in Independence, Missouri. The other material in my personal possession will be deposited in those Archives soon after this volume has appeared in print. Most of it is already there on computer disks I have sent to the Archives. Much of the material in my possession was given to me by Roy Cheville, especially in 1980 when he was moving into Resthaven. Wayne Zion and Ruth Zion, at whose home Roy lived from 1974 to 1980, gave me additional material.

Malcolm L. Ritchie, Dayton, Ohio
June 1997

List of Abbreviations and References

BoM—Book of Mormon. Published by the RLDS Church
D&C—Doctrine and Covenants. Published by the RLDS Church
pBull—Bulletin to the Patriarchs. In RLDS Archives
RLDS—Reorganized Church of Jesus Christ of Latter Day Saints, Headquarters, Independence, Missouri.
SH—*Saints' Herald*. Periodical published by the Herald Publishing House, Independence, Missouri.

References to Roy Cheville's Publications

The bibliography of Roy Cheville's publications is found in the first four appendices to this volume. An effort has been made to make these lists exhaustive to date. Appendix A lists his published books and unpublished book-length manuscripts; Appendix B lists his published hymns; Appendix C lists his pamphlets; and Appendix D lists his published articles. These publications are ordered according to a unique code assigned to each publication, consisting of four digits for the year of publication followed by one or two letters to indicate sequence in that year. Thus D:1950B designates his second publication in 1950. It is an article and is found listed in Appendix D. B:1950AC is his 29th publication in 1950. It is a hymn and is found listed in Appendix B.

Introduction

> As I walked through the gate and to the plane they were singing *Aloha Oe*... After the plane was in the air...a businessman...came to converse. We talked three hours. The send-off had stirred him... He wanted to know who I was and what I had been doing with that company of people. "In my years of travel out of Hawaii, I have never seen anything like it... I watched those people and saw tears coursing down the cheeks of men... What did you do among them?" [D:1960I]

Who was this man whose leave-taking produced such strong emotions? What did he do among those people in Hawaii? Was this unusual in his experience? Upon what foundation was this accomplished? This book attempts to provide some answers to these questions. This narrative will also raise many questions about the evolution of religious movements and the relationship of organizations to gifted persons.

The man was Roy Cheville. He was Presiding Patriarch of the RLDS Church, with headquarters in Independence, Missouri. He had been five weeks in Hawaii. That morning he had participated in dedication of the Makiki church in Honolulu. About the questions of the business man, Cheville wrote in his notes,

> I could not tell a stranger what made this so different. Here were native Hawaiians, Chinese, Japanese, Portuguese, and Haolis in one company. They and I had been together at the table of the Lord's Supper. We had been together when the Spirit of God ministered to us together. Some of my heart was still in Hawaii where my Hawaiian brothers and sisters and I had had our own Day of Pentecost.

Though the businessman had seen evidence of something powerful acting in the lives of the people there, the underlying dynamic was not easily explainable. Cheville could not tell the man in three hours what it had taken him more than 40 years to develop. Those 40 years had seen a progression in his intellectual and spiritual maturity that combined intense development of scholarly theory with equally intense laboratory exercise of group and personal experiences. In his notes Cheville had said that he and his Hawaiian brothers and sisters had had their own Day of Pentecost. He could have gone on to say that this did not happen by accident. It took significant preparation, and it required that they put themselves in personal readiness for spiritual experience.

One can deduce from this incident that Roy Cheville was a minister of great power. That had been true for more than 35 years, but it was only one of his many facets. He had been a college professor for 35 years and was at the time of this event in transition from professor to general church officer. He was a scholar whose thoughtful work deserves to be compared with that of eminent philosophers. That work is to be found in his 26 books, 100 pamphlets, 52 published hymns, and more than 300 published articles. He was often sought for personal counseling. He had a reputation for effectiveness and for being trustworthy. He could recognize thousands of people and call them by name. He usually could place their family's geographic location and ask about other members of the family.

The power that was present in his ministry could have been used to gain personal advantage in some way. But he would not allow that to happen. Instead, he taught that the power was available to every person who would qualify personally to receive and use it. He did not want those who were strongly influenced by him to praise him or to follow him. Instead he wanted them to exercise power in building quality and strength into their own lives. And he wanted to be their friend.

In 1974, at the time of his retirement from the office of presiding patriarch, one member of the patriarchal order, Franklin Schofield of England, wrote to him,

> Words are totally inadequate to express our love and great admiration for all that you have done for the cause of the kingdom. Your

> testimony has affected the lives of thousands of people, your enthusiasm, your utter complete dedication will always be a source of great inspiration.

The kind of experience Roy Cheville sought for himself and his fellow human beings could not be achieved by simplifying divinity in a catechism or simplifying the desired response into a decision for Christ. He sought an expanding understanding of divinity. He taught that divinity responds to persons as they reach out in pure motive and personal integrity. He taught that Jesus Christ represented that part of divinity which can be encountered in human form. He taught that the Holy Spirit is that part of divinity which is in interaction with humans and is the dynamic by which personhood develops. He believed that people become human through biology and become persons through interaction with other persons. He taught that humans are created with the ability to become persons and that is the sense in which we are created in the image of God; and thus the most important person with whom human beings can interact is the person of God.

Roy Cheville had four degrees from the University of Chicago, including the Doctor of Philosophy, earned in the School of Divinity. He was trained as a theologian and also trained as a social scientist. He insisted on rigorous thought processes and had no room for supernaturalism. In his view the issues of religion and divinity, as in other fields of human inquiry, consist of the understood and the not-yet-understood.

The career of Roy Cheville can be divided into three phases. As professor from 1923 to about 1941 at Graceland College, he was developing the powers foundational to his career. He was called "Unk" in this phase, and the students regarded him as a wise and friendly uncle. In the second phase, from 1941 to 1958 at Graceland College his abilities and accomplishments were in full flower. He was familiarly called "Doc," having completed the Ph.D. in

1942. From 1958 to 1974 he had the title "Presiding Patriarch" and from 1974 to his death in 1986 his title was "Presiding Patriarch Emeritus." Thus the three phases may be called *Unk, Doc,* and *Patriarch*. This book tells the story of his years as patriarch from 1958 to 1986.

BOOK IX

A New Calling

Anticipation of Mission

> I do not know what my life work will turn out to be. [Statement of Roy Cheville in presentation during Youth Conference of 1941]

After Cheville's death Clifford Cole, President of the Quorum of Twelve in the 1970s, recalled that statement. Floyd McDowell, who was on the platform near Cheville at the time replied, "When you find it I hope it amounts to something." Cole remembered this exchange partly because of the humor involved. That humor was determined largely by the fact that Roy Cheville was then a towering figure, a Graceland College professor and widely known religious leader. It was already hard to imagine a person who more completely fitted the image of the ideal professor of religion. Yet, here he was entertaining the idea of a call to another, perhaps wider and larger field of service.

In a college class about 1946, he had made a statement much like that of the 1941 conference. The essence again was that he was not sure what his continuing calling would be. He was not the only one to whom that thought occurred. Enid DeBarthe remembers a special experience during the Lamoni reunion of 1949. While waiting to talk to someone else, she saw Roy walking across the Graceland campus and was suddenly made keenly aware that Roy would soon be called to the office of evangelist and in time to the office of presiding evangelist. She had no difficulty with the first calling, but considered a call to be presiding evangelist "an impossible figment of my imagination, for like others I expected Lynn Smith to inherit that calling."

During that same 1949 reunion, Arthur Oakman gave voice to the following counsel for Cheville:

> You have done well in achieving depth in your thinking, in your loyalties. Continue to do so, for the saints will be needing the stead-

> fastness that your spiritual depth can afford. Another field of ministry lies before you. Continue and you will be ready.

Roy Cheville was ordained to the office of patriarch/evangelist at a special meeting of Lamoni Stake in the Coliseum on October 1, 1950. RLDS Church President Israel A. Smith presided. The ordaining ministers were Apostles Arthur Oakman and Charles Hield. It was unusual in those days for a man only fifty-three to be ordained to this office.

At the time of the ordination, Roy received several statements of counsel. President Israel A. Smith said, "You will live among the Saints in spiritual fellowship. You will receive confidences and confessions that only you and God will know." Elbert A. Smith testified to him that "through many preceding years God has been prompting you and guiding you for this ministry with specific expressions in counseling and encouraging adults, youth, and children with the guiding light of the Holy Spirit." Brother Elbert also said, "You will minister to the saints in the singing life of our people. You will provide hymns that express the Restoration gospel. You will vitalize the singing of the saints." Arthur Oakman said, "You are called and ordained to be a patriarch. As a patriarch you will minister as an evangelist, as a revivalist, as a father living with the saints."

Cheville entered into the activities of patriarchal ministry with typical full speed ahead. By the first of October 1958, he had given 592 patriarchal blessings. (The patriarchal blessing derives its name from the blessing on each of his children given near the end of his life by the Old Testament patriarchs. The current blessing is given once in a lifetime to a church member as spiritual guidance and assurance.)

Cheville continued to feel a mission which might take him beyond the Graceland campus. In August of 1957 Cheville wrote a letter to E. J. Gleazer, Jr. which contained the following statement:

I have a sense of theological mission which I question may have fulfillment here at Graceland. I say this so you will understand my attitude. I do not speak of this here—I would not be understood."

Presiding Patriarch

> You are to lead out creatively with ministry to your fellow ministers and to the saints. Lead out and keep us informed about your ministries. [W. Wallace Smith, 1958]

These words of counsel were spoken to Roy Cheville by W. Wallace Smith, President of the RLDS Church, October 8, 1958, as he ordained Cheville to the office of presiding patriarch of the church. In this role he was to be pastor to the president himself and leader of the quorum of spiritual fathers, called to offer patriarchal ministry to all members of the church.

The official designation of this office in the RLDS Church was then Presiding Patriarch/Evangelist. Roy Cheville preferred the shorter title Presiding Patriarch (in D&C 145:4b calling him, the office was designated Presiding Patriarch). The official designation was changed in 1995 to Presiding Evangelist.

The calling of Roy Cheville to this office was a surprise to a great many people. He had not moved into this office through the typical route of employment and service in the church headquarters structure. Instead, he had been a faculty member at Graceland College for 35 years. There he had pursued a largely independent role in teaching religion, history, philosophy and sociology. He had also directed religious activities on campus for 30 years.

Though the call was a surprise, the church members supported it almost unanimously. One of the best known and best loved ministers in the church, he was also the church's most highly regarded scholar in theology and religion. The Herald House had published 12 books by him. He had authored 34 published hymns, 35 published pamphlets, and 175 published articles. He had led the singing at all-church conferences for some 30 years, and had spent his summers ministering in regional reunions and youth camps throughout the church. He was in great demand to perform weddings, and in no less demand to provide marital, personal, and educational counseling.

Cheville's call to the office of presiding patriarch had some unusual characteristics. The call itself was presented to the RLDS General Conference, which began on October 5, 1958, by the president and prophet of the church W. Wallace Smith, who himself had just been called to his office in this conference. (His predecessor Israel A. Smith had been killed in an automobile accident shortly before the conference began.)

On the day after his own ordination to be President of the Church, W. Wallace called Roy into his office and told him that in response to guidance by the Holy Spirit, he planned to submit a document to the conference in which he would designate Roy as the new presiding patriarch. He wanted Roy's response and particularly his acceptance of the call. W. Wallace told Roy that he had not been thinking of him for that office. Instead he had assumed that the designee would be Lynn Smith, continuing the blood lineage precedent established in the old Testament. Without exception the Smith line had held the office in the Restoration. Lynn was Elbert A.'s son.

Lynn had been serving for four years as secretary to his father Elbert, who was presiding patriarch. Lynn had been designated by Elbert as his successor. As early as September 18, 1949 Elbert had written Lynn a long letter about the office indicating that, while he did not know what *would* happen, he knew what *should* happen. What should happen was that Lynn should be called to succeed him. On May 17, 1952 Elbert wrote Lynn, "I am quite sure as to your calling and I think the people now expect it." He had talked with President Israel A. Smith about the matter. In later talks, Elbert showed Israel a precedent in the church for the presiding patriarch himself to designate his successor. He also described personal spiritual confirmation of Lynn's call. In a letter to Lynn on January 7, 1953 Israel Smith stated that he had told the Council of Twelve, "that it had been revealed to me that you should succeed, upon your father's release . . to the office now held by him. I am positive that to this office you are called."

After Israel's death, Elbert had sent a letter of resignation (for health reasons) to W. Wallace and included a notarized letter indicating his conviction that Lynn should be his successor. He described his spiritual experience confirming that selection.

W. Wallace told Roy that the idea that Roy should be called began to emerge in his prayers and in his meditations upon potential calls to that office. He knew that Lynn Smith and others would be keenly disappointed if Lynn were not selected. But, he told Roy, the power of the Spirit was so strong that he could not deny it and the action it required. Roy said that in the process of relating the intensity of his experience, W. Wallace broke down and cried. Roy recalled in 1980, "I never saw him do that before or since."

Though there was no expressed opposition to Roy's ordination, the appointment of this strong-minded man to an important position in the church hierarchy stirred some anxiety. His theological outlook, powerfully integrated and powerfully expressed, was a threat to the ideas on which some administrators had based their faith, their beliefs, and their career activities. Their anxiety was increased by the recognition that their own academic backgrounds were weak in comparison with that of Cheville. While Cheville was at Graceland outside the main church structure and engaged primarily in ministry to youth, he was not perceived as a threat. But now he would be inside the church structure, highly placed, and charged to minister to all church members. He would bring direct competition on basic issues. Opposition preceded him and continued to grow. He was never to feel that he was accepted by the structure.

Cheville began his work as presiding patriarch with a rich understanding of ministry and of the nature of divinity. This understanding had grown in depth through his university training and personal study, and it had been augmented and evaluated in his laboratory of personal and group spiritual experiences. Most of his major concepts were already mature and laboratory tested. He felt a mission to teach the church at large that religion was a matter of individual and group experiences, and that theology was to be used to develop explanations for those experiences. He knew that progress toward his objectives would be slow, but he held what he had described as the "long view." In the long view one keeps doing what is fundamentally correct. Eventually, the position will be adopted if it is indeed correct. He had said that God always takes the long view, even if centuries are required for his way to prevail.

Cheville was to find rich and rewarding experiences among the church members. Among the general church officers he was to find increasing opposition to his ministry and to the theology on which that ministry was based. Church administrators moved steadily away from the initial instruction for him to lead out in his ministry and keep them informed. Instead they moved steadily toward increasing control over what he did and the way he did it.

BOOK X

In the Organization

Photo 7-1. Roy Cheville in his office as presiding patriarch *[Photo: RLDS Archives]*

Quorum Leader

> It has been a time (1) of exploring the nature of the ministry of this office, (2) of building a fraternity among men of the order, and (3) of cultivating the sound spirituality essential to this particular office. [Cheville's first General Conference Report, D:1960V]

When he assumed its leadership in 1958, Roy Cheville already knew most of the 100 patriarchs comprising the Order, as he had been a member of the quorum for eight years. Except for three in Australia, six in Canada, one in England, two in Germany, and one in Holland, the patriarchs all lived in the United States. Cheville undertook to get to know many of them, making it his business to be with them whenever possible and frequently staying in their homes as he traveled. During his final year of leadership of the quorum, it had grown to 240 persons.

His predecessor, Elbert A. Smith, had sent out a "Bulletin to the Patriarchs" once or twice a year. Cheville began immediately to publish an issue each month, 184 in all. They were usually four pages of text on two sheets of paper. His stated objectives appear above—to explore the nature of patriarchal ministry; to build a fraternity among the men of the order; and to cultivate sound spirituality. An examination of the content of the bulletins reveals a fourth objective—to publicize events and plans in the world church. The bulletins also attempted to integrate the order into the structure of church leadership. An examination of the content of a number of issues and the response of the patriarch audience reveals Cheville's success in achieving these objectives.

Characteristically concerned about historical context, Cheville traced the 100-year history of patriarchal ministry within the Reorganization. [pBull, Nov. 1958] He highlighted the growth in numbers and in understanding of the function. He noted that in 1900 the ratio was one patriarch to 40,000 members; in 1930 one to 4,080; and in 1958 one to 1,860. He suggested that an ideal ratio would be one to 1,000. Two functions—church father and revivalist—had precedence in history.

Many bulletins defined the role of the patriarch in the contemporary church. Acknowledging that each man would bring his own approach to the office, Cheville wrote in his first bulletin:

> Some of us will be *fathers* to the Saints through counsel, instruction, testimony, blessing and association. Some of us will be *evangelists* through our reviving ministries that enliven and assure the members of the Church.

He noted that "this kind of ministry cannot be assigned. The spiritual quality of the minister is basic. The influence of a godly man upon others cannot be listed in a report of ministerial activities." His advice through the pages of the bulletins covered a wide discussion of the patriarch's role, ranging from abstract theological principles to very specific suggestions.

An article entitled "Our Ministry for 1960" laid out a plan of action for individual patriarchs:

> 1. Associating with others so as to encourage them to live clean, complete, and competent lives with God and with God's people.
> 2. Communing with God so as to catch increasing vision of what he is and what he does and to devote themselves to what God is doing.
> 3. Counseling others so they see their situations in the perspective that comes from being with God.
> 4. Studying so consistently and exploringly that we expand our understanding of God, his universe and his people.
> 5. Witnessing to others with testimony of God at work in our lives and in the life of the Church.
> 6. Teaching others so as to develop in them comprehension of what God purposes to do and how he is going about it.
> 7. Preaching so others hear the affirmatives of the gospel of Jesus Christ and move toward the Christ.
> 8. Blessing others so they are enabled to sense themselves as

children of God and to be assured of God's support as they live his way.

9. Implementing our desires with achieved competence in fields suited to us and needed by his people.

10. Trusting God so hopefully and so healthfully that we rise above worry and use our powers in ministry. [pBull Jan 60]

Cheville identified the scope of patriarchal ministry in several issues. "Ministering to Ministers" [pBull Sept. 1962] described a unique mission for the patriarchs as being the minister to those who head up ministerial responsibilities, those who are "alone at the top." He urged patriarchs to be sensitive to those who were in need and provide brotherly and fatherly association and spiritual companionship.

In October 1959 he wrote an article on "Being Alone with Ourselves and God." He explained the value of spending some time alone as Jesus did in the wilderness and other times when he withdrew to be alone with his heavenly Father. In this, he said, "we seek to get straight on our values and to clear our perspectives so we can return to humanity better equipped... We can push aside social compulsions and pretense and can come clean before God."

The *Bulletin* for February 1969 was devoted to patriarchal ministry found in the *Book of Mormon*. The word *patriarch* was not used but many fatherly figures in the book gave patriarchal counsel. Among the ones quoted were Lehi; "If there be no righteousness, there can be no happiness," King Benjamin; "When you are in the service of your fellow beings, you are in the service of God," and "I would that you consider the blessed and happy state of those who keep the commandments of God," Alma; "See that you are not lifted up unto pride: yea, see that you do not boast in your own wisdom, nor of your much strength," and Helaman, who was a general and a father to 2,000 young soldiers.

Attempting to prepare the men for evangelistic outreach, in the *Bulletin* for August 1973 Cheville described 15 inquiries about our church. He developed these after a friend in another country had asked him how to identify his church. These were the questions,

1. Is yours a Christian Church?
2. Did your church rise out of some other church?
3. Does your church discount and denounce other churches, other religions?
4. Do you have church organization? What kind? For what?
5. Is your church mainly concerned with the hereafter?
6. Do you consider man to be good, bad, or otherwise in his own nature?
7. Do you consider material things to be evil or otherwise?
8. Does your church see all things coming to an end?
9. Does your church plan for family living?
10. Are individuals automatically related to God?
11. Do you open your church fellowship to people of all races?
12. How is your church managed? By priests or by people?
13. What scriptures does your church have and how do you use them?
14. Does your church promise anything, practice anything about the Holy Spirit in contemporary living?
15. What does the name of your church connote? It sounds unusual.

"Ministries in Many Languages," [pBull Nov. 1961] began by quoting the second chapter of Acts, "they . . began to speak with other tongues . . We do hear them speak in our tongues." Several instances of worldwide and cross-cultural patriarchal ministry described instances where individuals did not share the same language, such as in Germany and in French Polynesia. George Ventura of Barcelona attended the British Isles reunion, where he received his patriarchal blessing. Cheville quoted Joe Bayless as one who loved the German people, and had worked hard to master the German language. Once Bayless said to Cheville, "I am just fair in word language;

I do better with the language of the heart." The article described also the value of speaking the language of many vocations and of many age groups.

"When They Want to Get Out of Life" [pBull Oct. 66] addressed the challenge of ministry in suicide situations. The introduction stated that "A casual survey indicates that the problem is very much with us just now." Cheville identified three groups of people:

(1) those who contemplate suicide;
(2) those who attempt it; and
(3) those who do take their lives.

Ministry must deal with the society in which individuals think of, try, and/or execute suicide. In the third group "we are ministering to those who survive when suicide takes place." The discussion considered issues which might lead people to contemplate ending their lives, exploring the actions patriarchal ministers might take, ministering to those left behind, and seeking out the assistance of competent consultants. In the end Cheville suggested, "We do not dump the case on God. We work with God."

An item in the *Bulletin* for November 1967 noted that someone had told Cheville about a member of our church who had joined a smaller "faction." Cheville had known the family forty years earlier and knew that a traveling missionary, gifted in griping and faultfinding, visited frequently, creating a negative atmosphere. The faith of this family broke under this impact. No minister of evangelistic spirit presented an alternative to counteract this persistent complaining against the church.

"Designating the universals of the gospel in everyday living" was defined as one of the tasks of the patriarchs in the *Bulletin* for May 1966. The universals are the enduring essentials that apply to all the world. "This is a call to interpret the gospel in terms of the difference it makes in human living. We need to indicate how it transforms and aligns people with God."

Some instructions to the order were very specific. For example, the July 1960 *Bulletin* devoted a page to the ministry of letter writing, establishing its value with reference to the letters of Paul of Tarsus.

In the October 1959 *Bulletin* he described creative special ministries. The Reed Holmes family met with him for a few minutes in the worship room of his offices—the father, the mother, the five children in a benedictory service before they left for the Australian Mission. "It was significant that all the family came—all were going on the mission."

One patriarch wrote to Cheville that he had been asked to dedicate a home and he wondered if he should encourage this. Cheville responded [pBull June 1966] that such a service of dedication was an opportunity for effective ministry. Characteristically, he provided a complete program for such a service, including responsive readings and a hymn modified for the occasion.

Blest is the house where faith we find,
And all within have set their mind
To trust their God and serve him still,
And do in all his holy will

Blest such a house, it prospers well;
In peace and joy the parents dwell,
And in their children's lot is shown
How richly God can bless his own.

Then here will we and ours today
A solemn covenant make and say:
Though all the world forsake his word,
We and our house will serve the Lord. (tune Hursley)

In the September 1959 *Bulletin* there was a discussion of the practice of making a contribution to the patriarch who gives a blessing. He felt that individuals could contribute to defray the cost of recording, transcribing, and mailing.

A second, and highly successful, effort of the bulletins was to build fraternity and morale among the members of the order. To establish acquaintance within the group, Cheville would include excerpts from letters he received from individual patriarchs. He frequently added descriptive material about the letter writers. Occasionally he would print a list of all the patriarchs, noting the city in which each lived. When one died, he always wrote at least a paragraph about the person, probably from memory.

The *Bulletin* for May 1962 welcomed 27 new patriarchs. Twenty-two of them were ordained at the April conference. Just before the ordination service in the Stone Church, Arthur Oakman greeted Cheville with,

"Roy, how do you feel about all that is happening here this morning?" Cheville answered from the heart, "I am thrilled beyond words." He described them as "men of wide experience, honorable character, deep devotion, and wholesome spirituality." Much of the bulletin was given over to guidance to the new patriarchs in the several aspects of patriarchal ministry.

Stories about individuals provided inspiration and encouragement. For example, the *Bulletin* for June 1960 carried a story about British patriarch John Worth. Some years before he was ordained patriarch he was advised in a prophetic message that in time he would hold this office.

> He saw many of his co-laborers in the steel mill grow old with gnarled and stiff hands as a result of their hard work. He believed what he had been told about a future call and ordination. He would go home after work and massage his hands and anoint them with oil and other materials. He was seeing to it that when he should be ordained his hands would be in fit condition for the blessing of his people. They were.

In the December 1962 *Bulletin* was a note that Patriarch David Wilson and his wife had visited in the home of Patriarch Francis Bishop at Springfield, Mo. The four of them made a tape recording of a friendly greeting and sent it to

Photo 7-2. Cheville conducting a meeting in the chapel of the Auditorium. *[Photo: RLDS Archives]*

Cheville. David Wilson remarked, "I feel very close to the brothers in the patriarchal order. I am happy to be associated in such a great work with men of this quality. As I read their testimonies and greetings in the *Bulletin* I feel at one with them." Many other patriarchs expressed appreciation for what Roy did in person and with these bulletins. For example, one wrote, "It has been a real pleasure and a valued opportunity to work with you and under your leadership. It makes us feel like real brothers in Christ." Another wrote, "Perhaps most of all I have appreciated your personal concern for each one of us in the Order."

Spiritual growth and spirituality—both for the patriarch and for those to whom he ministered—received frequent consideration in the bulletins. One long-standing principle in Cheville's teaching was that a person should be able to define religious terms without using the terms themselves.

The October 1964 *Bulletin* gave the following definition of spirituality:

> Spirituality is two-way communion with God. Here is association of reaching out to God and receiving from God. We have learned that those who communicate well have common concerns, common background, common language. This is so with us and God. This means that the truly spiritual person *lives* God's way, *loves* God's way, *labors* God's way. Such communion transforms the communicant so he becomes more qualified to commune. And the resources of God come to him as he is ready for them.

He wrote in 1965 that "Our Call is to Spiritualize," and he defined what he meant,

> The gospel of Jesus Christ...looks to the transforming of the living of people so the living accords more and more with the life that is in God. Our calling is to spiritualize people and to spiritualize the use of things.
>
> Sometimes parents and ministers ask me to minister to individuals or groups and "give them" some spirituality. I cannot do this. The Holy Spirit like the light of the sun coming into a plant has to get into the growing process of a life and effect growth and fruitage. The Spirit cannot be plastered on as a veneer. The Spirit has to be absorbed. [pBull Feb. 65]

"Patriarchs and Prophetic Ministry" [pBull Apr. 1961] was introduced by a quote from a brother who said, "Here is something that is at the heart of our movement, yet we seldom confer about it." The first section of the bulletin posed the question, "Should we discuss prophecy and inspiration, or will discussion cheapen the prophetic gift and eventually dispel it?" In that section Cheville makes the following points:

> Nothing in the gospel of Jesus Christ is to be taboo from consideration. Nothing is to be relegated to the field of mystery. Everything that is sound and wholesome can be brought to the light. That which is left to ignorance may prove dangerous.
>
> One of the great needs in our Church today is understanding of the nature and functioning of inspiration and prophecy so we can qualify for a richer, sounder expression of it." [pBull Apr 60]

A related topic, "Spiritual Manifestations" [Oct. 1972], advised the patriarchs to evaluate such activities by the degree to which they "edify," as defined by the Apostle Paul.

Cheville had been receiving inquiries from patriarchs in the field wondering if speaking in prophecy had become "passe" in the Church. Some of the questions from the field were,

> 1. I realize that there has been a lot of thin stuff spoken in the name of the Lord, but I believe that we are needing some good solid counsel and I believe that God wants to speak to us. Am I out of step?
>
> 2. I have heard that some of our general church administrators are looking with disfavor at speaking in prophecy. Is this the case? Or have I misheard?
>
> 3. I spoke to our people at our reunion. I am not certain that some of the general church men who were there approved. What is a man to do in a situation like this? Does he speak or doesn't he?
>
> 4. It looks to me as if some of our study materials are not favorable to our speaking in prophecy. Or are they unenthusiastic about it. Where are we?
>
> 5. This idea of "pervasive inspiration" is bothering me. It is bothering many others. Does this mean that the day of "speaking in prophecy" has passed? Does it mean that from now on prophecy is replaced by dialogue? [pBull Sep 69]

Cheville described two precedents from the Bible. Isaiah, sometimes called the "statesman prophet," was in touch with trends in the Jewish nation. He saw a crisis developing as some Jewish officials were maneuvering with Egypt and breaking terms with Assyria. He sensed impending disaster and decided the responsibility lay with Shebnu, a royal official. Isaiah studied the situation and sought counsel from God. This direction came to him, "Thus saith the Lord of hosts, Go ... and say ..." (Isaiah 22:15) Isaiah spoke in specific prophecy.

Something like this happened in Jeremiah's ministry. He was directed to speak to Baruch this way, "Thus shall you say to him, Thus saith the Lord ..." (Jeremiah 45:4) Here was a specific message for a specific need.

Cheville went on to say that the kind of thing that happened in the lives of Isaiah and Jeremiah happened in the founding days of our movement. As with Isaiah and Jeremiah, it took a while for Joseph Smith to develop sensitivity, capacity, and reliability so that God could speak to him significantly. The Restoration movement could not have come into being without these prophetic directives that carried the tenor, "Thus saith."

> Several of us consider that the most fruitful days of the prophetic ministry of Joseph Smith was when he was diligently asking, "God, what is the word?" . . Prophecy had to do with identifiable problems with flesh-and-blood men and women on this earth. It was concerned with bringing God's direction into the living now... The Restoration movement still needs healthy prophetic ministry.

Cheville's fourth objective for the bulletins was to publicize events and plans of the world church. The future temple occupied a large part of his attention. "Our men listened with uplift and rejoicing as they heard this sentence in the message to the church, 'The time has come for a start to be made toward building my temple in the Center Place,'" he wrote. He described a tremendous responsibility.

This building is going to involve much more than raising money and drawing plans. This qualifying is requiring that we come to see what a temple is for and what we are going to do with it and in it. This is an exciting adventure in exploring... Now there is another objective that we may well add to this list. It grows out of the happenings of the conference. Number 6 would be, "To guide our people in developing a sound appreciation of the purpose and function of the temple." [pBull May 68]

The *Bulletin* for June 1968 was devoted to developing understanding of spiritual issues in temple functions. The major subject of the July 1972 *Bulletin* was the counsel by the prophet during the April conference (D&C 150:8) to "continue your study toward defining the purpose and selecting a place for erecting a temple in my name for the teaching of my priesthood." One brother had commented that the advice for him to continue was premature for he had not started his study of the subject.

With characteristic historical perspective, Cheville traced the development of temple thought. He noted that the early reorganization was busy with getting under way and expressing differences with the Utah church. The founders insisted strongly that the temple constructed in Nauvoo was never completed and did not have the sanction of God.

In 1871 and 1872 Joseph Smith III wrote a series of articles to present a comprehensive view of the church. In his presentation concerning "the temple" Smith wrote a historical review:

As an adjunct to, and necessary consequence of the gathering, the building of a temple has been attempted as a measure calculated to intensify the worship of the people; to foster their spirit of devotion, and to develop their love of God, their industry, patience, faithfulness, and their ability.

Joseph III wrote about the cornerstone for the temple being laid in Jackson County and the saints being driven out before the temple was constructed, about the Kirtland

Temple's building and abandonment, about the burning of the incomplete Nauvoo Temple. Then he discussed the place "a temple or its equivalent or representative" had had in nearly every important faction of the church since Nauvoo. Listed were the "Tower of Strength" of those led by James J. Strang, "the Secret Chamber" of those in western Iowa known as the Baneemyites; the "Rock of Refuge" of Gladden Bishop; the "Ensign of Peace" and the "Council House" of the followers of Alphaeus Cutler. At that same time the Mormons of Salt Lake City were planning on the construction of temples in Utah. (The St. George Temple was dedicated April 6, 1877, the Logan Temple, May 17, 1884, the Manti Temple, May 21, 1888, and the Salt Lake Temple, April 6, 1893.)

Cheville wrote that Frederick M. Smith stated in a message to the 1917 Conference that "Another two years should see a goodly start toward the temple fund." He referred to the temple again in addressing the 1926 conference when construction of the auditorium was under way, "And must I mention still before us the great task of building, ultimately, the Temple, to which we have looked forward? I have not forgotten it. I do not forget it. For in the dreams of Zion, it is always in a prominent place of perspective." [SH 1926, vol. 73, p. 317] Then Cheville quoted from a prophecy by Elbert A. Smith given in the Stone Church April 7, 1928, "When the time comes, in my way and in my manner, which is the way of law and order, I will command you further concerning the building of my temple in Zion."

Cheville referred to a paper he gave in a 1967 seminar on Zionic Living, entitled "The Function of the Temple in the Zionic Community." Richard Howard, church historian, observed that to his knowledge this was the first presentation on the temple ever made in the Reorganized Church. Cheville made the point that none of the counsels to the church was complete enough to give clear guidance. Adequate functioning of the temple would call for insight by members. Here would be a sanctuary to which the spiritually prepared saints would come to meet God. The temple would be the focus of the Center Place. It is to be a symbol to the Saints; it is also to speak to others.

In the Conference of the following April, W. Wallace Smith presented counsel that the time had come for a start to be made on building the temple. The functions of the building would be revealed through the prophet as the need for more specific direction arose. In an addendum to the counsel, it was noted that "full and complete use of the temple is yet to be revealed, but there is no provision for secret ordinances now or ever." [D&C 149, 149A]

Cheville went on to list seven questions members had been asking—what to study, how to study, with whom to study,

> 1. What take place in our temple? How can this take place here rather than in other buildings we shall have?
>
> 2. Did the Kirtland Temple include all the provisions for services that a temple is to have?
>
> 3. Is the Temple in the Center Place to have meaning and ministry for Saints in all parts of the Church?
>
> 4. Is the Temple to be only a "school for priesthood?" Or are there to be ministries for all our members? Is it to be for "men only?"
>
> 5. How is the Temple to be functionally "the house of the Lord?"
>
> 6. How is our temple going to differ in facilities and functions from the Mormon temples? Will anybody get in? Will it be a tourist place?
>
> 7. What is this idea of a "temple complex?" Is the temple just "another building?"

The *Bulletin* for June 1970 addressed the concerns of the saints about the temple. Cheville wanted very much for the saints to be involved in discussions about the functions of the temple to be built. He said that many of them needed assurance that what we shall be doing in the temple building will be advised by God. He recalled a discussion with a member of the Utah Mormon church about the functions of a temple. His summary statements of the issues went this way,

> Your temples have to do with status in the hereafter. Yours are life-to-come controls. I believe that we are to live life with eternal quality here on this earth. The temple should have function in enabling us to live here and now in this life. If we live well here, God will provide well in the hereafter. Certainly God is more concerned with the spiritual quality of our lives rather than with our getting secret means for enabling us to pass through portals.

Another major topic addressed in the bulletins was the concern many members felt for the future of the church. He offered a summary [pBull Apr 71]:

> Concern I. Many of us are wondering if there is going to be any Restoration church pretty soon. Or are we to become another ordinary church pretty much like all others? We are needing desperately to identify what our distinctives are going to be and how we are going to phrase them meaningfully today.
>
> Concern II. We seem to have been declining in missionary interest and expression. If this goes on, we shall be a dying church. In our present thinking, why should anyone want to become a member of our church?
>
> Concern III. This recent conference was a managed affair. Matters never got to the people. Many of us do not agree with the position of some administrators that some matters are administrative and are not to come before the conference.
>
> Concern IV. What has been done in religious education has been done in a corner. The "papers" threatened our very church. When these leaked out we wondered how many other things had been kept from us. We believe that in our educational program the people are to participate. There is need of mature individuals on the staff.
>
> Concern V. There is too much centralization taking place in the church. There is too much heading things in the First Presidency, in some cases in the Twelve and Presidency. Conference and common consent seem to be going out.
>
> Concern VI. Many recent gatherings of our youth have lacked soundness in purpose and in management. There has been consid-

erable negative spirit, with little enlisting of youth in the life, the program of the church.

Concern VII. We are troubled about the release of appointees. On what basis were the releases made? How were the appointees consulted? Is going under appointment like choosing a vocation or is God involved? Are these men employees or are they brothers in Christ?

Concern VIII. It looks as if this polygamy situation was kept secret. Some feel that the problem would have been met if there had been a frank presentation. Was it the intent to keep this matter secret? We feel that this leaked out without the administrators wanting it to.

Concern IX. In youth work, notably in college ministry, there has been a veering toward the vociferous leftists. We have paid more attention to them. Many reliable youth have been disregarded. There is need to consider all youth in a constructive program. We need leaders with spiritual maturity.

Concern X. We hear about reaching out into the community, into society. Many times this sounds as if we are to become a social service agency. We believe that we are to reach out in Zionic expression but that there should be a spiritual quality in this. And God should be in this.

Concern XI. There appears to be a tendency to water down the functioning of the temple, so it would be interpreted as only another building for holding priesthood and other meetings. If the temple is not going to stand for anything more than this, we do not see any need for building it.

Concern XII. Our theologians are weak in their interpretations and emphases of what is vital in our Restoration church. We hear a lot about grace and the like, but not much about the Holy Spirit.

Concern XIII. Our church leaders seem apart from the people. We are needing communication with them. They need to get out where the people are. Sometimes it looks as if they are saying, "This is our plan and we are going to push it whether you want it or not."

Following this list Cheville noted that many people needed ministry the patriarchs could offer as they faced these situations in the church.

The whole of the *Bulletin* for October 1961, recognized the ferment taking place regarding theology in the church. Patriarchs were encouraged to be aware of the issues and informed about ways to "share in this exploration . . We shall do well to join the company of searchers who want to discover improved interpretation of the Restoration gospel." Cheville went on to define theology,

> The word *theology* is formed from the Greek words *theos* (God) and *logos* (study). . Good theology seeks *consistency* . . Good theology is *functional*: it makes a difference in everyday living... Religion is the personal experience with God.
>
> The Restoration movement began with searching for God and finding response from God. Right away the experience of Joseph Smith in 1820 called for interpretation and confirmation.

He listed 12 questions as typical ones to raise in the exploratory discussions in the church. They ranged from a global question about picturing God carrying on his creative work, to evidences of the divinity of Jesus Christ, to intensive interpretation of the Nauvoo period in relation to the Utah Movement.

Anticipating problems that were to become acute in the church within ten years, he defined "seven dangers for us to avoid." They ranged from name-calling, party alignment, leaving it up to the leaders, to speculation apart from research and validation. He then noted seven things members could do to minimize the problems. These included keeping channels of communication open between those of differing views, bringing together in worship and fellowship those who might be alienated, and interpreting the Restoration gospel as expanding insight about God. He concluded with a note that this was an important time,

> This bulletin invites you to share in something of great consequence in the Church. Some are worried. I am not. I see the possibility of moving from yesterday to a tomorrow with a conception of the Restoration gospel beyond any we have known and used. Let's get the

thrill of exploring! I join you as one who believes so thoroughly in revelation and expects further light along the way.

The *Bulletin* for June 1962 again referred to problems in the Church. The headline was, "We Shall Be One!" Then followed part of the prayer of Jesus Christ during the Last Supper,

> I pray for them: . . that they all may be one; as thou Father, art in me, and I in thee, that they also may be one in us.

Cheville continues,

> Oneness does not call for identity. A ministry or a membership with all built on one pattern that produced identicals would be stifling, without initiative or creativity. We can have oneness of intent and concern as we function in our several personhoods.

He went on to say that

> we face growing pains in church administration, in theology, in religious education, in financial procedures, in world missions, in general evangelism. Certainly ministers of the Church of Jesus Christ can be big enough to tackle these problems together in the spirit of fraternity.

Responding again to developing problems within the Church, and seeking a way to address them constructively, Cheville's theme in the August 1962 *Bulletin* was, "We Build Morale."

> Morale building calls for (1) setting forth something worth living for, worth dying for; (2) seeing things as they are, however they may be; (3) identifying resources available for making the worthful cause come true; (4) living alongside those who stand up for the cause; (5) practicing the make-it-come-true policy; and (6) taking up and testifying up the basics of the cause."

The *Bulletin* for July 1970 addressed the need for ministers to be in significant contact with members of all the diverse groups that constitute the Church. Among the diversities described were the "legalists," the "liberals," college students, Americans, those outside the United States, ordained men, laity, elite, ordinary, youth, and adults. Patriarchal ministers should find ways to reach all types and to minister to them.

In the *Bulletin* for January 1971 Cheville describes his concern in the months before the 1970 conference, trying to see things as they were and to vision things as they should become. He wanted to "see with God" so he would be able to minister to the Saints. As the conference approached he felt that the Saints were not identifying areas on which they sought direction, and were not making the preparation leading to the possibility of consensus. As the conference closed he felt, as others did, that they had not tackled the major questions as a conference which could have led to "common consent."

In the April 1971 issue he wrote:

> Often I am asked if the tone of things has been improving during recent months. Here I refer to the 1970 conference which I consider our low spot. I would say, Yes. This does not mean that the anxieties and perplexities have disappeared. I believe that most are still with us. It does mean that the tone of things has improved. We have a healthier atmosphere. We can make a better approach to our problems.

One of Cheville's purposes in the bulletins was to keep the brethren of the order informed about the growth of the church. For example, the *Bulletin* for July 1968 noted that there was a branch of the Church where Black Saints and White Saints were meeting together,

> Something significant is taking place in Brainard Branch in Chicago. I know of nothing like it anywhere else in our Church. It is a pioneering project in bringing Negroes and Whites together in congregational living. This is more than sitting in rows in meetings in the same room... The first amalgamation meeting took place last fall. Since then this branch is exploring in biracial living... The outlook is promising.

The *Bulletin* for January of 1974 emphasized places around the world where the good news was being shared.

In addition to the previous four objectives, Cheville occasionally extended patriarchal greetings to other church leaders. The *Bulletin* for March 1969 contained a letter to the Joint Council members. Included were these statements,

> This Christmas time I wrote 150 letters, in longhand. No duplicates. Many went to brothers in other lands. They went to all continents. They went to all racial colors. They ranged from a letter to our prophet to a letter to a prisoner in a state penitentiary. Replies were not expected, but they came. The messages expressed world fellowship in action.
>
> In the field of religion many people are weary of negativistic and faultfinding approaches. They are wanting something constructive.
>
> Yes, brothers, we have problems, lots of them. And we have needs, many of them. But we have good news and good hope and good personnel. And the Good Spirit is ministering.

Through the bulletins ran a thread of optimism, hope, and proclamation of the good news of the gospel so characteristic of Cheville. At Christmas time (1959) he wrote of the need for the message of hope in Jesus Christ. Like the angelic heralds, people can say there is good news of a great joy.

> Our times are more spiritually weary than men know. Our life is more meaningless than many suppose. As is usual, when people of civilizations lose sight of purpose and sense of direction, they tend to get busy. Hurrying to get somewhere, not clear as to what to do after arrival. Anxious to keep in motion, lest we be bored in the quiet of being with ourselves. Boisterous in sound lest the silence tempt to look inwardly. Mingling with others, often to the point of losing identity, thus avoiding the necessity of thinking our own way through. We moderns are on the march or on the go or on the merry-go-round... We are to tell men the glad tidings of Christ who can make life meaningful and hopeful.

"With Hope and High Expectancy" was the title of the *Bulletin* of January 1970. "Here is a summons to all of us to look forward with intent to work together, to expect together with God, to help him bring to pass the good thing he has in his plans for us on our earth." Cheville referred to Isaiah's word from the Lord to go, set a watchman, then ask him, "Watchman, what of the night?" Cheville presents a hymn for watchmen, who see the star of hope,

Watchman, tell us of the night,
What its signs of promise are.
  Watcher, o'er yon mountain height,
  See that glory-beaming star!
  Let its beams so clear, so bright,
  Lift the darkness, spread its light!

Watchman, does its beauteous ray
Aught of hope or joy foretell?
  Watcher, Yes! It brings the day,
  When its light shall guide you well.
  Let its beams so clear, so bright
  Lift the darkness, spread its light. (Dix)

He quotes a homespun philosopher who once observed, "When I do some honest-to-goodness hopin', I'm bound to do some hoppin', too." And he went on to say, "And when I hop, I have to have something to stand on." [This may be one of the best short expressions to be found to describe the life and outlook of Cheville himself.]

He presents another hymn text for moving forward into the new year.

We rise and move together
  With joyous, hopeful song,
As on our Christ's own highway,
  We bravely march along.
We face the unfolding future
  With confident, good cheer,
As dawns with solemn brightness
  Another glad new year.

O God, enlarge our insights,
  Build our foundations sure;
Expand outreaching friendship,
  Prompt us to motives pure.

Renew in us the vision
  Of building Zion here,
And send us forth to build it,
  Throughout this coming year. (Webb)

The theme of the *Bulletin* for August 1970 was "Let's Nurture Hope!" Cheville quoted from John Gardner, "A prime function of the leader is to keep hope alive." Gardner explained that "Hope is out of style today." Cheville observed that many people parade themselves as living on hopelessness. They sit in the bleachers and point out what is wrong with the game. Because of the need for sound faith with radiant hope, we can bring hope into style in our world. Ministers must acknowledge the existence of absurdities and evils. Cheville believed that honesty requires that we see all this; courage requires us to rise above it. Ministers will be alert to sense qualities of resiliency and response to what is good. God never surrenders to evil that appears to be sitting on the throne. Cheville listed a number of grounds for hopefulness and closed with a hymn that stresses the words "arise" and "hope" and "courage" and "pioneers,"

Men of the Church, arise!
  Here stand today as one,
Strong in the Spirit of our God,
  As promised by his Son.
From strength to strength go on,
  Together work and pray,
And see in hope the coming morn,
  The dawn of a new day.

Men of the Church, move on!
  Let those about you feel
The courage of your valiant faith,
  The fire of youthful zeal.
Like pioneers of yore,
  United, brave, and strong,
Move on to fields ne'er trod before,
  And raise our marching song. (Diademata)

The significance of the biblical Christmas greetings was the subject of the *Bulletin* for December 1972. Cheville noted that gloom, futility, and lack of meaningful purpose are in the atmosphere of the times. Then he said,

> Jesus saw so much corruption and sensuousness and self-centeredness. He saw the force of military power, of priestly institutionalism. But he did not build his life on these. He rose above all this and brought to men then and now the gospel of hope and love. When in his closing days it looked as if everything was going against him, he said to his men, "Be of good cheer!" and "Let not your hearts be troubled!" Brothers, this Christmas let us speak confidently the salutation heard at Bethlehem, "Fear not: I bring you good news with great joy, for all people!"

Many expressions of appreciation came to Cheville for his work with the bulletins. Typical was a message from W. Wallace Smith,

> Dear Brethren: We have been interested in reading copies of the monthly letter sent out from the office of the presiding patriarch. The information, the suggestions regarding procedure, the words of encouragement are a source of inspiration, not only to you men, but to the church through you.

In addition to the bulletin, which of course had wider outreach, Cheville used quorum meetings at general conference for the same four purposes. During the six days of the General Conference of 1960, for example, the Quorum of Patriarch/Evangelists met together 11 times. Each session had been planned carefully for brotherhood, instruction, and for quorum action on church business. They began with a session in which pairs of patriarchs introduced each other to the group, giving identifying information. Next, there was a session in which each one was invited to give a short statement of, "This good thing has happened to me" since last conference. Experienced patriarchs made presentations in instructional sessions.

On 4 April 1974, in a message to the church through President W. Wallace Smith, Cheville was released from the position of presiding patriarch. He was honored on the conference floor. On that day also the Quorum of High Priests wrote to him,

> Your rich, able and enthusiastic ministry at Graceland College and in the Lamoni Stake had already brought you to the favorable attention of the Church prior to your ordination to the high priesthood in 1925. Since that time you have grown steadily in the affection and respect of church members throughout the church-world.
>
> The time has come for you to retire from the heavy responsibilities you have borne as presiding patriarch-evangelist. We remember with deep gratitude your informed and dedicated ministry with and for generations of young people, both as teacher and leader, your pioneering in breaking down national and racial barriers, your musical contributions in song-fests, at Conferences and conventions, as a hymn writer and as a member of the Hymn Committee, your leadership in administrative and departmental affairs, and—permeating all—your faith, your friendliness, your dedication and zest for life.
>
> Despite the excellence of your services in so many other fields, your experience, judgment and fatherly concern pointed you toward the Evangelical Order. Your ordination to this ministry in 1950 coincided with a growing awareness of the importance of this calling in the life of the church. This was registered more deeply in the revelation of 1958 in which you were designated presiding patriarch. Your service in the past sixteen years has led to greatly enriched evangelical ministry throughout the church as the Order has grown under your guidance in both numbers and understanding. We congratulate you on the record you have made and count ourselves especially fortunate to have been the beneficiaries of your varied services.
>
> You provoked us toward better discipleship through your books and hymns and we sincerely trust that you will continue these contributions to our basic resources, and will find joy and peace in so doing. You have also extended the fatherly hand of love and concern to God's people in the performance of your duties as presiding patriarch and we pray that this fatherly ministry will continue to strengthen and guide the church as you move about in your new role as Presiding Patriarch Emeritus.
>
> Your brethren in the bonds of the everlasting gospel,

The Quorum Of High Priests, G. F. Spencer, President, Paul A. Wellington, Secretary.

selves especially fortunate to have been the beneficiaries of your varied services.

You provoked us toward better discipleship through your books and hymns and we sincerely trust that you will continue these contributions to our basic resources, and will find joy and peace in so doing. You have also extended the fatherly hand of love and concern to God's people in the performance of your duties as presiding patriarch and we pray that this fatherly ministry will continue to strengthen and guide the church as you move about in your new role as Presiding Patriarch Emeritus.

Your brethren in the bonds of the everlasting gospel,

The Quorum Of High Priests, G. F. Spencer, President, Paul A. Wellington, Secretary.

On April 4, 1974 after the announcement had been made that Roy Cheville had been released from the office of presiding patriarch, almost 100 members of the order sat down and wrote testimonials to him. James R. Cummings, Sr. wrote, "No man in my life has made an impact so forceful as you . . You will always be my spiritual father." Ed Buckley wrote, "30 years ago you married Alice and me. We find our life enriched by the concepts shared with us then and over the years through your writing, teaching, and worship leadership." Jay Doty wrote, "I don't have words to tell you the influence you have had and still have in my life. It's a blessing to know you as my brother." Gerald L. Giles wrote, "I appreciate your contribution to my life and pledge to continue in the direction you have guided." Charles V. Graham wrote, "Your ministry has strengthened me and many others throughout the world in our church." Alan D. Kelley wrote, "Words are not sufficient to express the love and respect held for you by the Patriarchs of the Church."

Roscoe Davey, who as an apostle in 1961 had made critical remarks about Cheville's ministry in Germany, wrote,

> I have been very appreciative of the very fine leadership you have brought to the Order of Evangelists, succeeding in making out of a

group of dedicated men a real brotherhood, and an organization with meaning and purpose.

Photo 7-3.
Cheville greeting Roscoe and Mabel Davey in the offices of the presiding patriarch at open house during World Conference.
[Photo: RLDS Archives]

Evangel

> The words *evangel*, *evangelism*, *evangelist* are characteristically Christian. They are at the heart and center of the Christian faith. What they express is indispensable in the Christian life and message... *Evangelism* is the process of bringing the good news of God's promise and provision to man, every man... We need to keep up on the "Modern Book of Acts of the Saints" that is being written, as well as on Dr. Luke's "Acts of the Apostles." [pBull Nov 66]

In the revelation of 1958, Cheville was called to be "Presiding Patriarch." He understood that there were two major functions of his office; patriarch and evangelist. As "patriarchs," he and his colleagues were to be fathers to the church members. As "evangelists," he and his colleagues were to be revivalists in the church, bringing the "good news" of the gospel.

Cheville shared the good news in his monthly bulletins and in his other contacts with members of the Order of Patriarch/Evangelists. He continued to write books which were designed to define and illuminate the good news. He wrote articles regularly for the *Saints' Herald*, and other church publications. He wrote letters to hundreds, perhaps thousands, of people. And he preached and taught in congregations all over the world. Appendix E provides a listing of the travels of Roy Cheville in sharing the good news of the gospel with the Saints. The following pages provide some specific examples.

For Cheville, the good news of the presence of Jesus Christ included actions of the Spirit at work in the lives of people in present time. He could see the effects of spirituality at work changing the lives of people across the world through the influence of the Saints . He called the account of these events "Today's book of Acts."

On a Saturday evening in 1960 in East St. Louis, IL, Cheville spoke after a branch supper, "I talked to the congregation about good things taking place in the church today, with attention to stories from India, Brazil, Korea, Japan. A Book of Acts is being written in our day." [D:1960J] He believed that these events are like those described in the New Testament Book of Acts. In the older Book of Acts and in the modern Book of Acts the Spirit of Jesus Christ is at work.

Cheville believed that, in order to report the good news, individuals had to establish a personal relationship with Jesus Christ. At times he took a historic approach. At Easter 1966 Cheville invited the youth of the Port Huron District in Michigan to meet Jesus Christ in a series of settings; *on the Jerusalem way*, *in the Temple courts*, *in the Bethany home*, *in the Upper Room*, *on Golgotha Hill*, *in Zarahemla land*, and *on the Emmaus Road*.

In Lamoni and in the Spring Branch congregation in Independence Cheville conducted two series of meetings in 1976 with the theme, "Meet Jesus Christ in His Friends." He invited the Saints to understand Jesus better through the friends he chose and the relationship he had with them. He believed that modern disciples like the disciples of old needed to pay more attention to what Jesus said and less attention to the interpretations of his work by other people, including the writers of the scriptures. He stressed the words and actions of Jesus as key data in understanding Christianity. Using the example of the relations between Jesus and his friends he said,

> God does not want man to follow commandments out of fright and apprehension. God wants man to line up and *covenant*. God's way is not that of "scaring," of getting man to "surrender!" Rather with Christ Jesus I make covenant!

At Easter time in 1973 in Columbus, OH, Cheville chose the theme, "We Meet and See Jesus Christ in Diverse Life Situations." Again he focused on what Jesus actually said and did. He made the point that we need to get down to basics to interpret Jesus Christ in ways that are not distorted by the many commentators who have written about the fundamentals of Christianity.

To the Liahona encampment in Nauvoo, IL, Cheville spoke October 6, 1977 in counsel, pointing out ideas that masquerade as the good news,

> Hear again, today in Nauvoo, the salutation of the angelic gospel messenger to the shepherds near Bethlehem, "Fear not: I bring you good news with great joy, which shall be to all people." . . Today there are some of those called to be saints who are not responding to this salutation. Some are inclined to focus attention and to give emphasis on conditions, on happenings in the social order and in people that do not accord with what they conceive as the designs of their Eternal Father. They are not evangelists with good news.

Cheville understood that the good news required a worldwide fellowship. Though he traveled North and South America, Europe, Africa, Asia, and many Pacific islands, Cheville was never a tourist. He was always on mission and always in the company of his fellow covenanting friends. In congregations he made a point of introducing them to some of their brothers and sisters in other lands. In 1972 Cheville and Wayne Zion spent ten days in Kenya, six days in Germany and four days in England, returning to Kansas City December 3. Richard Mbeche wrote Cheville in January 1973, saying, "I maintain that you were sent here to Kenya by God, especially for the assignment of performing the baptisms." He had received a letter from the congregation in Middletown, OH, signed by 71 brothers and sisters. They had sent $1 to pay the postage of his response to them. They also sent him a copy of the *Book of Mormon*.

Sam Agwanda wrote Cheville on February 20, 1973 stating that it was wonderful to have this fellowship while in Nairobi. He said he was happy and his spirit strengthened by letters from Sudbury, Middletown, and Camdenton congregations. He had already replied to "these greetings of fellowship." The Saints at Camdenton had sent him a copy of the *Book of Mormon*. Then he said,

> I do keep you in my prayers always, to be a living witness of the resurrected Christ... Do extend my hand of fellowship to all the brothers and sisters in that great continent of yours. One in Christ, Sam E. Agwanda

On October 18, 1975 the Saints of Wenatchee, WA, sent a letter to the Saints in Nigeria, West Africa. This letter speaks of hope about "bringing to pass a worldwide fellowship, the Church of Jesus Christ on mission." It says, "here is a song that our Saints are singing here,

> Let us sing a worldwide anthem,
> Mingling saints of many a land,
> In the gospel motif joining
> At the leading of God's hand.
> Though diverse, we blend together
> In a symphony divine,
> As we vow unto our Father,
> "We are one, for we are thine."
>
> Let us have a worldwide chorus,
> Every kindred, tribe and tongue
> Singing of God's love outreaching,
> Of his ministry far-flung.
> Let us sing how every person
> Can by love be well enticed,
> And be blended by his Spirit
> In the Church of Jesus Christ.

This hymn was first published in 1979, appears in the 1981 Hymnal, and continues to express a basic principle of the good news for many people.

Related to the essential presence of a worldwide fellowship as a component of the good news was the principle of inclusiveness. Cheville believed that there is one gospel and it is for all, whether member or nonmember. Any person can qualify for contact with and ministry by the Spirit of Jesus Christ. People have done so throughout the ages and throughout the world. His sermon on July 4, 1965 at Kirkwood, MO, declared that "He has made of one blood all nations of men . . Have we not all one Father? Has not one God created us? We are many members, but we are one body in Christ."

He gave the keynote address at a meeting October 1971 in Seoul, Korea with the title, "The Gospel is Inclusive and Incessant." He said that he could have used the traditional words and said, "The gospel is universal and eternal," but he wanted to focus on continuing quality, dynamic quality. It is for everybody and for all time.

On the Asian trip in 1971 Cheville went with Hiroshi Yamada to the headquarters, near Kyoto, of a Japanese religious group called Tenri. Hiroshi said, "The reason I took him was that some of the beliefs of this Japanese indigenous religious group share some similarities with the Restoration; such as God (the Parent), revealed truth, the concept of Zion, etc."

Inclusive evangelism, Cheville taught, should not only reach out to Saints in other cities, other states, and other lands. All members of the congregation should be involved in establishing and maintaining activities of sharing the good news. Cheville made regular efforts to involve all ages and all groups in congregational good news activities. Among his song sheets are several with lyrics designed for juniors, teenagers, middle-agers, oldsters, and other groupings of the Saints . In the five weeks he spent in Hawaii in early 1960, for example, he ministered in several priesthood, women's, and Zion's League meetings, then participated in dedicating the new Makiki Church in Honolulu.

He taught that inclusive evangelism was more than being extrovertive and social. He connected outreach to his concept of a living laboratory for testing the validity of spiritual experience. In Atlanta in 1976 Cheville's theme was "We explore the ministering of the Holy Spirit." He

Photo 8-1.
Cheville lecturing to Korean youth group. [Photo: RLDS Archives]
Photo 8-2.
Cheville and Hiroshi Yamada in front of headquarters of Tenri religious group in Japan.

used the word *explore* to emphasize that Jesus conducted a laboratory school in gospel living. Theory and practice went together. Jesus ministered with his men, and he sent them out into the working field.

At the Blue Valley Stake Youth Encampment in 1977 Cheville spoke in spiritual counsel including these words,

> My sons and daughters, your Father is calling you to explore, to experience, to explain the ministering of the Holy Spirit. So many see this in partial ways, in emotional response only... The Holy Spirit is to enlighten perception and understanding as well as exhilarate the emotions . . you are advised to explore what it means to be endowed by the Holy Spirit.

In a meeting he called a "laboratory school" in Ridgewood, NJ, in 1977 Cheville declared,

> 1) The inspiring and unifying spiritual force in the Church is Christ Jesus, who is the living revelation of God to us on earth, in human terms.
>
> 2) The church is a fellowship of people who covenant to live with God, to work with God in bringing to pass God's intent of good life for all.
>
> 3) The Holy Spirit is the endowing, personal presence that God affords for enabling covenanting people to achieve spiritual living as these line up with God.

Another principle of Cheville's understanding of evangelism was his belief that the Spirit of Jesus Christ is active with all those who put themselves in the right condition to receive such contact. In his sermon at the 1966 World Conference he said that "we shall search for spiritual reality . . We are needing a new tongue to identify and interpret the Holy Spirit."

In Lancaster, WI, in 1972 he asked the question, "What's The Good News of God Today?" The daily themes were, God Is on the Job Today, Man Is Designed for Good Living Today, Jesus Christ Reveals Good Living Today, Spiritual Dynamic Is Available Today, and The Church Is on Mission Today. As he did so often, he composed a hymn for the series that captured the theme:

God is moving through the ages
    For a life of noble worth,
Calling us to nobler living,
    Through the promise of new birth,
Ever working, ever working
    To restore God's way on earth.

We are called to stand with courage,
    With a faith that will not yield,
Confident that in God's program
    Weakness, illness will be healed,
Ever hoping, ever hoping
    For united worldwide field.

So with God we stand together
    To live forth good news today
Sharing how our Christ is wanting
    To help us with guiding ray,
Ever singing, ever singing,
    Good news of the Light, the Way. (Regent Square)

In his own ministry, Cheville described spiritual events in the lives of the Saints across the world. His personal sharing of the good news included his own testimonies of profound experiences in contemporary lives in the church. He told several times of a special experience in ministry with Humberto Salas, a national minister in Saltillo, Mexico in 1967. In preparing for the patriarchal blessing, he felt that "this sacrament was to reach out and see Jesus Christ as our universal Friend, not limited by land boundaries or language barriers." The result he described as "a Pentecostal experience."

He was in Lima, Peru in June of 1972, to which he had felt a spiritual pull. The Good Spirit prompted him "warmly and clearly" to bring to the Lima congregation a prophetic message. "They needed to experience this inspired and inspiring ministry in their home land," he said. The message had such power that Darrell Mink wrote him later that he used it for teaching his congregation during the weeks that followed. [Cheville letter to M. Ritchie 6 Jul 72]

Another recurring theme for Cheville's ministry of evangelism was the concept of sharing the good news. He was convinced that a person who comes to the point of friendship with Jesus Christ is a changed person. The changes are such that the world is richer and fuller. The good news of fellowship with Christ works in such a way that the person wants to share it with others.

A specific form of sharing the good news of the presence of Jesus Christ is through testimony. Cheville was always clear that the person whose life has been changed by the Spirit of Jesus Christ should speak out in testimony of that effect of the Spirit. The two disciples who met Christ on the road to Emmaus, when they realized they had been talking with the risen Christ, went straightaway to Jerusalem to tell the good news. They could not refrain from bearing their witness. In a *Herald* article, Cheville wrote, "It is the calling of every Saint to interpret and express the distinctives of the Restoration in 1968—then go on to loftier insights in the years ahead." [D:1968B]

Another characteristic of the good news is that the lives of people are transformed under the influence of the Spirit of Jesus Christ. This principle ran through the theology and the teaching of Cheville, and it permeated his preaching ministry. In a sermon at the 1960 World Conference, he gave the good news that there are spiritual forces available for personal development to lives of eternal quality. [D:1960M]

In Pittsburgh in 1969 he conducted four evening meetings with singing, socializing and sermonizing. His evening titles were, 1. God is on the job, today!, 2. Man has good potentials!, 3. Jesus Christ helps man become!, and 4. God's Spirit is available today! This emphasis on personal development was expressed also in a series of meetings in Osceola, MO, in 1976. Cheville explored the theme statement, "God's continuing business is developing individuals of worthy, eternal quality!" The bulletin said, "The teaching, testifying minister for this good news project will be Roy Cheville, of Independence, Missouri, church patriarch, college professor, worldwide friend."

The theme of personal development stood out in Olathe, KS, in 1976. There Cheville gave a challenge on the night that the area's high school graduates were presented. He described some undesirable reactions by young people:

1) Hippies, these withdraw;
2) Yuppies, these get rid of what is;
3) Yappies, these talk up and blurt out;
4) Softies, apathetic, no guts.

He described youth qualities that are needed today:

1) Adventure, spiritual adventure;
2) Team Spirit,
We're the youth, We've got a date,
To be on the team in Sunflower State;
3) Enthusiasm, Zip and Zest for what is worthful;
4) Hero appreciation, needed today—heroes, Coach Jesus—dynamic, "Give us a virile Christ."

Cheville recognized that the work of the Holy Spirit in the life of a person is such that the person grows in understanding and in companionship with the Spirit. He called this spiritual growth. Such spiritual growth requires nourishment of the person's personal development. He taught that one important aspect of that nourishment is the prayer life of the Saint. To be effective, prayer should be a conversation with God. Conversing is a two-way activity in which the Saint aspires to see the choices of daily life from the perspective of divinity. At Easter time 1969 in the Norton Heights congregation in Kansas City he emphasized that Christ often went off by himself to commune with his Heavenly Father. He said that all Saints should spend some time alone in worship and prayer.

As saints achieve personal communion with the Holy Spirit, they come to achieve spiritual healthiness. Being spiritually healthy, they have qualities in their bearing and in their being which radiate to those about them who are observant of personal qualities. He wanted to identify these processes and help the Saints develop toward this state of spiritual healthiness.

To the Liberty Street congregation in Independence in January 1976 he stated, "We believe that Jesus of Nazareth lived on earth with zest, with ministry to enable others to live with zest, with hope." His theme was, "An Adventure in Gospel Enthusiasm!" One evening a trio of youth and adults interviewed Cheville with questions centering on "What in our Restoration Church generates enthusiasm in you?" He emphasized a similar theme and approach in North Platte, NE in March of 1977.

To the Saints at Brush Creek reunion August 5, 1977, Cheville spoke in spiritual counsel including these words,

> Today, my Saints, you are counseled to look to and to desire the cultivation of the fruits of the Holy Spirit. See these spiritual fruits as essential qualities to be developed in the inclusive living in all your relationships. These fruits come into realization through endeavor and exercise... Then to those who cultivate spiritual fruits your God will grant extra endowments as spiritual gifts. This endowment will come as there is need and readiness . .

Taking the possibility of individual personal growth one step further, in Weyburn, Saskatchewan in 1968, he invited the Saints to think that God designs every person to be somebody. He referred to the Last Supper when Jesus said, "Henceforth I am not calling you servants, for the servant does not know what his Lord is doing. No, I am calling you friends, now, because I have told you what I have heard from the Father."

Another of Cheville's evangelistic principles expressed itself in a spirit of concern. He wanted Saints to be concerned with others, particularly those with shared covenants who needed to be nourished. In November of 1974 he had the Willowdale Branch in Toronto send to Richard Mbeche in Kenya a message of "the good hope, the good cheer of the Restoration gospel." In December of 1977 he had the Saints in Orem, UT, send a letter to Russell Fletcher and family in Sao Paulo, Brazil. This letter noted that in a sense the Utah Saints were pioneers in Mormon land, and the Fletchers were pioneers in that Portuguese-speaking country.

As Cheville had encouraged each patriarch in the Order to identify "concernees," so he encouraged the Saints in the congregations he visited also to identify "concernees." In the Malvern Hill congregation in Kansas City Stake in March 1966 he urged the Saints to identify our evangel to moderns in terms of transformed living. He wanted them to select *concernees* with whom they would live evangelistically.

Another of Cheville's principles of evangelism was that the Saints should sing the good news. He frequently found new ways to encourage musical fellowship. One classic occurred at the British Isles Mission Reunion at Swanwick in Derbyshire early in July 1961. At the Saturday evensong, Cheville delivered a recorded singing message that had been made by the Zwaagwesteinde congregation in Friesland, the Netherlands, where Cheville had been shortly before the reunion at Swanwick. On Monday morning the British Saints prepared a return greeting. The singers crossed the North Sea in spirit and extended their hands and hearts to brothers and sisters in the Netherlands Mission. Cheville wrote, "We are building this world-wide spirit among my people through projects more than through preaching." [D:1961O]

Another musical event had its setting in Tahiti. Cheville arrived in Papeete February 16, 1971. Cheville had learned some songs in Tahitian. He visited an elderly church member in the hospital who knew only Tahitian, so they could not converse. Cheville thought of the song, "We've a story to tell to the nations," and he could sing the first verse in Tahitian. He began to sing that song. The Tahitian face

Photo 8-3.

Cheville being met at the Rairoa Tuamotu airport in Tahiti. Everett Graffeo is on the far left, Aberahama Fauura is fourth from left, and Cheville is fifth from left. [Photo: Ruth Zion]

Photo 8-4.

Cheville and friends traveling between Avatoru and Tiputa on the island of Rairoa. Left to right are Timi Bennett, Aberahama Fauura, Heenui Tepehu, Cheville, and Tu Mauri. [Photo: Ruth Zion] first registered surprise, then joyful approval, then friendship, brothership. He motioned to start again, then joined in with a joyful baritone voice. By the time they finished the stanza at least twenty people had come in the room to listen.

What might be called a musical reprise took place in Hannover, Germany in November of 1972. Cheville and Wayne Zion had been in Africa. They flew from Nairobi to Frankfurt and on to Hannover, arriving on the 24th. That evening Cheville asked the congregation to sing a song he had taught the German Saints to sing in 1961 in their Pfingst Conference, just before the Berlin wall went up. He said,

> How they sang, "Auf, denn die Nacht wird Kommen, Auf mit dem jungen Tag! [Work for the night is coming] The walls rang. I was in a spiritually alive, evangelistic congregation, Zionic colony in Germany."

Cheville identified the church as a joyful fellowship of those who have made a covenant with God. When the saint achieves the ability to converse with God in prayer, the result is joyful and friendly interaction with the divine person. He chose to speak and to teach the joys that derive from association with the divine friend. To the Center Stake women on October 15, 1965 he spoke of the word picture Zechariah gave of the community yet to be,

> There shall yet old men and old women dwell in the streets of Jerusalem, and every man with his staff in his hand for very age.

And the streets of the city shall be full of boys and girls playing in the streets thereof.

Then Zechariah challenged his people to get to the business of living the kind of life that would characterize such a Zionic community. Cheville called for the same activities in 1965.

The Bureaucracy

> The church is more than an institution, an organization. It is a fellowship of covenanting members on mission with God. (Roy Cheville, unpublished 1980 manuscript *Sayings*.)

> I was his contact in the Presidency. Anybody that ever has known Roy, knows that you don't direct him to do anything. (Couey, Duane E., *An Oral History Memoir*. RLDS Archives, 1993, p. 455.)

Despite Cheville's achievements and his stature in the church, or perhaps because of them, not every church official welcomed him to church headquarters with open arms. Even before he became presiding patriarch, a movement had begun in church headquarters to counter his thought and his teachings. That occurred with the founding of the School of the Restoration shortly after Graceland initiated its four-year program in religion. The momentum of that movement increased and expanded.

When Cheville was ordained to the office of presiding patriarch, he expected that he would be invited to regular meetings of the Joint Council as his predecessor had been. That attendance would have brought regular contacts and association with colleagues of the Presidency, the Quorum of Twelve Apostles, and the Presiding Bishopric. But he was not invited to participate in Joint Council meetings or other significant deliberative institutes, conferences or committees. He would say later that he could have been a more effective presiding patriarch if he had been in closer contact with the governing processes.

It should be made clear that what began to happen was not a conspiracy and not the actions of people who were deliberately hostile. All the people involved in these actions were honorable and sincere, and they all were and remained Roy's good friends. All were dedicated to doing things for the good of the church. All respected each other as brothers. They would have been surprised to hear it said that they were less than brotherly to Roy Cheville. But it did happen, and the effects became far-reaching for the church. For Cheville the pain was deep because "he was wounded in the house of friends." He was committed to positive service, and he bore his wounds for years with very little external evidence of them.

We can trace some of the significant problems beginning with the announcement in the *Lamoni Chronicle* of February 28, 1957, of a new four-year program in religion at Graceland College. That announcement noted that Dr. Roy A. Cheville would head the instructional staff for the program. It also stated that his "creative thinking has stimulated the church around the world," and that his academic training "insures that Graceland's courses in religion will be accepted by other colleges and accrediting agencies."

When Graceland established that degree in religion the church responded by opening up the School of the Restoration. According to Duane Couey,

> . . when Graceland opened its religion major, the church and particularly F. Henry Edwards thought that the college should not get ahead of the church. So the church opened up the School of the Restoration. [Couey, Duane E., *An Oral History Memoir*. RLDS Archives, 1993, p. 441.]

F. Henry Edwards, a member of the First Presidency, was the prime mover in this action. Edwards was a brilliant man. He was a charismatic leader and a scholar of considerable achievement, though he did not have a college degree. He suffered under comparison with Roy Cheville, who had earned the highest degrees given by one of the most prestigious schools of religion in the country. Edwards believed in supernaturalism (that is, that there is a sharp dividing line between that which is human and that which is divine), which was assumed by the writers of the Bible. Cheville believed that direct contact with the Spirit of God was the basic stuff of religion, and that supernaturalism interfered with the development of testable ideas of the way the Holy Spirit works with people. A direct comparison between the thought of Edwards and Cheville can be made by comparing books by each on "authority" in 1956. Edwards' title was *Authority and Spiritual Power*. Cheville's title was *By What Authority*?

As a self-taught scholar Edwards would have had difficulty understanding the full dimensions of Cheville's thought. He knew there were real differences between Cheville's thought and his own, and he promoted his own. Thus, when Cheville moved into church headquarters, he was not included in the Committee on Basic Beliefs, which Edwards chaired.

This exclusion was noticed by many members. There was no official explanation. Those who discussed the matter informally heard some reasons Cheville's ideas were not sought. One was that Cheville's thought was "dated." Another was that Cheville represented the University of Chicago "process theology" approach which was not widely accepted by the church. With regard to committee appointments popular wisdom had it that Cheville would have been appointed to more committees but he was always busy out in the branches of the church and not readily available to attend meetings in headquarters, or that Cheville would have been appointed to more committees if he did not always want to run things.

This pattern of exclusion and the oft-repeated explanations for it became conventional wisdom at church headquarters. The effect was such that Don Landon could say in 1966 with sincerity that Dick Lancaster was "the only professionally trained theologian in the headquarters environment." [Donald Landon, *Oral History Memoir*, RLDS Archives, p. 89] This pattern of exclusion and down-grading within headquarters took its toll on Roy Cheville. It eventually affected his ministry and even his emotional balance.

Patriarchs in the RLDS Church do not hold positions of administration. They are thus unencumbered by the decisions and responsibilities of business and personnel matters, leaving them free to counsel and minister. The presiding patriarch has no section of the church to supervise. In theory, he is free to go anywhere in the church and minister to the members there. At the same time all branches, congregations, and missions of the church are a part of a supervisory structure. At the top of that structure are the Twelve Apostles, and the whole church is divided up among them. That means that whenever the presiding patriarch travels to some branch to minister that branch is supervised by one of the Apostles.

When Cheville was ordained to the office of presiding patriarch by W. Wallace Smith, he was told to "move out in ministry and keep us informed of your activities." As notions of administrative control increased, he was expected to obtain permission of the administrators any time he went anywhere to minister. Frequently he was expected to obtain rather detailed information about what the administrative programs and objectives were, and was expected to conduct his activities in such a way as to serve those objectives. Because of this expectation friction sometimes developed between the Patriarch and some Apostles.

Cheville was not excluded from everything. W. Wallace selected Cheville as one of ten people to help plan the High Priests' Conference to be held in Kirtland Temple in October 8-11, 1959. Consistent with his long-held belief that the Holy Spirit blessed efforts of private preparation as well as immediate presentation, Cheville reported that from the first planning session of this committee "the Holy Spirit prompted me to start making ready for prophetic ministry during the conference." [C:1983] There was a significant precedent for this kind of ministry in a powerfully effective prophetic message delivered at the High Priests' Conference of 1950 by Presiding Patriarch Elbert A. Smith.

Cheville did deliver such a message at the 1959 Conference. The text is contained in Appendix F. It began,

> Even as I, your Master, walked in Galilee and called men to follow me, and to go out and minister for me, so I have called you to be my ministers and have sent you out to serve my people and to witness for me... [D:1959I]

This introduction suggesting that he was speaking for Jesus Christ was unusual for Cheville. For many years, he had taught that it was better to let the quality of the message speak for itself, rather than to say in words that it came from the Holy Spirit. Dr. George Shoemaker opined that this 1959 message was the first time that such a statement had come from a highly educated minister in the church.

Immediately at the close of the message, W. Wallace Smith stood and spoke in testimonial affirmation and approval. The message was printed in the *Saints' Herald* with the following endorsement:

> The Kirtland Conference of High Priests was very richly blessed. Several veteran high priests described it as the most outstanding group experience of their lives...
>
> The shared insights, the steadily growing fraternity, and the many individual resolutions for wiser and more sacrificial service were all related to each other. There were no star performers. The message received at the Saturday morning priesthood meeting through Presiding Patriarch Roy A. Cheville, and attested by the President of the Church, would not have been possible except for what had gone before and the spirit in which all shared...
>
> We feel that the Saints who supported the conference so earnestly and so generously are entitled to share this message as fully as they can. Printed below is what was said.
>
> The First Presidency [D:1959I]

Though Cheville had not often declared that he was speaking in spiritual counsel, such counsel became more frequent. That posed some problems for the Presidency. It was one thing for people to seek the guidance of the Spirit and to speak when they felt so impelled. It was quite another for these utterances to be written down and circulated among the saints. After one such event, W. Wallace responded on May 18, 1964 to a letter from Cheville,

> Our decision not to reproduce "the message" of the service on Sunday morning, Apr. 12, was arrived at soon after the meeting on the basis that it was a communication for a specific time and group which of course was very beneficial... My feeling is that it is similar to what I gave in 1962 and has its greatest benefit for those who were in attendance.

Cheville's relations with the administration continued to be complicated. He once stated that he had always been disinclined to centralization and hierarchical procedure in the church. He believed that the church should not be run with the interests of the organization taking precedence over the development of individuals. The work of the church inheres in the mutual teaching and learning relations among the ministers and the saints. A letter of January 1977 to Bot Otiene of Nairobi, Kenya put that thought in this form,

> The church can be pictured as a living organism that expresses this good life. Paul, the apostle referred to the church as "the body of Christ, in which every member affects every other member, in which all members are designed to function together in mutual support" (Romans 12). Like the human body, the church draws on resources that God provides for the health, for the vigor, for the functioning of the church in action.

Church structure should serve to enable those relationships. He believed "ever so much" in developing enlightened consensus.

Many church leaders who had administrative responsibility chose to put their ministerial efforts where they would have the greatest effect on serving the church, local and general. Cheville always put ministry to individuals first. He put his efforts where he felt he could have the greatest effect on the development of individual people.

It was his view that the church would be served best in the long run if the eternal qualities in individuals were maximized.

Cheville felt a strong calling to extend his ministry to others worldwide. In traveling abroad, he encountered some conflicts with the apostles in charge, even though Cheville felt he took considerable pains to coordinate with them and learn what the local situations were. He was in Hawaii for five weeks in early 1960 and that trip seems to have gone very smoothly. He gave 11 patriarchal blessings in Honolulu and Hilo. Richard Reid reported to the *Saints' Herald* that Brother Cheville brought prophetic counsel in the prayer service and then spoke at the dedication of the Makiki church. "There were more than three hundred people in attendance, and in every way it was an outstanding service," Reid wrote.

The warm reception for his contributions to the High Priests' Conference and the Makiki church dedication marked the high point in his reputation among his peers at church headquarters. There were more complex responses to Cheville's trip of three months to Europe in 1961.

Apostle Roscoe Davey was in Europe in 1961 during part of Cheville's trip. Upon his return, according to Duane Couey [Oral History Memoir], Roscoe, who was normally kind and gracious to his colleagues, offered an observation that was to have far-reaching consequences for Cheville. In a Joint Council meeting he said, "Do you know what that man did, he completely reorganized the whole European Field without even consulting with me."

That report by Davey seems hard to substantiate. Every priesthood member in the church knew that a patriarch had no administrative function or power. Furthermore, throughout his career Cheville always avoided administrative position for himself. He always taught that people who are moved to serve should do so within the established structure of the church. When he was in Europe he always traveled with the local officials in charge. On that trip one of the officials was Clifton McArthur. He wrote about Cheville's 1961 visit to Wales in glowing terms, "The church members of Wales feel that Brother Roy belongs to them in a rather special way." [SH 1 Oct. 1963] McArthur did state that Cheville told him and Harry Black they should acquire property there as "God has a work yet to do in these places." McArthur went on to say that he and Harry had been working individually on these problems, but they looked hopeless before. Later McArthur and Black went back for two weeks and arranged the purchase of three properties.

Joe Bayless, a new church appointee, was in Germany during this trip. He had been trying to get some guidance from Apostle Davey. When none was forthcoming, he wondered if Davey had sent instructions for him to Lou Zonker, his immediate superior. Lou Zonker said in 1997 that there were no instructions, and that was typical of the way apostles operated at that time.

Lou Zonker remembers a great deal of tension between Davey and Cheville when they were together. He felt at the time they had not talked to each other before the trip began. On a trip from Hannover to Berlin Davey, Cheville, Zonker, Anton Compier, and Bayless were in a car together for some hours. Both Zonker and Bayless remember that Cheville was unusually quiet during the whole trip. Bayless recalls, "Up to that time in our travels Roy was always talking, sharing experiences and so forth. But he was very, very quiet on that trip going into Berlin. He was conspicuously quiet." Expressive of the tension Cheville was feeling was his remark to Betty Zonker one evening, "I don't know why he's [Davey] here when I'm here." Davey was relaxed and somewhat low key in contrast to Cheville's dynamic approach to ministry. He said to Joe Bayless once that they needed to be serious about each meeting—"we may never have this group of people together again."

Bayless said that he heard later that Cheville could "kind of take over," but that was not the case in his experience. He said that Cheville's three weeks in Germany brought a lot of encouragement. He recalls feeling just a little bit uneasy early when Roy asked what plans had been made and what were the goals of the activities. Sometimes Roy would initiate a discussion about some of the things Bayless and his colleagues wanted to accomplish. But he never directed. Instead Cheville's visit there produced some outstanding experiences.

One of these experiences occurred at a youth gathering. After a period of singing, Roy drew aside during testimonies to consult an English-German dictionary. After about 30 minutes he came back with a song to teach the German youth. In that 30 minutes he had written a hymn in German to the melody of the "Battle Hymn of the Republic." Bayless said,

> In German we sang, "We see a gathering of an army strong and large." There were several verses and a chorus. I am sure those who remember Roy can visualize his leading the chorus, "The youth are leading the way." I stood there in amazement. In less than half an hour this man had written a song in German which captivated the youth and became the theme of the bond between East and West. It gave them the feeling that they were a part of a movement with real meaning. It became a theme song with German youth. We sang it at the conference and they would sing it later every time they got together.

Another experience Bayless remembers as outstanding occurred a short time later. Cheville asked the church appointees to gather. The six of them included Alfred Urban, who had spent all his appointee life behind the Iron Curtain. During the sharing, Cheville said that sometime before he had been walking on a beach in Hawaii when he was impressed by the Spirit that he would have a message to share in Berlin, Germany. He did not know what the message was, but now he knew.

He walked up, stood behind Alfred Urban, put his hands on his shoulder and asked me to interpret. Roy told Alfred that the next weeks and months of his life would be the most trying he had ever gone through. He told Alfred that there is no power on earth that could separate him from God. He and his people should know that God would be with them. I remember thinking, "What more can these people go through? They had gone through the takeover and occupation of their country. Alfred had been warned and threatened about his church activities." Six weeks later the wall went up. There was total isolation and separation. A lot of people called it the imprisonment of 17 million Germans.

Of this time in Germany, Cheville made these notes:

In the summer of 1961 I was again in Germany. This time I spent four days in West Berlin. That Sunday afternoon I experienced again the Day of Pentecost. Again I spoke in prophetic words. This was the last time these German Saints from East Germany came in to West Berlin before the wall went up on August 13... The next morning Alfred Urban, our appointee in East Germany and I met with three other brothers in an upper room. Joe Bayless was our interpreter. God was with us as I spoke words of counsel. Then Brother Urban spoke, "I have been lonesome and discouraged. Now I can go home and say that God is with his Church, for today I have received prophetic ministry. This is the mountain-top experience of my life." Alfred Urban could not speak English, and my German was too limited for conversation. That day, however, we spoke the language of the Spirit of God. We were brothers in a brotherhood of worldwide dimension.

There is a letter about that same trip from the "Saints from Scandinavia" in the *Saints Herald* of August 21, 1961. They reported on Cheville's visit in this way,

> We here in Scandinavia are very appreciative of the ministry we receive from the visiting ministers from church headquarters. The visit by the church's leading evangelist, brother Roy Cheville, was a rich experience for us, and we feel rewarded because he and other church leaders travel so far to give their ministry to a handful of Saints...
>
> Brother Cheville's ministry brought to us the understanding that there can be some spiritual advantages in a small group. We see some things more clearly now than before, and we are anticipating a period of spiritual and physical growth. We anticipate this

Photo 9-1.
In Sweden in 1961. Left to right: Dick Andersen, Fred Banta, Roy Cheville, Jim Everett.
[Photo: RLDS Archives]

because now we believe that we can do more for ourselves than we had previously expected that we could do.

The statement of Roscoe Davey that Cheville "had reorganized the whole European mission" was repeated often and remembered by people in church headquarters to this day. Though it seems unsupportable, it became common knowledge and had a strong negative effect on Cheville's reputation in the administration.

In January of 1962 the First Presidency issued a bulletin to "Administrative Officers and Evangelists." This document grew out of conferences between the Presidency and the presiding patriarch and it stressed communication. Cheville described the document in his *Bulletin to the Patriarchs* of February 1962. He gave this statement,

> During recent months I have had situations in which brothers in administrative positions and I have not seen alike. Nor do we yet in all things. Sometimes there has developed lack of understanding. I believe that in every case things that could have brought on division have been faced in brotherly spirit.

He quoted the closing paragraph of the message from the First Presidency:

> These are days of great opportunity for the Church of Jesus Christ. These are days which call for technical skills, especially in the field of communication. But, most of all, these are days for which we need endowment such as comes only when the people of God remember that they are the people of God.
>
> God bless you for such a time as this.

It seems clear that Cheville and W. Wallace had somewhat different views on church administration. Roy frequently noted that one of the problems the church should address was the tendency toward centralization of church administration. He felt that ministers should work as colleagues rather than hierarchical employees. In the *Bulletin to the Patriarchs* for February of 1963 he wrote that patriarchs are not to be concerned about prerogatives and protocol, but concerned about achieving conditions conducive to effective ministering. He went on,

> We shall achieve these good, agreeable, relationships as we and our brothers in administration converse together, explore together, work together, for the good of the Saints. We are to work through *common consent* in all fields. This consensus comes through wholesome interaction. This common mind and heart involves administrators, ministers, members and patriarchs.

In his *Bulletin* for April 1963 Cheville listed twelve concerns for members of the order. Three of the ten dealt with administrative matters,

> 1. Spiritual fraternity among administrative ministers, a fraternity centering in Jesus Christ, with common commitment to ministry with him.
> 2. "Common consent" in administrative relationships and procedures that permits a common front in the work of the church, a common mind that transcends printed directives...
> 4. Resolution of tensions that have risen out of matters involving prerogatives, protocol and priorities...

In that same *Bulletin* he suggested communication "to our brothers in leadership,"

> Let us speak in spoken word or in written message to presidents, apostles, bishops, seventies, fellow patriarchs, district presidents, pastors of our expectancies, of our confidence, of our support. It does something good to a man when he realizes that others expect ministry of good quality from him and that others support him in this good ministry.

Some kind of interchange between the First Presidency and the presiding patriarch occurred in 1964. One bit of correspondence survives to give the flavor. On December 28, 1964, President W. Wallace Smith wrote to Cheville,

> We all appreciate the frank and forthright spirit in which you wrote your letter of December 22. In it you indicate that our conversation on December 17 was distressing to you. As we read it, it became evident that we did not get over to you the point which was under consideration. The problem very simply stated is that the men who

> have responsibility for general direction have not always known where you were... No one has any intention of restricting you in your "person-to-person contacts." We feel rather deeply, however, that a lone wolf approach by any one of us would be confusing and oft times irritating to the administrative personnel.

Cheville felt that the reason the First Presidency wanted always to know his whereabouts was their feeling that they should be in control. However, if the negative connotation could be removed from the "lone wolf" phrase, Smith's words would be a fair description of Cheville's office as the single "patriarch to the whole church." Cheville was confused by this discrepancy.

Cheville met with the Council of Twelve October 21, 1965 to consider together the calling and the ministry of the patriarch-evangelists, the first such meeting to be held. Cheville set forth three issues he thought were primary: introducing new patriarchs, including patriarchs in the program of the area, and giving patriarchal blessings within the context of the total program of ministry. The discussion included facilitating contact between patriarchs and administrators about problem situations, using older men in various ministries, and lowering the average age of ordination to the office of patriarch. Cheville described the meeting in the *Bulletin* for December 1965 and noted that "The atmosphere was brotherly. The topics were pertinent. The conferring continues."

When Duane Couey succeeded F. Henry Edwards in the Presidency in 1966 he was assigned the function of coordinating matters affecting the presiding patriarch. He had great respect for Cheville. As a kind and resourceful administrator, he understood Cheville's strong motivation and dedication. He understood also Cheville's dynamic work pace and the inner vision which drove that work pace. Couey said that "nobody manages Roy Cheville;" Cheville felt that his assignment was such that nobody was supposed to manage him. He was on a prophetic mission which really began when he was 16 years old. His view of his mission had frequently enlarged, but otherwise had not altered.

Couey had warm feelings toward Cheville. He tried to visit man-to-man but felt he could not get past Roy's reserves, which had resulted from the deep wounds inflicted by decisions of the First Presidency excluding him from important deliberations. Because he was committed to bring a positive ministry to church members, he did not complain publicly. He would not, and perhaps could not, engage in private discussions which came close to those personal wounds.

Cheville supplied members of the Joint Council with his monthly bulletins to the Order. All four pages of the *Bulletin to the Patriarchs* for September 1968 were devoted to a pastoral letter to members of the Joint Council. It endeavored to present an inclusive picture of the concerns and outlooks of the church membership. These were representative,

> Our people believe that we should have "unity of the faith." For many this means identity in everything. They have not discovered how there can be harmony with diversity.
>
> Some believe that we have been moving toward centralization in our church administration... As most of you know I am not a disciple of centralization. I shun it. So I can give members a lift in this concern.
>
> Our people are needing both interpretation and cultivation in the ministering of the Holy Spirit. I consider this a foremost need and opportunity in our church life today. Our people respond when we combine examination and experience.

Cheville frequently experienced considerable delay and frustrations in trying to arrange for his visiting ministry. He wrote in 1969 that, "I volunteered to go to the branch in Weyburn, Saskatchewan, for a few days... It took almost two years to arrange my going." [D:1969A] Had he been a participant in Joint Council meetings, he might have developed an appreciation for the problems faced by church administrators.

Since he was not a part of the Joint Council he also did not have an opportunity to discuss there considerations of structure. But he did find ways to make his views known to some extent. On April 9, 1969, Cheville wrote to President W. Wallace Smith noting that the statistical report of baptisms for 1968 was disconcerting to many in the church. "Many are saying that we are needing a fresh creative approach to the whole field of evangelism. And so do I." Cheville stated that he had turned to the counsel W. Wallace had brought to the Church in April 1966 freeing the Twelve from detailed administrative duties to,

> give more attention to their primary work of pushing the work into new fields at home and abroad.
>
> As I read and reread this direction, I sensed with clarity the application for the Church today. It was an uplifting experience.
>
> Then I turned to the counsel spoken to the Church in 1958. I noted the direction that the Twelve were directed "to spread the gospel into all the world as special witnesses." Again I sensed the timeliness of this counsel for today as I had not sensed it when given.
>
> I write this with the intent to encourage you, to sustain you. I realize the guiding light that came to you in 1958, in 1966. May the Good Spirit guide you today in instructing and inspiring us all in evangelistic expression with members, with nonmembers.

Administrative issues were just a part of the communication between the Patriarch and the Presidency. For example, Couey, for the First Presidency, wrote to Cheville August 27, 1969, expressing

> our appreciation for the excellent ministry which you gave recently in reference to the gathering of Professional and Vocational Associations. The good spirit that seemed to prevail was due not only to the high caliber of the people who participated but to the spiritual preparation which you made and your sensitivity to the needs that prevailed.

In that meeting, Cheville had delivered a prophetic message which the Presidency endorsed by having it printed in the *Herald* with their own introduction. [D:1969E, reproduced in Appendix G] (Cheville could accept, without administrative approval, invitations to minister at events such as the Professional and Vocational Associations because they did not fall directly in an apostolic administrative territory.)

Cheville finally described to Couey in a calm three-page letter of December 24, 1969 a summary of some of the administrative matters that had been on his mind. In one section, he noted that he thought when he was ordained presiding patriarch he would have contact with and association with brothers of the Joint Council, and he had not had any such contacts in meetings. "I presumed that this was the way you wanted things to be, so I adjusted to this arrangement. I confess that at times I could have been a more effective presiding patriarch if I had closer touch."

In other sections of that letter he wrote,

> Right now I am concerned with developing our people for informed participation in working on our church problems and strains. And I am concerned with developing the quality of saintly fraternity that will enable us to work on these matters together. And I am concerned that our people grow in fitness for the divine guidance that we are needing so very much. I believe ever so much in developing enlightened consensus.
>
> I admit that I am concerned about the trend we are going to be taking in church administration. It is likely that I may veer to one side. I have always been disinclined to centralization and hierarchal procedure. This is nothing new. President Frederick M. Smith smiled once and chided me a bit about this. I do not believe in a church administratively operated by either the First Presidency or the Joint Council, or any other group. There is no animosity in this. This is my conviction.
>
> ... Men have said to me that they could not converse with you men, that your minds were made up... And now it looks as if I am in the same relationship that these men have said they were. It troubles me that this is so. I am not angry; I am troubled...
>
> I assure you that I shall minister constructively and hopefully. Through recent months members have said that they have needed

so much the hope and the enthusiasm that I express. I want it to be so these coming months.

Facing the problems of the Church with "Clarity and Charity" was the theme of the *Bulletin to the Patriarchs* for February 1970. He was pointing toward the coming World Conference. He offered these items to define the desired attitude of the patriarchs,

A vital, functioning church is going to be facing problems of consequence.

A church without awareness of problems is either dead or deaf and blind.

We shall not lament the presence of problems.

Rather do we address ourselves to seeing them and solving them.

Some vision a Zion or a heaven that has no problems.

A person or a group that does not engage in healthy problem solving deteriorates.

A healthy life has problems its size, has resources for tackling them, has skills and dispositions for problem solving.

A healthy church will designate those problems of such importance as calls for priority in consideration.

A weak or neurotic church will give undue attention and energy to tidbits.

A healthy church learns how to achieve harmony with diversity, how to harmonize "together with God."

As the church began to narrow its definition of acceptable theology, Roy was increasingly accused of promoting positions that did not agree with the established positions of the Joint Council. One example of this was a two-page interoffice memo written to him April 13, 1971 by Geoffrey Spencer, who stated that he was "considerably disturbed" about the most recent of Cheville's Bulletins to the Patriarchs. In that Bulletin, Cheville described some of the "foremost concerns" of church members. These were reports of what he heard as he ministered around the church. Spencer went on to say,

> I can not see how this can do anything else than increase the uncertainty and polarization which plagues the membership.
>
> Roy, I have the feeling that these may not only reflect your own wording but your own sentiments at many points. I know that you have serious questions about the curriculum and the manner of its preparation: observations of yours elsewhere reflect the point of view stated in concern No. 4. Again I note that the observation, in my opinion quite unfounded, that we hear too much of grace and too little of the Holy Spirit appeared many months ago in your new Book of Mormon manuscript.

Cheville's "Concern No. 4," referred to by Spencer read as follows:

> What has been done in religious education has been done in a corner. The "papers" threatened our very church. When these leaked out we wondered how many other things had been kept from us. We believe that in our educational program the people are to participate. There is need of mature individuals on the staff.

Cheville responded to Spencer two days later with a three-page memo that was also explicit. Spencer had used the word "inflammatory" in describing Cheville's Bulletin. Cheville said that he considered it "unsound and unfair" for Spencer to use that word as there was no intent to raise heated and troublesome matters in an inflaming way. He said further, "The concern of mine was that my fellow ministers be sensitive to the anxieties of our people, all of them not of any segment." In reference to what he considered exclusionary editing by Spencer's Department of Religious Education Cheville stated, "I question that you are to be the determiner of the thinking of our people."

There was some justification for the increase of hierarchical administrative actions in this era. The controversies which were alluded to above in the interchange between Cheville and Spencer had led to overt actions by some disgruntled members. Some of these members were using their status as priesthood members to speak and work against the church in whatever ways they could. It was necessary for the administrative structure to develop ways to manage situations which posed threats to the church. But Cheville continued to place primary focus on ministry to individuals.

The *Bulletin to the Patriarchs* for February 1972 looked forward to the coming World Conference. Cheville began with noting that the Restoration had a century and a half of exploring and experimenting with "conferencing." He defined the words *confer* and *conference*, noting that the fundamental meaning was *coming together* for *carrying together*. The criteria of a good conference involve interaction out of which common mind and common heart can emerge.

> In a good conference members are searching together, exploring together, and God is in this seeking and investigating and deliberating and concluding. God lives among the Saints in our conferring through the ministering of the Holy Spirit.

He discussed the first vision of Joseph Smith as "conferring," and the organization meeting of 1830 and the conferences of June and October 1830 as group decision meetings. The latter conference raised the problem of church procedures in the context of Hiram Page's personal interpretations. This problem was handled in brotherly fashion. In that context came this counsel,

> All things must be done in order and by common consent in the church, and by the prayer of faith. [D&C 25:1]

"This stands as foremost direction to the church in the holding of conference. The way of conferring is the way of common consenting. This calls for free and considerate interaction so that enlightened consensus might emerge."

In contrast Cheville pointed out the developments in Nauvoo. For a number of reasons cited (including increasing centralization in administrative matters with hierarchical operations) there developed a pattern of little conferring and little consenting. "This Nauvoo period was not conducive to healthy conferencing and to the functioning of enlightened common consent, and to qualifying for divine direction."

Next Cheville described events leading up to the first conference of the Reorganization movement. A small group met June 12, 1852 and a somewhat larger group met in October of the same year. They sought to ascertain who should preside as they went ahead in effecting reorganization. "They sensed confirmation in their endeavors, but sensed need for further direction. This was to the good: no man stood forth as declared leader to be." They were proceeding with enough humility to qualify for spiritual guidance. A conference was set for April 1853.

During the preliminary meeting in March H. H. Deam wrote down what came to him as guiding directive. This was the heart of the counsel, "Let three men be appointed by the Conference to select seven men from among you, who shall compose the majority of the Twelve" (apostles). He kept this counsel except to show it to Zenas Gurley.

In the April conference perplexity prevailed. The conscientious Saints did not go ahead. They needed more direction, more assurance. They came together in prayer. In an atmosphere of humility and urgency a transition came. The darkness lifted. H. H. Deam read the counsel that had come to him and asked his brothers and sisters to pray for light and confirmation. J. W. Briggs wrote about the transformation,

> The evident proofs of divine direction were so strong that doubt disappeared, while the light was so clear to all that diversity of opinion ceased, and the whole were truly of one heart and one soul...
>
> The next morning the revelation of March 20 was presented to the conference and was accepted by unanimous voice. The conference closed with testimonial assurance. And there were seven

> apostles to carry on the work of the Restored Church. Here was true conferring...
>
> These conferences speak for themselves. Ever were there needs and problems to be met. Ever was there need for the Saints to consult and confer. Ever was there need to seek wisely, consistently for divine direction.
>
> So do we find guidelines for our church today as we move toward and into the general conference of our church in April 1972.

The coming conference was the subject again for the *Bulletin to the Patriarchs* of March 1972. Cheville described four significant conferences in which he had participated. They were: The Exacting Conference of 1919, The Strenuous Conference of 1925, The Transition Conference of 1946, and The Clarification Conference of 1968. Some conferences were not very contributive as they turned into forums for argument and debate. Some conferences did not get very far because the problems needing consideration did not get identified. Some conferences did not include God in the preparations, the deliberations, and the concludings. In some there was little sharing for consensus, for carrying together. Then he wrote, "let us build to make this conference of April 1972 a carrying together with God!"

Cheville's difficulties with administrators was felt not only in conference actions but in his evangelical ministry. In his *Bulletin to the Patriarchs* for January 1974 Cheville described the development of our church in Africa. Then he tells about his going to Africa himself in November of 1972, his baptizing Sam Agwanda and Richard Mbeche and giving Sam Agwanda his patriarchal blessing the next day in the home of George Ngangira. Three days later he discussed with Charles Neff in a hotel room the outlook for ministry among these people in Kenya. Apostle Neff was not happy with Roy's activities on this trip, and he let his feelings become known. He felt that Cheville, by these actions, was enhancing the status of Agwanda and Mbeche above that of other members of the small group there. That would counteract some of the careful plans he had made about orderly development in the area. Cheville felt that he had ministered effectively to the people involved and increased considerably their personal commitment and their understanding of the Church.

Photo 9-2.
Cheville baptizing Richard Mbeche, top, and Sam Agwanda, bottom, in Lake Victoria near Kisumu, Kenya. *[Photo: RLDS Archives]*

Cheville had more to say about these events in the *Bulletin* for January 1974, which emphasized places around the world where the good news was being shared. He quoted a letter from Sam Agwanda,

> First, I shall tell of my own experience. Sunday, November 19, 1972, is a date which I shall never forget. On that bright peaceful day in the waters of Lake Victoria two black men of Africa, my brother-in-law Richard Mbeche and myself were baptized into the Restoration Church. Roy Cheville was the minister. Since then I have been blessed in so many ways. My wife who had been ill for six years was healed. Our Baby daughter was born eight years after our first daughter. The Spirit of God has sustained us…
>
> Then on October 23, 1973 was another wonderful day. That day 12 more Kenyans were baptized in Lake Victoria, with Apostle Charles Neff officiating. My wife, my daughter, and my mother were in this group…
>
> The Church has brought me brothers and sisters on all continents. My circle of fellowship is widening. Here we are wanting to share the gospel with others. We are exploring the translating of the Book of Mormon into Swahili. We are working on the registration of our Church.
>
> Let us pray together, go forward together with the Good News. *Harambi!* Sam Agwanda

This bulletin could have been interpreted as Cheville's taking undue credit for the developments in Africa. Neff's feeling already had been that Cheville was getting in the way. Neff was focused on the organization and Cheville was focused on people.

There was general agreement among the church administrators that the ministry of Roy Cheville in the 1970s was not as effective as it had been in former years. He had lost some of his ability to capture and hold the interest of people of all ages. In late 1973 the First Presidency sent him a directive letter which Cheville described as setting forth "the policy of church administrators concerning my procedures and patterns of action, particularly in fields outside the United States."

Cheville, "at long last," responded to the letter on January 1, 1974. He carefully explained how he identified himself as patriarch to *all* the church, and came to perceive his work as patriarch to the saints in all lands. He had tried to minister in as many lands as he could. His correspondence had reached many individuals in many lands. He had gone to several fields, sometimes at his own expense. In home territory he had endeavored to use these relationships with those of other lands to develop a sense of fellowship among our people here with those of other cultures. And he had appreciated so much the response of the people.

Cheville went on in the letter to say that, though he seldom speaks of it for it is too sacred, too personal in witnessing, that there had been a vitalizing direction of the Holy Spirit in this ministry. He had been directed much as Paul had been when he was advised to go over into Macedonia. He felt a sense of frustration and said he felt hemmed in with respect to what he considered his field of ministry. He would be going later in the year to visit his daughter in Japan. As he saw things now, he would not be making contacts with the saints in Japan. "An invitation from the apostle to do so would not be acceptable, receivable now," he said.

Three other stances of Cheville's were troubling to the administration. He was continuing to push by all quiet means available to him for more conference consensus on matters of theology. He regularly made the point that the Church should have unity in seeking guidance by the Holy Spirit and enjoying fellowship with diversity of viewpoints. He continued to define problems needing to be faced by the church, particularly by the conferences. It was easy for some administrators to interpret this as inciting contention. He also wrote regularly that the Church should develop its future with its past as the foundation, paying due attention to its distinctives.

Cheville was released from his assignment as presiding patriarch on April 4, 1974. The World Conference Bulletin for that day noted,

> In recognition of past and continuing ministry through the years we honor Roy A. Cheville for service which is distinctive by the nature of his gifts and personality. In response to the word of the Lord, as acted on by this World Conference, and by action of the Joint Council of the First Presidency, Council of Twelve, and Presiding Bishopric, we pay tribute to Brother Cheville in his retirement... Many lives have been influenced for good by the personal ministry of Brother Roy Cheville. His concern and interest in the individual goes beyond race or creed and know no bounds. As pastor-at-large of the church he has indeed served as one of God's chosen ministers in these last days.

On the evening of the day of his release Cheville gave a sermon in the Conference chamber entitled "Enthusiasm in Living Zionically Today!" He noted that there is considerable apathy in religion and described that condition as "the bland leading the bland." He noted that there are other movements in which fervor has precedence over foundational factors, and he described that condition as "the blend leading the blended."

Cheville received a great many letters from Saints who heard that he was no longer presiding patriarch. The number of the letters and the degree of praise, respect and warmth they show makes it clear that his reputation among the Saints was much stronger than it was in headquarters.

The revelation which released Cheville from the office of presiding patriarch stated that he should be given the title of "Presiding Patriarch Emeritus,"

> Thus in retirement he can make his contribution but in a less demanding way and without the stress of presiding authority in the order or assignment to the field. [D&C 151:1]

Cheville was given desk space in the office of the presiding patriarch and had available the services of the staff and the facilities. He would prepare no more *Bulletins to the Patriarchs*; he would prepare no more conference plans for the Order, and he would lead no more meetings of the Order. He could preach, write, conduct correspondence, give patriarchal blessings, and travel with some restrictions. These he could do as he felt motivated and able.

He continued writing books. Three were published after 1974, *Spiritual Resources are Available Today*, [A:1975A] *Joseph and Emma Smith, Companions for Seventeen Years*, [A:1977A] and *Humor in Gospel Living*. [A:1978A] He had increasing difficulties with the editors of church publications. Three unpublished book-length manuscripts are described in Appendix A.

He continued writing hymns. He wrote many after 1974, but only one, "Let Us Sing A Worldwide Anthem," [B:1979A] was published during his life. He continued writing articles for church publications. Eight of these were published after 1974. He continued giving patriarchal blessings, 326 of them after he became "emeritus."

The extent of the directive (to which he responded on January 1, 1974) limiting his ministerial activities is not clear. He did continue to minister in his local area and to travel to some extent. He continued correspondence with friends all over the world. He increased the pace of sending letters by the congregations in which he ministered. These went to individuals and to groups where he thought contact would be particularly useful. Many responses echoed the thoughts in this message from Cecil Robbins that appeared in Cheville's January 1974 Bulletin. He wrote from Northern Ontario, Canada,

> More and more we are feeling and seeing the Church as a worldwide fellowship of people who care, who desire to share. We believe that gospel living will bring meaning, understanding, forgiveness, love and peace... We of North America greet our beloved associates all around the world. We share with you the prophetic insight of our beloved Roy Cheville who has said to us here, "We are to make

> and share good news with the whole church, with others. Good news is now happening among us." The Spirit is ministering. God strengthen you, direct you this coming year and on. Amen.

On November 7, 1975 Roy Cheville and Wayne Zion made a trip to Africa at their own expense. Cheville gave three patriarchal blessings in Monrovia, Liberia and two more in Abak, Nigeria. They attended the Nigerian Mission Conference in Abak. In Kenya they visited with George Seda, George Ngangira, and Richard Mbeche. In Barcelona they met with George Ventura. In London they stayed with patriarch Franklin Schofield. After several days with T. Ed. Barlow and Marjorie in British Isles Mission headquarters in Birmingham, they flew back to Kansas City on the 19th of November.

On December 1, 1975 Charles Neff wrote a letter to Cheville marked Confidential. He complained in scathing terms about Roy's November trip to Africa. A particular problem was that Neff had visited with Ochieng on the day before Roy gave Ochieng his patriarchal blessing. Neff stated that Ochieng felt pressured by Cheville to have the blessing and Ochieng decided he would not have it. Cheville wrote a response on December 20 saying that Neff's tone and charges were not merited. Neff had sent copies to the Joint Council and Cheville sent a copy to the Presidency.

Ochieng' himself seems to have had no negative feelings. On February 19, 1976 he wrote a newsy letter to Cheville which said in part,

> Your visit here in November last year is still fresh in my mind and I will continue to be thrilled when I remember the delightful time we had together all along from your time of arrival to departure... I would assure you that that divine mission which you undertook to visit us here left a mark which we will live to remember happily throughout our life.

On February 4, 1976 Charles Neff wrote Cheville a memo noting that the Nigeria Mission Conference in November had elected Cheville to serve as their delegate to the 1976 World Conference. He said, "We shall be pleased if you can represent Nigeria." He must have received a letter from Cheville, for he wrote again on February 25 noting that Cheville had declined to serve as a Nigerian delegate. Then he said it was disappointing to him personally and he felt sure that the people of Nigeria would be disappointed also when they heard. He went on to say that a greater concern for him was the hurt that Roy was experiencing. At some length he described his understanding of what it means to be hurt,

> Therefore, I want to apologize for the harshness of my letter, the poor choice of language, or whatever it was about the letter that was offensive to you, resulting in the wounds you describe. It was not my intention then, nor will it ever be my aim, to do anything which will hurt you or to cause a breach in our relationship. Please accept the apology.

This interchange is significant. It is probably true that no one in headquarters knew the effect of their collective actions on Cheville. At last Neff had begun to understand. When that happened, Neff's caring side came to the fore and he responded with the basic friendship and respect that he felt for Cheville. He tried to undo the damage he could now sense.

Duane Couey, for the First Presidency, wrote to Cheville on September 30, 1976 in response to some earlier correspondence about a Cheville trip to Africa. Apparently Cheville had written about a proposed plan and the Presidency had responded, raising some questions and issues of concern. In this letter of September 30, Couey said he was "very sorry for the note of disappointment and frustration which is apparent in your letter to me of September 29, 1976." He went on to explain that he understood the passion with which Roy had pursued his ministry in many places. He said, "We deeply respect this desire...but the very nature of the church is such that from time to time it is necessary for each of us to evaluate what others may feel is appropriate ministry." He had interpreted Roy's letter as asking the advice of the Presidency about his proposed trip. Then he said,

> I would like to say clearly, however, that we have not said that you may not go to Africa. This would be an inappropriate direction for us to give ... We deeply appreciate the thought which you have given to this matter and know that in many ways it has been a traumatic experience. Please be assured of our continued support and fraternity in your ministerial endeavors.

Cheville did not go again to Africa, though he maintained extensive correspondence with his friends there.

Cheville continued to look for opportunities to support church leaders. President Wallace B. Smith wrote him a letter on July 6, 1976 thanking him for his letter "and for the inspired ministry that it contained. The words of assurance and counsel are most welcome, and I thank you for the concerns that you have had and your willingness to bear part of the burden."

Phillip Caswell remembers a trip that he and Cheville made to the Orient in 1978. Apostle Sheehy told Caswell that Cheville would like to go to the Orient at his own expense, and Sheehy wanted to know if Caswell would include Cheville in his trip plan. There was some hesitation, for Cheville was then 80 years old. But they concluded Cheville could walk and keep up with younger men. They went to India, Korea, the Philippines, and Israel—all the places Caswell was responsible for. In India they had to walk long distances to reach some of the church people. They ate all kinds of food. They slept sometimes on bare floors. Once when Cheville was weak with diarrhea and tired from a long walk, showing signs of exhaustion, a group of 50 children came out from a village to greet Phil and "grandpa." All at once Cheville seemed no longer tired. He visited engagingly and shook hands with every one of the kids.

On March 6, 1980 Cheville wrote to President Wallace B. Smith to express some outlooks and viewpoints "in the light of the official directive that you and your counselors expressed to me a few months ago." He had not mentioned that directive to any person, especially deciding not to mention it to his son and his daughter. He went on to say that he did not use the term "emeritus" since he felt that, in the opinion of the Presidency, he did not have meritorious standing. He wrote,

> Your directive has struck at my convictions about my ministry. When I was a young man of about twenty-two, a minister with significant spiritual insight once spoke to me in "the gift of tongues." He said, "In your lifetime, your voice will be heard in many lands across the waters, in gospel ministry." I was told that I would mingle with those of other lands and cultures as a friend and brother. This counsel was renewed when I was ordained a patriarch. Through these several years I studied cultures, notably religions of several lands. Often my ministries were not understood or appreciated by church administrators. Now I feel that I have been dropped from this stewardship.
>
> As I have indicated, my reaction has not been one of resentment and denunciation. Rather have I had a sense of deprivation of expression in my God-called expression and assignment.
>
> Another counsel was set forth to me. As a young man, I was told in a very straightforward message that I should be a spiritual explorer. This applied especially to theology, to the designation and interpretation of our distinctive theology. Most of the time I felt a "loner," but was not lonesome. More recently I sensed the calling to express this Restoration Gospel in words and concepts meaningful to our members and to others. I dropped much conventional terminology which many retained. I sense the need to speak in terms meaningful to our people. I sense, too, the need to live with our members in laboratory expression and interpretation, rather than in seminars and the like. I see an urgency in this respect for "any new program."

Although Smith's directive to him was not among his papers, it apparently instructed him not to minister beyond a certain area. Except for one trip to Topeka, Kansas in 1981, the rest of his ministerial activity was limited to Independence.

Closing the Church's Mind

> Latter Day Saints have never been much concerned with drawing up creeds and then forcing them upon others... They said that men who were led by the Holy Spirit would come into a unity of understanding. Consequently they taught men to seek this inspiration. Men were not to be argued or compelled into a single belief about God: they were to follow certain principles and *find* God for themselves... The church has given us a wonderful heritage in this field of her teachings. [C:1933D]

> Each member [of the Joint Council] had his beliefs and assumed that they were as good as anybody else's and he was going to continue to teach those. The problem was the people out in the field would hear one and then hear another and a certain amount of confusion developed. [Clifford Cole, *Oral History Memoirs*, 1985 p. 127]

> Our people believe that we should have "unity of the faith." For many this means identity in everything. They have not discovered how there can be harmony with diversity. [pBull Sept. 68]

It started with the purest of motives—to reduce confusion among the church members by encouraging leaders to talk out their differences and reach consensus on major principles. In time, a single approach to theology emerged. It soon became exclusionary. The sequence of events could be described from Roy Cheville's viewpoint as closing the church's mind. It would lead to a great deal of conflict and then to the loss of a great many church members. Protagonists in the conflict described it as a conflict between liberals and conservatives. Cheville described it as a conflict between two approaches to theology, both of which were narrow and exclusionary. He offered a healing approach based on a refined but humble theology, but his counsel went unheeded.

Clifford Cole remembers that the story began when Presiding Patriarch Elbert A. Smith wrote an article on the nature of God, which contradicted an article by Apostle Arthur Oakman. Cole and other apostles began to hear that people out in the branches of the church were concerned—they were hearing mutually exclusive views from church headquarters. Cole knew that it was generally true that members of the Joint Council had their own views and they felt free to express them. Little or no effort had been made to get these various ideas discussed by the leadership. He felt that steps should be taken to bring some unity of understanding and mutual support among members of the Joint Council, and that was to be a first step in helping to unify the rest of the church.

A committee of the Joint Council was formed about 1956 to study the basic beliefs of the church. F. Henry Edwards became chairman of the committee and he guided it for ten years. Roy Cheville was in church headquarters for eight of those ten years. Despite his credentials and accomplishments, he was not named to this committee. In addition to his other duties in those eight years, he wrote six books, *Ten Considerations for Family Living* [A:1958A], *The Field of Theology* [A:1959B], *Meet Them in the Scriptures* [A:1960A], *Did the Light Go Out?* [A:1962A], *Spirituality in the Space Age* [A:1962C], *Scriptures From Ancient America* [A:1964A], and *Spiritual Health* [A:1966A]. He wrote 122 published articles and 97 *Bulletins to the Patriarchs*. He gave 536 patriarchal blessings. These things he did in addition to his regular duties.

Duane Couey has said [1996 letter to Ritchie] that "Two engines drove the cultural and theological task of the church" in this period. "The first was the cultural revolution which occurred in this country and in much of the west. The other was the missionary expansion of the church into non-Western, non-Christian nations." He went on to say that some members now in the leading quorums of the church had traveled widely during World War II and had learned the need to reinterpret much of the message of the church to encompass a larger field than the American church.

One landmark of the cultural revolution to which Couey referred was the disruption of the 1964 Democratic National Convention by a radical group calling attention to its own political position. In the Church World Conference of the same year there was a proposal which had the potential of producing long-term divisive disruptions within the Church. The proposal was that all appointee ministers of the Church be required to sign a statement that they believed in the virgin birth of Jesus Christ. The antagonists pro and con on this issue had marshaled their arguments and their political forces for a conference showdown. Cheville recognized a very real threat to the church and resolved that he would have to assume intellectual leadership. In doing so he gave the Church a lesson in "unity in diversity."

The issue came to public attention when the *Saints' Herald* and the *University Bulletin* carried dialogue articles on the validity of the virgin birth. As the controversy generated heat but little light Cheville recognized the threat to church integrity should a resolution requiring doctrinal unanimity pass. In a thoughtful *Bulletin to the Patriarchs* for November 1963, he pointed out the folly of trying to solve theological problems by legislation. He cited historical precedent, including the experience of the Nicean Council in 325, in which church leaders voted certain beliefs which the state imposed throughout the Empire, thus replacing freedom to think with institutional compulsion.

In the time before the conference he listened to the "agitations and perplexities" of the church people in many places. Several were inclined to bring in resolutions of one kind or another. About the preparation for his conference presentation he wrote later,

> But one resolution did come in. I was sick at heart when I read it. I sensed at once that we were facing a troublesome situation. To

> refer would give the impression that the issue was being shunted aside. I realized that attitudes would be tender and definite.
>
> I refrained from other participation. I came to realize that I would need to stand up and speak on this situation. Many would not do so. It is my conviction that a minister who places security and standing and approval by others ahead of spiritual integrity is not worthy of being a minister. I was quite aware of what the cost of speaking would be. But the future of the church was at stake. [Letter to Editor of the *Saints' Herald* 20 Apr 64]

As the issue came before the conference for discussion he said, "Saturday morning [April 11] I sat in the business session and sensed what I should do. Calmly I outlined what I should say. I was well aware of what the reactions would be." [Letter to *University Bulletin* editor Barbara Higdon 29 Apr 64] He rose and gave a masterful presentation which was not reported or recorded. Much of the content, however, is outlined in the November issue of the *Bulletin to the Patriarchs*. He said that the church should not try to legislate matters of fact. The saints should focus on the great vision of the divinity of Jesus Christ and not create distress on details. Because of his cogent logic and of his stature among the delegates, his recommendation prevailed and no resolution was passed.

Though he was calm in manner and precisely in control of his thoughts and speech, there is evidence of the great strain he was under. He said in the April 20 letter to the *Herald* editors,

> After the Saturday afternoon meeting one man asked me, "Are you willing to take the responsibility for what you have done this afternoon?" I told him quietly that I was quite aware of the responsibility and had made my choice calmly and deliberately. I sensed clarity and assurance as I proceeded. I would do it again.

But he went on in that letter to raise the question of why the *Herald* editors chose to print the virgin birth materials. He said that he considered he was "reaping fruits from the influences growing out of those articles in the *Herald* and in the *University Bulletin* and by discussions and forums in classes and campus circles." He said he was not advocating muffling the press or covering up issues, but felt the editors should be very discriminating in the treatment of such matters. "The price is too high. The gain is too low." He sent a copy of that letter to Barbara Higdon with the note added to the bottom, "This is my view. I share it. I don't mean this as a pity-me approach. I did what I did of my free choosing."

Saints' Herald editor Paul Wellington responded April 22 with a sensitive and beautifully written letter. He began with,

> I received your letter yesterday and noted the great stress you must be experiencing as a result of recriminations you have received for your stand on the Conference floor relative to the Virgin Birth issue. May I apologize for not taking the time to tell you how much I appreciated the stand you took; for I realize it placed you in a position contrary to the many who don't mind speaking their mind bluntly, and it must have been a difficult experience. I hope others take the time to tell you how much they appreciate the courage it took for a person in your position to take this stand.
>
> Your present distress is understandable, and I probably should admit being responsible for pulling the trigger which brought this issue to the Conference floor. But I don't feel I should feel basically responsible for the tensions that have built up during the years preceding this event.

Paul went on to liken his position as editor to that of Roy Cheville as Graceland professor in the many years he introduced advanced issues to his students. He said that Cheville was often criticized for being entirely too liberal and he knew that some students would become confused. He noted that Cheville had asked what was gained by bringing up the issue in the *Herald*. He said the answer was the same as Cheville's bringing issues up in the classroom—the imparting of knowledge. Paul closed the letter by suggesting they have lunch soon, and added,

You're one of my favorite people. You have always asked more questions in your teachings than you yourself could answer; but I've liked that. And I hope I'll someday have the wisdom to do what you've done in leading some people out of a shell of prejudice and ignorance.

Cheville wrote back immediately,

Your letter just came in. It is a masterpiece. I wonder if you have ever written anything better. It states your outlook with a gentle cynicism and forthright response.

My concern was not about printing materials but about adjudging time and theme and treatment in the light of the contemporary pulse.

I am not talking about the matter. You were honest and so was I.

Barbara Higdon wrote Cheville on April 23 in response to the letter he had sent to Paul with a copy to her. She said that she was probably more responsible than Paul because the article by Lynn Weldon in the *University Bulletin* (which she invited Lynn to write) came first and may well have touched off the whole discussion. She went on to discuss the charter ideas for the *Bulletin*. Church officials had criticized the way the issue was presented but supported the basic charter of free and liberal discussion in the *Bulletin*. She closed with these thoughts,

Your speech on Saturday at World Conference was inspired and I deeply appreciated your effort and the results that flowed from it. It was a unique opportunity for you to exercise patriarchal ministry.

I believe that the whole controversy was good for the church, however. We need to reaffirm the principles that you stated so well in your speech. It was encouraging to a lot of us to know that the kind of repressive fundamentalism that was represented in the resolution and its support does not prevail in the church.

In his response Cheville thanked her for her letter and said, "I felt the life of the church was at the crossroads. It was... Someday we'll meet and look ahead together."

A part of the reason that this experience was so painful to Cheville was both sides represented positions he could not support. One side was requiring belief about a fact that could not be supported. The other side was making an issue of what they did not believe. Making an issue of what one does not believe was against his principles. He had described several times a basic operating principle that he did not talk about the things he did not believe. His reason was that one cannot build a life on what one does not believe. His clearly stated intent was to talk and write about things people can build their lives on. He chose, instead of parading disbelief, to describe positive ways of looking at those same issues. When people subscribed to his positive ideas, the incorrect ideas began to drop out by their own weight.

This non-confrontational approach had worked well for him over many years. It was a part of the reason he was so effective in his writing and his teaching. It allowed him to teach advanced concepts to those who would learn, and still allow personal fellowship with those whose minds were fixed. The cost to him of the virgin birth discussion was his feeling that his conference speech might well jeopardize his personal relations with this latter group.

That conference left some imprints on a number of thoughtful members. The comments of three patriarchs were later reported,

> (1) If there is any topic that we Saints should be able to consider without rancor, without rage, it ought to be Jesus Christ. I fear we did not discuss this matter in this way.
>
> (2) I saw ministers get heated and hostile when the matter of the Virgin Birth came up. When this happens, we are disqualified to discuss the question.
>
> (3) Ministers called of Jesus Christ ought to be able to talk about him without getting riled up. We do not need to call names. We ought not threaten to quit. [pBull Feb 66]

Cheville addressed another aspect of the developing tensions in his *Bulletin to the Patriarchs* of August 1965.

He noted that he was deeply concerned about members and congregations directing their energies in speculating on "prophecies,"

> in sending materials hither and yon to people who are likely to accord with their views. Some of these "prophecies" forecast impending doom and destruction and stir up members to flee, to gather. Some of them imply denunciation of the church as it is, without constructive counsel for getting out of this presumed lethargy and lack of direction. Some of them look to the coming forth of materials hitherto hidden, that will explain "mysteries." On the whole this kind of emphasis turns out to be negative and nonproductive and dangerous.

His instruction to the patriarchs was, "Let's encourage our people to use prophecies prophetically. This means that we shall search for the mind of God and the heart of God. God wants to speak to us on the higher levels. Let's become the people who will see prophetically and use prophetically what we see."

At the Church's World Conference in 1966 a set of six objectives for the Church were presented. The first of these was "To clarify the theology of the church and unify the membership in their faith." At this Conference Edwards was released from the First Presidency and Duane Couey replaced him. Clifford Cole became chairman of the committee on Basic Beliefs. Couey began to work with Cole in implementing the work toward clarifying the church's theology.

Cole took the lead in working out "some kind of seminars that would help us discuss matters which had been dividing us." He and others felt that they should not be just talking with themselves, but have some outsiders who could listen in and advise on the soundness of ideas and their logical consistency. Cole stated that some of the church men had gone to St. Paul's Theological Seminary and had become very well acquainted with Professors Carl Bangs and Paul Jones. "It was thought that maybe these men would be good men to help us."

One can raise a question at this point about the reason Cole did not turn to Roy Cheville, who was at least as well qualified as Bangs and Jones, and had the additional advantage of knowing the RLDS church. There is no question that Cole (a 1942 Graceland graduate) knew Cheville well, loved him, and had great respect for him. At the time Cheville was released from the office of presiding patriarch in 1974, Cole wrote him a letter of appreciation saying that no one had a more positive influence on his life except his wife. At that time also Cole was surprised and rueful to learn that Cheville felt he had not been included in the Joint Council's sphere of concern, but had remained an outsider.

A committee of Presidents Maurice Draper and Duane Couey and Apostle Clifford Cole (sometimes joined by Apostles Reed Holmes and Charles Neff) began developing a series of seminars for the Joint Council. In the summer of 1966 Don Landon began work in the Department of Religious Education and soon became the arms and legs of the committee to work out a contract with St. Paul's to provide a series of seminars on theological issues. These seminars were well received by the Joint Council members, though Landon realized later that they did not reach any formal conclusions. [Donald Landon, *Oral History Memoirs*, RLDS Archives, 1971 p. 99]

Landon and his colleagues in the Department of Religious Education proceeded to develop study materials based on the content of the seminars. Some of these materials were known as "position" papers, intended to be "straw man" studies to illuminate a point of view. Some of the papers were clandestinely spirited out of the department, circulated among certain church members, and described as new dogma of the church. This action was taken by people who felt that the effect of this deconstruction process was neglecting and belittling important church principles. When this work of the Department of

Religious Education became known among church members, there was a great deal of agitation and outcry. Much of the animosity was expressed against Landon and his family. He was threatened personally. His children were attacked verbally at school and on the playground. Several times garbage was strewn across his front yard. He was surprised as well as dismayed by this response; no one had expected this kind of result. He could have used the counsel of Roy Cheville, who already had more than 30 years of experience in delivering advanced thinking to RLDS church members. And he had done it while gaining increasing respect throughout the church.

Landon had been a student of Cheville's at Graceland. He reported that Cheville stimulated a great deal of excitement in him with his courses in Latter Day Saint history and the Bible. He saw Cheville as a person he wanted to be like, and his own interests in serving the church full time were crystallized under Cheville's influence. He stated that Cheville generated creativity and did not generate skepticism. When Landon later called into question some of his earlier thought patterns he realized that there was no fault in what Cheville was doing—the fault was that Don did not understand Cheville adequately. It appears that Landon associated the thought of Cheville with his own relatively immature ideas as a Graceland student (1950 graduate), and therefore he did not think to seek Cheville's counsel.

Cheville observed that in looking to new directions the church should not abandon its past. A strong future for the church could only come out of a refining of its strengths and distinctive characteristics. Toward that end he wrote an article outlining what the church might look forward to accomplishing in the next ten years. [D:1967A] He stated that both hopeful and doubtful people were asking questions such as these:

> Where is the church going? What will the church be doing ten years from now? Such questions *ought* to be asked in an honest, searching spirit—and considered with clear insight and large overview. Tackling such questions . . should draw on large funds of human experience in many fields. It should draw on fresh inspiration from God who is ever expressing himself in new forms, in extending creativeness.

He proceeded to describe 30 issues for the direction of development of the church. These 30 items defined constructive ways of looking at many basic issues in the church such as, God, Jesus Christ, Man, the gospel, atonement, the Holy Spirit, the church, congregations, Priesthood, health, Zionic living, families, education, church quorums, common consent, revelation, worship, scriptures, etc. A description of each of these analyses is found in Appendix N.

On April 7, 1968 he delivered a prophetic message to the Melchisedec Priesthood which contained this statement:

> Again I bid you guard against viewing your own conceptions and conclusions as fullness of understanding. This counsel is directed to all my sons...

In his *Bulletin to the Patriarchs* for May 1969, Cheville presented material the patriarchs could use to help understand the issues and to counsel those they could reach.

> In our theological probings we tend to move into contrasting directions. One side preaches revelation but they want God to use the framework of yesterday. By such insistence they limit God. Often they stand against enriching the framework of thinking...
>
> On the other side some of the "free" way of thinking tend to stress pervasiveness and to discount specificity. The largeness of the revelation of God in the life and person of Jesus Christ prompts them to discount specific utterance. These will do well to remember that the all-inclusive, eternal God ever expresses what he is in specific situations and therefore in specific utterances. The eternal is expressed in the situation, in the utterance. It needs to be said again and again that God operates in eternal and universal dimensions but he expresses himself in specific, identifiable situations.

All this applies to specific prophetic expression in the living now. Leaving out the specific expression can make revelation nebulous and abstract apart from validation in the laboratory of living... [pBull. May 69]

In a 1969 letter to an editor in the Department of Religious Education, he made some of his observations rather explicit,

I veer from the legalistic, fundamentalistic, finalized theology of my conservative brothers in the church. On the other hand I feel that some of you at the head of the department are about as finalized in your brand of theology, which seems pretty nebulous to me. And I believe that some of you are as inconsiderate toward the extreme right as they are toward you. I am perplexed not so much at the differences, but at the strains and sometimes at the attitudes.

By the time of the 1970 World Conference of the church there was widespread opinion that the major conflict within the church was between liberals and conservatives. William D. Russell wrote a summary of actions at the conference, defining two issues that had become prominent in the church,

...its relationship to other Christian churches and its stand vis-a-vis social problems... Greater contact with Protestant scholarship has led to a de-emphasis of some Mormon teachings and greater stress on central Christian themes. [Russell, William D. "Reorganized Mormon Church Beset by Controversy." *The Christian Century*, June 17, 1970, pp. 769-771.]

Roy Cheville did not agree with Russell's assessment that the basic issue before the church was liberalism versus fundamentalism. For him the basic issue was whether or not the church would adopt Protestant characteristics. To do so would give the church no reason to exist, and it probably would not for long. Nor was he content to side with his fundamentalist brothers who were fixed on a different set of assumptions. He feared that in deconstructing these assumptions the church would lose sight of the bedrock foundations upon which its theology should be built, utilizing the best scholarship available. To make that point, he chose for his 1970 World Conference sermon the topic "In Palmyra Grove Today."

In that sermon he described the 1820 experience of Joseph Smith. It had its genesis in the confusion of the religious revivals on the frontier. There were many counterclaims about the way to salvation. Joseph Smith sought guidance in prayer with the result that he was directed to hear Jesus Christ. Cheville went on to say in this sermon,

> I often designate this experience of Joseph Smith in Palmyra Grove, with the divine salutation directing him to listen to Jesus Christ, as the foundational experience of the Restoration movement. This is the core of the Restoration—the restoring of personal communication with the ever living Christ... We need to place in secondary position our doctrinal notes and scriptural references and encyclopedic quotations while we get with Jesus Christ. Yes, we need to interpret him, but this requires being with him. [D:1970C]

Thus we have his appeal to church members to put doctrinal differences in a secondary position. So doing allows even conflicting interpretations to coexist. The point of unity should be in seeking to be guided by the Spirit of Jesus Christ. Those who would be guided by the Spirit would in time come to a unity of understanding. He expanded these thoughts,

> Some conditions today are very similar to those of 1820. There was clash between frontier doings and seminary-born procedures. There were weaknesses and strengths in both. A difficulty was that each side presumed it was lined up with God and had priority and proof. It is somewhat the same now. In our day, however, with pluralism functioning in so many fields, the situation is more complex, more confusing. But this much is the same: We need a core group of searching Saints who will go into the grove and ask for light. This does not mean vindication of our own formulated positions, of our own quorum protocol, our own wings of thinking. The times call for competent, conscientious, cooperative men who will be sensitive to the salutation, "Hear him!" and will respond accordingly. It is high

time for us to pray not, "God, give me vindication!" but "God, help vision grow within me!" [D:1970C]

Despite his eloquent appeals for unity in diversity, Cheville felt that the 1970 conference itself did not come to grips with its problems. The polar positions remained polar and there was not enough humility to seek divine guidance toward consensus. The problems were left to the administration for action. For those reasons, he came to view the 1970 conference as a low point for the Church.

In 1973 Cheville addressed the relationship of distinctives to survival. [D:1973C,D] He noted that the question is not "Should a church have distinctives?" but "Are these distinctives indispensable?" He called these "vital distinctives" and noted that they indicate what is happening in the life of the church. They are beliefs that are functional in the lives of the people. He went on to say, "What we think—what we do about God, Christ Jesus, man, the church, the Holy Spirit, Zion, and 'the end'—does make a difference. What we set forth as our distinctives is vitally important. And how we do this matters tremendously."

In the years since 1970, the church has moved rather consistently toward the position which Russell described above as that of the liberals. The theology which appears in church publications has been increasingly like that taught in Protestant seminaries. The experience and careful reasoning of Roy Cheville have been largely ignored or rejected by the church administration. For example, in 1980 he received a letter from the 1981 Hymnal Committee telling him that the texts of five of his hymns had been altered by the committee "to reflect the best present understandings of the church theologically and linguistically." Since the church owned the copyright, the committee did not feel it necessary to ask his permission, and they already had the approval of the First Presidency.

Some of the changes in his hymns were of the type that he would probably have agreed to. That had happened with prior publication of some of his hymns. However, in scholarly circles, it is an affront and an insult to a living author to make any changes in material to be published without the author's permission. That is undoubtedly the way Cheville felt about the action described in that letter.

BOOK XI

Macro Religion—Community

Photo 11-1.
Cheville in thoughtful mode speaking to a group in Center Stake in 1966. *[Photo: RLDS Archives]*

We Here Assembled

> Ten days after Jesus' final departure—on the Day of Pentecost—the disciples came into a full experience of this promised power. This day has often been called the birthday of the church militant. Notice carefully the conditions under which the Holy Spirit was given to the Early Church. There was perfect accord; the disciples were waiting together in prayer. When they were ready, the gift was given them... Under this added power the disciples were transformed. Their influence was magnified; their words were with power. The effect of their preaching was miraculous. [C:1935C]

This chapter is intended to introduce the series of chapters constituting Book XI, Macro Religion—Community. It deals with ministry in groups of people as opposed to the chapters in Book XII—Individuals, which deals with ministry to people one at a time.

Cheville understood that wonderful things can happen to a group of people who gather together with a common purpose. One of the most dramatic accounts is the story of what happened in the gathering of the saints on the first Day of Pentecost after the ascension of Jesus Christ. The story is told in the second chapter of the Book of Acts.

Cheville looked at the events of the Day of Pentecost to examine the conditions under which the empowerment occurred. "As explorers we need to work at finding out as far as possible what happened on that day. Then we need to designate with some soundness what should happen on a present Day of Pentecost." [A:1975A]

One of these conditions was a sense of unity. The scripture says "they were all with one accord in one place." Another condition is that they united in their mission as Christians. They were expecting guidance and were praying in preparation. Under the power that came to and among them their unity increased in that their different languages ceased to be a barrier between them.

In this context let us look again at Cheville's use of music in ministry to groups. He wrote,

> It is a fascinating experience to stand before a group of people and see them welded together into a social unity. It is a rare technique, and I have marveled at the ability of certain song leaders to accomplish remarkable res genuine song leader has precious possibilities in his baton. [D:1927E]

This description of one who stands before a group of people and welds them together refers to a song leader. Roy Cheville was one who could and did do that on a regular basis. When he planned and conducted a service he could make that sense of unity extend throughout the various parts of the service. It was clear to him that the singing was thus an intrinsic part of the service. He was very careful about the words and the tunes that were being used so that all parts of the service worked together.

A sense of unity by itself was not adequate preparation for the ministry of the Holy Spirit. It was essential that there be a beneficial aim for that sense of unity. The singing should impart cognitive content challenging the people to higher aims in their personal living. Prayer was another element of achieving that beneficial aim in the group experience.

Throughout most of his career Roy Cheville was a shining star when he was in front of a congregation of people he knew, leading their singing, praying, conducting a service he had designed, and speaking the words he had carefully prepared. When all of these were true, the members of the congregation usually reported a very impressive and effective meeting. And the experience usually energized and inspired Cheville himself. He always prepared to make *this* meeting a special experience.

Until he was nearing the age of 80 Cheville could hold the interest of all ages of people in a group in the speaking role alone. He had a very impressive ability to be understood by young and old, by liberal and by conservative.

His religion was applicable to everyday living and he was always ready to establish the connections.

Cheville was not limited to stories in the Bible for descriptions of group meetings with the presence of the Spirit. In the *Bulletin to the Patriarchs* for December 1959 he referred to the October meeting of High Priests held in the Kirtland Temple,

> Our men went out from the Kirtland conference of high priests with uplifted spirits. They could declare the Christmas message of Immanuel, "Go with us." The endowing blessing of the Holy Spirit was more than something told out of the distant yesterdays: these men knew that they had felt this promised blessing in the living now. They sensed it alone; they sensed it together.
>
> The message of Kirtland was a message of hope and expectancy and promise. It was intended that the men who felt so deeply the cheering presence of the Holy Spirit should go out and share their experience with members all over the Church. They were to go home with a message of hope. Here were some of the counsels.
>
> This was the word concerning their association with the priesthood members in their home regions: "There is need that you reach out to under shepherds to extend cheering encouragement to them through the brotherly hand and helpful word."
>
> These high priests were advised to converse in their own homes in constructive spirit and to tell their own sons and daughters of encouraging things. "I send you to these homes to bear testimony of me. Speak of the good things taking place in the church."
>
> All ministers were to return to their congregations with a testimonial report of what had been taking place in the temple. "Tell them the Spirit that leads to do good in functioning, that this Spirit has been with you in this gathering."
>
> There came a ringing call to all to go out with a message of hope. It was to be a call to repentance. This part of the message rang out with conviction: "Dwell not on terrors and disasters to come on lands and peoples, but concern yourselves with tempests of men's souls. Tell how with repentance there is available redemptive power which can lift and heal. This is a message of hope."

The following eight chapters will describe group ministry activities of several varieties which were a part of the overall ministry of Patriarch Roy Cheville.

We Sang of the Restoration

> It has been said that music makes everything go. It makes a peace meeting more peaceful; it intensifies the spirit of courage in soldiers; it makes drunkards drink more; it seduces; it uplifts, it stimulates workers; it soothes and it heals. It can touch every phase of our life. [C:1933H]

> This singing of the Restoration message is not some extra added to the regular program: it is an integral part of this seven-weeks' program. [Cheville to Franklin Weddle, 26 June 1961]

Singing was a basic in the personhood of Roy Cheville. It has been said that his hymns will still be teaching and uplifting long after much of his other work dims. He understood clearly that words of truth can be given wings of song. He dedicated a life of study to refine the truth in his words. He further refined that truth with a life of close interaction with his eternal friend Jesus Christ. Then he matched his words with tunes that would give them wings. And finally, he taught his people how to sing them.

His use of songs was not limited to those with significant content. He was at home with youth around a campfire singing simple songs with catchy tunes and rollicking rhythm. He could build enthusiasm with such songs and gradually move to songs with enduring meaning. In such settings he would remark that it was easy for youth to "transish."

His use of music was always planned to help him accomplish the purpose for which the group had assembled. In planning any meeting he always addressed first the question, "What do we want to happen as a result of this meeting?" Then, he would make all parts of the meeting flow in the direction of accomplishing those purposes. He knew that music was used to "warm people up." He observed that frequently the people were warmed up by the music and then left to cool down after the meeting with no

Photo 12-1.
Cheville leading the singing in a meeting in the lower Auditorium. *[Photo: RLDS Archives]*

Photo 12-2.
Cheville leading the singing at a youth mixer in 1958 Conference. *[Photo: RLDS Archives]*

significant changes in their lives. He wanted to make sure that the warm-up resulted in the possibility of new insights and new resolves.

The high period in his singing was in the "Doc" period at Graceland College. His skills and abilities had been developed in the "Unk" period. In the "Doc" period he wrote most of the hymns that have been widely used and published repeatedly. In this period he planned and directed the religious services on the Graceland campus, enlisting help from students, faculty, and visitors.

His ministry in these services was directed primarily at the college students. What he wanted to have happen with the services was aimed at the issues in life the students were facing. They were putting together the foundation for their careers. They were choosing the associates, including marriage partners, who would influence the way their lives developed. They were enlarging their view of the values on which these lives would be based. He wanted them to have a growing approach to religion that would keep growing as they matured in other aspects of their lives. That would involve an appreciation for the continuing use of the Bible. It would involve an enlarging understanding of the nature of divinity. It would involve an appreciation for the growing function of the church in their lives. It would involve a continual rededication of their lives to these principles.

It was in this context that "Doc" wrote his hymns. "Open My Eyes" [B:1941J] is a hymn prayer of readiness for enlarged insight and understanding. "Hast Thou Heard It?" [B:1950I] is a hymn of adventure in spiritual exploration. "All Things Are Thine" [B:1950K] is a definition of the principle of stewardship. "Conviction" [B:1953D] defines the lifelong student exploring the wonders of knowledge with the confidence of continuing exploration in companionship with the spirit of Jesus Christ. "The Christ of Every Age" (Afar in Old Judea)

[B:1955G] celebrates the universality of the mission of Jesus Christ. "Send Forth Thy Light O Zion" [B:1956W] illuminates the nurturing community in development. Each of these hymns was written out of need, for a specific purpose, in a specific program.

During the "Doc" period Cheville was regularly on committees to choose hymns for church headquarters. He had membership on the committees which produced the 1950 *Youth Hymnal* and the 1956 *Hymns of the Saints*.

The setting for Cheville's ministry as presiding patriarch was quite different. He was now minister to all the members of the church. Most of them had already established a life pattern. There was less commonality among them than with college students. He no longer had the opportunity to meet with the same group over a period of a year. Now he seldom had the opportunity to plan and conduct whole services. Instead he would serve a function in a service planned and presided over by somebody else.

He did continue to write hymns. He frequently included hymn texts within articles and books he wrote for publication. When he had meetings lined up at several places over a period of weeks or months, he prepared sermon topics complete with song sheets to be used in the several places. The song sheets would be saved at one location to be used in other places. These song sheets would frequently include original hymn texts. One of the hymns that began this way has been widely published,

"Let Us Sing a Worldwide Anthem." [B:1979A] For that hymn he used the tune "Nettleton," and he fought a losing battle to have that tune used with his text in the 1981 Hymnal.

Cheville wrote in 1959 [B:1959O] of a hymn he had written for use in the Kansas City Stake in several days of emphasis on evangelism through congregations. He said, "At the first general meeting of workers we sang this

Photo 12-3.
Cheville leading the singing during a seminar at Coe College in 1975. *[Photo: RLDS Archives]*

hymn to the tune 'Sutherland.' Each stanza has a place of emphasis—(1) the general church, (2) the congregation, (3) the family, (4) the person."

Speak thou today, O Lord;
  Speak through thy church restored!
Let Pentecostal power
  Upon thy Saints be poured!
Thy living church
  Thy witness speak
That needing men
  Thy way may seek.

Speak thou today, O Lord;
  Speak clear above world strife;
Help us show fellowship
  In congregation life.
Let deed and word
  Be well combined,
And work abound
  For all mankind.

Speak thou today, O Lord;
  Speak through our home today,
That those who tarry there
  May take thee on their way,
Our family shrine
  With altar bright
Reflect thy love,
  Send forth thy light!

Speak thou today, O Lord;
  Speak clearly now through me,
That friends who come my way,
  Thy gospel's power may see.
I'll use my strength
  To tell of thee,
And witness what
  Thou dost for me. Amen

When he ministered abroad he made every effort to have hymns available in the language of the people. He tried to learn in may cases how accurate the translations were. He did learn to sing the songs in the local language, working hard to get the pronunciation right. In that way he could come closer to his brothers and sisters in their land and in their culture.

Cheville sang with the Saints in Wales in 1961 and Clifton McArthur reported that "the Wales saints feel that Brother Roy belongs to them in a rather special way:"

> After the services of the evening we were to have supper with one of our church families. Our host asked if we minded if a few Saints dropped in for a visit, and we said that we would be glad to have them. Shortly our visitors began to arrive; each brought a song book, and one member brought his guitar. Soon the living room would hold no more and the "few" visitors spilled over into the dining room. Hardly before everyone was seated the singing had started. To have never been present when the Welsh Saints sing is to have missed something. I'm sure Brother Roy still has visions of heads thrown back, eyes closed, and deep emotion pouring forth as hymns and Welsh national songs were sung. Knowing that these were working people and that we ourselves had a very heavy schedule, Brother Roy wisely suggested about midnight that we sing one verse of "Blest be the tie that binds," and he would offer a closing prayer. [SH 1 Oct 63]

Cheville conducted a service on Good Friday in 1964 at the Eden Heights Congregation in Independence, with the theme Life Triumphant on the Cross. Included was the following poem which Cheville noted was his testimony:

Hymn of Recognition

Beside Gennes'rat's waters
  With brothers of the Way,
I meet the gracious, teaching Christ,
  Alone, at close of day.
I see how rugged fishermen,
  Who with him miles have trod
Become transformed: and I affirm
  "This is the Son of God."

Within the courts of Zion,
  I meet the daring Christ;
I sense the eternal worth in him,
  By which the soul is priced.

The way of priestly, grasping men
Fall down before his rod-
His strength beyond the strength of men:
I see the Son of God.

Before the cross on Calv'ry
I meet the lonely Lord;
I hear him pray forgiveness for
The men of scowling word.
And as he dies unflinchingly
I stand on holy sod,
Beside the soldier who confessed
"This is the Son of God."

Today in my own homeland
I face the Christ anew.
Each hour affords some larger light,
Some risk to prove him true.
Above the maze of words and creeds
Communion deep and broad
Reveals with insight born of love
How Christ is the Son of God. (St. Christopher)

On a Sunday in March 1974 the following appeared on the back of a Sunday bulletin of the Walnut Park Congregation in Independence: "This hymn voices the concerns and the hopes of our people as we look forward and into our coming General Conference. This speaks our intent to endeavor to achieve spiritual readiness before we convene and during our conference." Words written by Evangelist Roy Cheville.

Thy church, O God, now stands in need
Of thy directing light:
We need discernment, clear insight
To guide our way aright.
Draw us to climb to mountain view,
Where we behold with thee.
Help us remove the obstacles
That blind when we should see.

Unto the world we've testified
Of thy prophetic will:

Enable us to witness now
  That thou art speaking still.
With fervent faith and lifting hope
  May saints unite as one.
By thy restoring help, we pray,
  Thy work through us be done.

We trust the promised Spirit's power
  Will come and bless today,
Enlight'ning us, uniting us,
  With sure directing ray.
Amidst confusions, strains and doubts,
  Grant us assurance now,
That thou wilt guide thy Church on earth,
  Thy searching saints endow. Amen
    (Tune No. 328 The Savior at the Door)

Throughout his long life, Roy Cheville demonstrated that music provided an additional channel of communication with the Saints. It spoke of covenants and joys shared. Saintly fellowship soared on wings of song.

Of One Blood

> He has made of one blood all nations of men. . Have we not all one father? Has not one God created us? We are many members, but we are one body in Christ. [Cheville, sermon notes 4 July 1965]

Many people express a belief in the world brotherhood idea that we are all created of one blood by God. A good many of these people have difficulty applying that belief to people of a different color or culture. This was not true of Roy Cheville. He saw himself as a brother to every person. There was no exception. In his career he had occasion to demonstrate that brotherhood with many different kinds of people. In his personal and writing ministry he did a great deal to enhance the actuality of worldwide brotherhood among his people.

In his relations with people of multiple colors and multiple cultures, he was at once a minister and a social scientist. He stated that as a minister he spoke for good will and brotherhood. As a social scientist, he insisted that good intentions were not enough. "Programs of action must be constructed on the data of research; they must gear to the natural laws of social relationships." [D:1947F]

In his 1971 book, *The Book of Mormon Speaks for Itself* [A:1971A], Cheville addresses severe problems in that book's treatment of skin coloration. He tells about a young couple, both with dark skin, who came to him in 1967 for their patriarchal blessings. He had come from Ohio and she had come from Jamaica. They had met in England when each was undergoing training in the U.S. Air Force. They had been baptized in Alaska. He learned that they had great personal problems with portions of the *Book of Mormon*. They were reluctant to bring their friends to church if the *Book of Mormon* was to be discussed. They had gone to some study classes in which the darkness of the skin of the disobedient Lamanites was interpreted as representing the darkness of their souls. These two black people came to feel that they could not hold out this book to their friends with black skin. And what was their own standing with God? Were they second-rate Saints?

Cheville explored two issues with them. In one the couple came to see that many things had been read into the book in matters of race and skin color. The records of long ago had been concerned with identifying the people who had strayed. If the prevailing color had been black the identifying mark might have been whiteness. The difference was what had interested the first narrators.

The other issue he explored was an experience of fellowship that transcends racial barriers. The giving of their blessings was a Pentecost Day experience.

> As on that first day in Jerusalem (Acts 2) all fences of race and color went down. Two blacks and two whites met in spiritual fellowship, bonded by the Spirit of God. There was "one accord." Here the two of darker skin met the Universal Christ of the Book of Mormon. [A:1971A]

In his benedictory blessing to them was the message that they would minister in other lands. They were Shirley and Willy Phipps. Among Cheville's notes is one that says Shirley wrote to him saying that, "During the blessing this fear and anxiety was lifted from me. The four of us were one without consciousness of color difference. In this Spirit there would be no place for assigning any to inferior positions. I experienced the oneness of peoples."

Cheville once pointed out that Jesus did not go to minister to the Samaritans. Given the cultural climate of Israel at the time, such a venture on his part would have cut him off from the possibility of ministering with his own people. When Cheville contacted people of another culture, he tried to be aware of the attitudes in that culture which might affect his presence with and among them. He wanted to make sure that no artificial barriers might arise as a result of unintentional offense. He would take steps, for example, to help show that he did not fit the stereotype of the condescending American tourist.

Cheville believed that there was some element of divinity in all individuals. Spiritual experiences are natural to all beings now and in the past. These fundamental ideas went a long way to equip him to minister to other cultures and to people with no previous understanding of Christianity. He could say that the Spirit has been active among all peoples, but that the Christ of Judea is a more complete revealment. He could and did demonstrate the effect of the Spirit of the Christ in the contemporary acts of ministers today. That was validation.

A certain young man from Africa came to the United States in September of 1963 to earn teaching credentials at Iowa State College in Cedar Falls. His name was Anthony Jude Chindi Onumajuru. His home was in Ubulu-Ihejiofo, via Orlu, East Central State, Nigeria, Africa. He had left his wife and three small daughters at home while pursuing his studies.

At Iowa State "Tony" met a young man who had attended Graceland. From him Tony learned about the Church and about Graceland. After three semesters at Iowa State Tony transferred to Graceland. He wanted to have face-to-face, firsthand exploration with other members. He arrived at Graceland in February of 1965. There he met Roy Cheville,

> The Sunday after this young man came to Graceland, I chanced to be ministering on the Graceland Campus. I was drawn at once toward this man. His honest, exploratory spirit and his desire to help those in his country were caught up in his basic integrity. His name was Anthony Jude Chindi Onumajuru. At once he became "Tony" to me. [D:1981C]

Tony was baptized May 30, 1965. In December Cheville and Tony took a trip to Minneapolis in company of Wayne Zion and George Ngangira, another African student at Graceland. On the return trip, in State Center, Iowa,

Cheville gave Tony his patriarchal blessing. Of the blessing Cheville wrote,

> The blessing expressed approval of Tony's integrity, of his honest motivation. It pointed with assurance to happenings that he would be facing and to the commission that should be his in the evangelistic mission of the church. [D:1981C]

On January 12, Tony was ordained a priest in Lamoni. A few months later he returned to his home in Africa.

In the summer of 1967, civil war began in Nigeria. The Biafran tribe in southeastern Nigeria pushed to set up their own Republic of Biafra. Tony was of the Ibo tribe, which had no status with the Biafrans. He and his family were in the heart of this struggle. They lost their home and had to flee for their lives, though they all survived. After 31 months of civil war Biafra came to terms with the federal government and the Onumajurus returned to the site of their demolished house. They began building a new home on the site.

During the war no mail was transported in or out of Nigeria. In November of 1970 the first letter from Tony arrived. He told of their deprivations and dangers, how they had lost all of their material possessions, how they had fled from place to place.

> In his pocket he had kept "next to my heart the copy of my patriarchal blessing. It spoke assurance and promise to me and to my family," he said. "It has been a precious message to me and has carried me through many dangers. God must be wanting me to do something for him..". He closed the letter with "From Tony, your loving son with Jesus Christ." [D:1981C]

In January of 1971 Tony wrote to Cheville thanking him for his letter which included a dollar (to finance reply postage). He said that his children listen very attentively to the stories he tells about our "Great Dad In Jesus Christ Dr. R. A. Cheville, who has written to us and has sent a dollar to us." He said his gratitude for the patriarchal

Photo 13-1.
Roy Cheville with George Ngangira.

Photo 13-2.
Anthony Onumajuru and his family in Nigeria.

blessing really knows no bounds. "It is a miracle that is real in life... I did all that was humanly possible to save it in the midst of insecurity and uncertainty."

Cheville had planned to visit Tony on the African trip he made with Wayne Zion in 1972. At the last minute they learned that their visa had not been approved and that they could not stop in Nigeria. Tony learned about that after meeting plane after plane at the Enugu airport from November 20 to 24. He reported that as a "great shock." After the 24th he had to go home. There he received Cheville's letter telling him of the visa problem.

In 1975 Cheville and Wayne Zion did make their way to Tony's home in Nigeria.

> So it was in November, 1975, after the ninth mission conference in Nigeria that my friend Wayne Zion and I made our way to Tony's new home. There in an "upper room," the three of us sat at a table and partook of the Lord's Supper. In the quiet atmosphere we remembered and we covenanted. "God has guided me and protected me and mine," Tony said testimonially. "May he guide me now in using this house of mine in sharing the gospel with others and in making this a living home for Jesus Christ."
>
> We clasped hands in covenant and left the room in silence. In this spirit-endowed moment I remember the salutation and the closing phrase of a letter which Tony had sent me in November 1970. "My dear Dad in Jesus Christ," read the salutation, and he closed the letter with "From Tony, your loving son with Jesus Christ."

Cheville told of an experience at the 1967 reunion in Saltillo, Mexico. As he arrived for the week, Apostle Earl T. Higdon talked with him about giving patriarchal blessings to national ministers Juan Reyes and Humberto Salas. After three days of "*consociation*," Cheville scheduled the blessings. In those three days he sensed that Humberto viewed himself as a son of Latin America and the church was arranged and conducted in the land to the North, an English-speaking country. Cheville was a "gringo." He gave prayerful thought to preparation for Humberto's blessing.

Apostle Higdon and Clair Weldon were present for the blessing. Clair ran the recorder. After the blessing, he translated into Spanish for Humberto. Then,

> As soon as Clair Weldon was finished, I stood before Humberto and extended the hand of covenanting fellowship. I knew enough Spanish to enable me to say, "Mi hermano, Humberto, en Jesucristo" (my brother in Jesus Christ). My brother hurried to his feet and threw his arms around me in what I called "a football tackle embrace." Now I was no longer a *gringo*. We were spiritual brothers in the Church of Jesus Christ. We had had a Pentecostal experience and we were going to be brothers on a gospel mission. [D:1981C]

At the World Conference of 1970, Humberto Salas was ordained a seventy.

When Kisuke Sekine arrived at Graceland College from Japan in 1950, Roy Cheville met him at the train. They quickly became good friends. Seki was three when his natural father died. He said that in Cheville he found a new father. In time he was part brother and part father. Seki came from a Buddhist background, which Cheville understood. Cheville undertook to help Seki expand his views. Seki said in 1986 in notes after Cheville's memorial service,

> Brother Cheville worked with me very patiently and brought into my life "awareness" of the eternal nature of life and made my life profoundly meaningful. He enabled me to see God and Buddha not as some "beings" dwelling aloof in some remote heavens, but representing the fundamental entity, fundamental life, that created the universe and keeps it alive and operating, linking the East and the West. Brother Cheville introduced me to Christ, and Christ to me, leaving Christ with me and me with Christ. This was my first encounter with Christianity which eventually resulted in my conversion.

Cheville baptized Seki in 1951, ordained him an elder in 1957, officiated in his wedding to Saku on the day they were graduated from Graceland, and later gave each the patriarchal blessing. Seki still remembers the vibrant spirit of elation and fulfillment that he experienced when

Cheville said to him, "Seki, you have come into this world to share and spread the joy of God's love."

Seki was ordained an apostle in 1980 and served in that duty until 1992. He and his wife Saku now live in Ginowan on the Japanese island of Okinawa. Seki describes Okinawa as the "paradise island of the Pacific."

At Cheville's memorial service in 1986 Seki used an image from his former faith in this way,

> In my former faith, the wisdom of an enlightened one is often called THE WISDOM OF A BIG ROUND MIRROR. I can best describe this most influential man in my life, Brother Cheville, by using this analogy. Big Round Mirror—the circle is a symbol of this big perfect mirror. The mirror is thoroughly egoless and mindless. If a flower comes, it reflects a flower. If a bird comes, it reflects a bird. It shows a beautiful object as beautiful, an ugly object as ugly. Everything is revealed as it is. There is no discriminating mind of self-consciousness on the part of the mirror. If something comes, the mirror just reflects it; if it disappears, the mirror just lets it disappear. Whether it likes or not, no traces of anything are left behind. Such non-attachment, the state of no-mind, or the truly free working of a mirror, the precious lesson I learned in my early training was once again beautifully demonstrated in and through the life of Brother Cheville. Yes, he treated everyone and everything equally just like the mirror in the analogy. For Brother Cheville, a big mountain and a tiny small stone are equal. A diamond and a piece of glass are equal. Everything was equal—and that's the way Brother Cheville treated me for the past 35 years of my close association with him. Such an immaculate and lucid mind, thoroughly fair and impartial with no discrimination at all—symbolizes THE WISDOM OF BIG ROUND MIRROR.

Cheville maintained correspondence with close friends in Tahiti, Japan, India, Nigeria, Kenya, Spain, Germany, England, Holland, Mexico, South America, and Denmark. They were of many colors. Here is an event he called a "treasured simple happening."

> A few years ago I ministered in the Stone Church congregation for a week. At the closing meeting on a Sunday evening we were considering together how the congregation could reach out with good news

Photo 13-3.
Kisuke and Saku Sekine at home in Okinawa in 1997.

Photo 14-1.
Roy Cheville with Sam Kumar at the pulpit of the Choolamedu congregation in Madras, India.
[Photo: Ruth Zion]

into all the church and also how it should be receiving from congregations around the world. In closing, four of us stood together—three black men and one white man. Each prayed in his own language. One man was from Nigeria, one from the Caroline Islands. The high point for me came after the meeting when a mother told me what her small daughter had said while the four of us were standing there: "Mother, Brother Cheville and those black men love each other, don't they?" This little girl had caught the spirit of Zion. [D:1974B]

Photo 14-2.
A service in Tiona, Tahiti. Behind the pulpit left to right are Patriarch/Evangelist Denis Pioi, Everett Graffeo, Cheville, and Manua Niva. **[Photo: Ruth Zion]**

World Fellowship

> My ministry through correspondence has reached to many people in may lands. I have gone to several fields . . In my home territory I have endeavored to use these relationships with those of other lands to develop a sense of fellowship among our people here with those of other cultures... I have sought to further a sense of church-wide fellowshipping. I have appreciated so much the response of our people. [Cheville letter to the First Presidency 1 Jan 74]

When he was at Graceland, Roy Cheville had worked for decades on a program of world fellowship. He had talked and written at length on the desirability of outreach around the world. He had also taken a number of steps to implement such a program. He involved the students in an outreach program, which included having groups of them write letters to particular congregations of Saints in other lands. He publicized the return letters so that all could be a part of the warm responses that come from those who had thus been recognized and cheered.

Cheville also made a trip to Europe himself in 1949, fulfilling a long-standing dream to do so. He was warmly received and his rich ministry was highly appreciated. He also made many lasting friendships on that trip.

As presiding patriarch, he understood that he was to be patriarch to all the world. He knew that was more than one person could do, but he did what he could. What he accomplished was considerable.

He already had a number of personal friends abroad. Some had been students at Graceland. Some were the friends he had made on his trip to Europe in 1949. And he had made it a point to meet many Saints from abroad over the years at the General Conferences of the Church. His affinity for worldwide outreach extended back to childhood experiences. It was augmented by his conviction of world brotherhood in the Spirit of Jesus Christ. He had said,

> When a person and God get together in working companionship, something constructive takes place in the life of the person. As this happens, the person comes to live with all others in brotherly relations. [D:1947C]

He had held a number of weekend youth institutes at Graceland which introduced students and visitors to various cultures. Some who were students then were now appointee ministers serving in the lands to which these institutes had introduced them. They had appreciated Cheville's outreach interest and efforts, and they kept him up to date on people and activities in their various fields of ministry. When a number of ministers from the Asia/Pacific area held a conference in Hong Kong in 1975, one of their number, Howard Sheehy, wrote Cheville a letter of personal appreciation. He said he could not help reflecting upon how many of the men there had been touched by Cheville's life and ministry. He himself could date his interest in communicating the "universals" of the gospel to his participation in Cheville's Sino-Japanese Institute in 1953. About Cheville's influence he wrote in 1992,

> Roy's own enthusiasm and interest in students "from abroad" gave all of us a sense that this was a very important dimension of the life of the church. There would be no question that his influence upon a number of individuals who now serve as general officers of the church would still be bearing fruit in this regard. [Letter, Howard S. Sheehy, Jr. to M. L. Ritchie]

Cheville used every means he had to emphasize the importance of world fellowship. In "These are My People" [D:1959F] Cheville mentioned a young man from Spain (George Ventura) whom he had met in 1955 in Salt Lake City. In a similar column [D:1959K] he told of a baby son born to Kisuke and Saku Sekine in Hanno, Japan, where they were translating church materials into Japanese. The son was named Kiyoshi Arthur, Roy's namesake. In that same article Cheville tells of asking Etienne Vanaa to give a communion prayer at Graceland in the Tahitian language.

In "These Are My People" [D:1960E], Cheville mentioned a letter from Bill Horn, serving in the Dutch Mission. He first heard Bill's name when a girl at Graceland told him she was dating a fine young man who was then a Catholic. Cheville admired his ability to search and to take a stand.

In his column [D:1960J] he tells of describing for the saints of East St. Louis the good news of happenings in Japan, Brazil, Korea, and Japan. He said a Book of Acts is being written in our day.

In his column [D:1960N] Cheville again talked about George (Jordi in Spanish) Ventura of Barcelona. That summer George was translating church materials into French. (George is also fluent in English, Spanish [Castilian or common Spanish], and Catalonian [Spanish of the region around Barcelona]). In another column, he tells of a melting pot meeting in Independence:

> Sydney Jacka of Australia preached the sermon. . . At the close of the service I bade "Wiedersehen" to Franz Beil who was to leave the next day for his Germany. I shook hands with Arthur Butler, a young man from Nuneaton, England, who will begin study at Graceland. I chatted with the Directo sisters from Hawaii, greeted Christa Tegtmmeyer from Springe, Germany. I had spent the afternoon with Hae Joon Lee of Korea. [D:1960O]

In another column [D:1960R], he described receiving a letter from Marilyn Sorden at Offenbach-am-Main, Germany. She was studying in Germany and qualifying to translate our materials (particularly those for children) into the German language. She wrote that three members from East Germany were able to attend the Pfingsten conference in Berlin. They were advised not to take any conference materials back with them, not even a scrap of paper describing the conference program.

Another column [D:1960S] told of some experiences of Hae Joon Lee working in the Auditorium on translating selected materials into the Korean language. He was having trouble with the phrase "the dispensation of the fullness of time." Cheville smiled and said he might as well leave it out as most of us do not know what it means in English. Hae found a way to translate "stewardship" by using a Korean phrase which expresses how one man takes care of the land of another.

In another column [D:1961B], he described an exhibit in an institute for the women of the St. Louis District. It had a map of the world with a light glowing for each country where we have members.

A whole column [D:1961M] was devoted to a meeting of seventeen appointees in the fellowship room of the church in Rotterdam, Holland. It included descriptions of the fellowship activities of the group and of the programs and issues studied. Representatives from Scandinavia, from Germany, from Holland, and from Britain attended. A picture accompanied the column showing Richard Andersen, Fred Banta, Roy Cheville and Jim Everett. Two more columns [D:1961N, D:1961O] were devoted to aspects of Cheville's 1961 trip to Europe.

There were some remarkable events reported on that trip. Joe Bayless remembers an experience in which Cheville reached across the language barrier:

> Roy was preaching. I am not sure how all of this came about. I was his interpreter. For the closing hymn of the conference we were singing from the German hymnal. All of a sudden he dropped his half of the hymnal and bolted down from the rostrum toward the back of the church. A young couple was leaving the service early and Roy went to intercept them. Roy said later that he felt he just had to give this man a brotherly hand. They spoke for a bit and then Roy gave him a typical bear hug embrace. The only words he could say, and he said them from the heart were, "Mein Bruder."
>
> The man Roy thus embraced was Siegfried Filinger. Roy did not know Siegfried's story, but I had met him during my military days and we maintained contact. He was the leader and spokesman for a family of very good farmers in the East, which had been the breadbasket for Germany before the war. Within a few years after the

war this family had developed one of the most successful farms in Germany which was a showplace with the latest techniques and machines. When the Communists began to take over they invited the farmers to join collectives. For his family Siegfried declined. Then it became very difficult for them to get parts and supplies. A communist ideologue was sent to explain how the Soviet system would lead to world peace and plenty for all. Siegfried explained that he believed that goal but that it would come through the teachings of Christ. The result was that Siegfried and his family lived with a great deal of difficulties. They were forced into one of the collective farms. Siegfried had a strong faith, but that assurance that the presiding patriarch was a brother meant that he would not just be prayed for but he would not be forgotten. I am sure that he remembers that event to this day.

In another column [D:1961T], Cheville told of a song being recorded during family night at the Stone Church to be sent to the German Mission. They sang in German "The Spirit of God," "God Be With You," and "Redeemer of Israel." In the same column, he told of George Seda from Kenya moving into a Graceland dorm room with a student from Alaska and another from Peru.

Cheville maintained contacts with Saints all over the world. He noted that the Nigerian Mission held their first Mission Conference at Abak on a Sunday in November of 1975, and he described their business meeting as a miracle. For the first time the president of the mission was nominated and elected by the conference. He also noted that Apostle Neff had been laying the groundwork for this to happen.

In his sermons, he not only described the good news of active members in lands abroad, but he frequently had members of the congregation sign a letter addressed to specific groups or specific congregations abroad. He would tell why they were sending the letter to these specific people and would encourage his audience to grasp the idea of worldwide fellowship among all peoples who had the same spiritual Father and the same covenant with him.

The international character of today's church has not always been so common place. It is an important part of Cheville's legacy.

Our Families

> ...if God is personal and we are to be like him, then we are to become people... No other institution can do what the family can do in developing people... Happiness is a by-product. We do not get it by aiming at it. It comes as we achieve harmony in ourselves. This is brought about as we have a single, enduring purpose that unifies life and gives direction to what we do... The modern family needs something at the heart of their living to focus their energies and interests on the same goals. God can be this common center. [A:1958A]

The core interest of Roy Cheville was in the development of people. He believed this was God's central interest. This view was connected to his focus on the family, for he believed that the family can contribute to personal development in ways that no other institution can match. He wrote in 1955 that "The major objective of the church and the family is the same. They both set out to develop personalism of eternal quality." [A:1955P]

For many years at Graceland Cheville taught a course on marriage and the family. He taught it as a sociology course and the texts were written by sociology professionals. He was a professional member of the National Council on Family Relations. He sometimes invited the executive secretary of that Council to give special programs at Graceland.

In this field, as in others, Cheville's science and his religion were in mutual support. He believed that "Good families do not come by chance; they are planned." He also believed that good families do not come by merely praying for them. In 1939 he wrote a pamphlet for use in RLDS adult church school on the history and significance of the family in the work of the church. The editor noted that the material in this pamphlet was based on Cheville's Graceland College course on the family. To state the objectives, Cheville proposed setting up an inscription,

This tablet is dedicated to
the family of the future.
Lamenting over the passing of yesterday's
family is useless.
It is gone.
We cannot return to it, for conditions have changed.
We should not want to return.
Let us rather analyze the situation, see things as
they are, and
In the methods of science,
In the idealism and spirit of religions
at their best
Lay the foundation for the family that is to be. [C:1939B]

Cheville rejected the popular wisdom of his day that told a young woman that she did not need to go to college because she was just going to get married and raise a family. He assumed that the woman was taking on the most important job of all. To meet that challenge she needed all the education she could get. For the course of study on the family he wrote, "Can you select any area of study that more definitely touches your life than the field of marriage, home, family?"

He defined the family as a little society with members who live together in codes and assignment of positions. This little society is more than a collection of individuals but includes interaction between family members, if nothing more than a smile or a scowl. Individuals literally become people by these family inter-*reactions*. Through shared activities the family builds solidarity. The family must do things together—with enjoyment. "We are pulled toward the fellowships in whose activities we find satisfyingness," he said. Thus it takes planning and execution to develop and maintain those activities which strengthen each member and keep the family ties important for all.

The family is a part of a larger society that is made up of these small units. The family and the larger society strongly influence each other. The two may be in harmonious relations or they may conflict with each other. The principles involved in the relations among individuals, families, and the larger society are the subject matter of Zion, according to Cheville. That complex of issues was the subject of the chapter, "Onward to Zion" in the 1939 pamphlet.

Cheville wrote a historical account of family life among the Latter Day Saints. [A:1955P] He gave a history of the early beliefs and practices of the church, and he discussed how the views of the Utah church on polygamy had their origins in Nauvoo. During the year 1843, much attention was given to doctrinal development:

> Especially noticeable is the marked concern with the hereafter and the speculation about it. This involved both preexistence of man and his existence after death. The Saints seemingly responded to questions about their status in the world to come. Ideas appear which express concern that conditions initiated in this life, such as marriage and ordination, would need some "sealing" if they were not to cease at death. Such an atmosphere would create a responsive setting for such an idea as the "spiritual wife system." Let this celestial marriage theory take hold of someone and the next steps that lead to a rationalization about plural marriage follow easily. It is very simple to say that if plural marriage is practiced in heaven it ought to be practiced in earthly life. Especially could this be done when stories of the patriarchs of the Old Testament were brought to its support. Later, in 1851, James J. Strang in his *Book of the Law of the Lord* was quite explicit in saying that those who objected to plural marriage here would have to adjust to it in the celestial regions as they met the patriarchs and their several wives. [A:1955P]

About this Nauvoo development, Cheville noted that "social trends that seem sound and clean in their beginning can go on until they become socially dangerous; society needs continuous examination and evaluation of what is going on." He pointed out that those with a literal view of the Bible could find support for plural marriage. There is no question that the patriarchs of the Old Testament were polygamous. There is also no question that God used them and recognized them as his representatives. But it does not follow that if God uses a man as his priest everything this man does becomes 100 per cent exemplary. If that were the case then war and slavery can be sustained as patterns for today's life.

Family relationships are used to describe our relation to God. In our church we address God as our "Eternal Father." This derives from the scriptures,

> ...the Hebrews referred to God as their Father: it was the highest conception of human relationship that they knew. In the good Hebrew family the father and his child had a happy, helpful relationship. Love and trust and honor were involved. There was security, too. They tried to say that this was the kind of relationship that existed between God and his children, when the children would permit this kind of relationship to develop. Jesus used this same pattern of thinking: he addressed "Our Father." [A:1955P]

Cheville wrote another book on the family in 1958, *Ten Considerations for Family Living*. [A:1958A] It was, "An exploration by family builders, concerning the kind of families we are setting out to achieve and the characteristics that will identify them as Zionic in quality." Emptiness in marriage will always be a threat, he said, until those marrying develop a rich background of interests and a sound picture of what marriage is to be.

He cited a study which showed that many functions formerly carried on by the family have gone from the family, and will likely not return. Two major functions remain in the family: the development of personality and the expression of affection. The functions that have gone from the family are the more specific, the more tangible. The ones remaining are more intangible and spiritual.

One of the things a family can do is to introduce their children to people of quality. Cheville said,

> Many a time I have been invited into a home for a meal or for a visit or for overnight or for some social gathering, when a parent had indicated to me a reason for inviting me. Said one, "I want my boys

and girls to meet men and women who will give to them some impression that the church is worth while and has interesting people in it." Said another, "It makes a lot of difference in our family if we bring in the right kind of people." Commented another, "The soul of our family expands as we bring in individuals with big souls." [A:1958A]

Cheville had reviewed family texts and research on the family and discovered that the general run of them had nothing to say about God in the family. His own findings were that God is always with his people in their homes to the degree that they are receptive to and qualified for his presence. Home should be for people the sanctuary that sustains in good works and inspires to become.

For a meeting of families at Temple Grove in 1975 wrote this benediction,

> God, bless these families of ours,
>   That they may live together
> With thee, in thy great family
>   Through every kind of weather.
> Help them confer and pray and work
>   In varied, full expression,
> That they may go along with thee,
>   And move in thy direction.
> May every family henceforth
>   Live in consociation,
> And share the good news born in thee,
>   Of Love, of Restoration.
> With handclasp now we covenant
>   To live in worthful ways,
> With joy and satisfaction
>   Well blest by Spirit's rays.

Onward to Zion

> Many of my people came to this region that Zion might come to be. But most of them saw only in part; they did not vision the total picture of the Zionic community. They did not see the requisites for a well-rounded community in this place. Nor did many realize the necessity for righteousness as the basis for the city of their hopes. Too many sought their own safety and security. Not many understood how my Spirit is to function, to minister to them in the total process of building. [Cheville counsel to Center Stake Camp 16 Jul 66]

The idea of establishing Zion has been an integral part of the Restoration movement since the early 1830s. Throughout his career Cheville thought and taught about Zion. He sought to increase his own understanding of the concept and to share with other Saints the result of his personal search.

The concept of Zion appealed to the 16-year-old Cheville in his introduction to the Church. Although the idea of present-tense contact with God was the primary appeal, closely associated with it was the idea of personal development being conducted in the society in which the Saints lived.

Through the years Cheville enlarged his understanding of the aims for society in the work of the church. He recognized that society helps shape the individual and the church works to help shape the society. These objectives lie deep in the nature of the church and the distinctiveness of its programs. One of Cheville's presentations giving church programs and distinctive approaches was reported by Bill Russell in 1963 under the title, "Report on the Older Youth Conference:"

> He described the church as a fellowship and listed its seven basic functions:
> (1) a laboratory for developing saints,
> (2) a clinic for furthering spiritual health,

(3) a witnessing community,
(4) a dynamic nucleus in the social order,
(5) an evaluative commission in contemporary life,
(6) a fellowship of the committed, and
(7) a prophetic company of saints who speak forth for God.

Dr. Cheville also outlined eleven distinctives of the Restoration church:
(1) contemporary divine direction,
(2) specialization of function in multiple ministerial offices,
(3) theocratic-democratic theory and operation,
(4) congregational centralizational functioning,
(5) administration of sacraments,
(6) social gospel with the program of Zion,
(7) present-life salvation,
(8) identifiable experiences in restoring the church,
(9) structure for spiritual functioning,
(10) the dynamic of the church—the Holy Spirit, and
(11) the guidance through multiple and continuing scripture. [SH 15 Aug 63]

In a prophetic message to a conference on Zionic Community in 1969 [see Appendix G] he stated that the concept of Zionic community has always been in God's eternal program. "Ever is it designed to bring into realization the quality of person in my design for man. Ever is it intended to express my gospel in corporate living. Ever is it needed to provide testimonial ministry to the many millions of people in all the world."

The message went on to say that many have not understood. Some have wanted Zion as escape from turmoil. Some have expected deliverance from responsibilities. Some have hoped for security and ease. Many looked for benefits for themselves as they interpret benefits. Some have presumed that one day a glorious city would be set up that could be exhibited to draw others to the church.

> I say again that Zion does not come by such observation, that it does not proceed with exhibition. It cannot be pointed to with designation, "Behold! Here is Zion!" The Zionic way of living can be appreciated as people dwell with those who live Zionically... [see the chapter on Perception of Divinity]

I charge you to return to the congregations of your residences and work to bring to realization Zionic living among my Saints. Encourage them to work together in happy, worthful community.

Fred M. Smith had written a hymn about Zion in 1922 with the title Onward to Zion. With the recurring line, "Zion the beautiful beckons us on," it expresses optimistic expectation, but it did not have the how-to-do-it content that Cheville preferred in hymnody. For his ministry in the 1950s. Cheville wanted a hymn with more functional content. The result was his hymn, "Send Forth Thy Light O Zion,"

Send forth thy light, O Zion!
Out from thy towers shall go
The radiant beams a people
In tune with God can know.
Upborne by higher concepts
Of God's eternal call,
Let shine afar the guide-lights,
Revealing God to all.

Send forth thy love, O Zion!
Thy call is from above,
To make on earth incarnate
Christ's sacrificial love.
For by the saints outreaching
To those their lives can bless
Shall come Zionic witness
To heal earth's brokenness.

Send forth thy life, O Zion!
Not for thyself alone
Have come life-giving powers
By which the soul has grown.
Thy promise builds a people
Well-skilled in mind and hand.
Thy life is like a leaven
Of hope in every land. [B:1956W] Lancashire

For a series of meetings in Canada Cheville wanted to describe a contrast to those living in Zionic relationships of eternal quality. He looked to the description of the Israelites wandering back and forth in the desert between Egypt and Canaan. They were in the wilderness of Zin. Cheville created the adjective "Zinic." It denotes wandering with an attitude of complaining and hopelessness. Here is his contrast with Zin and Zion,

> In this complex world of ours
>   In this wilderness of Zin,
> Let us build up mission centers
>   That transmit light from within.
>
> Here in our Ontario mission
>   We can plan this buildup now,
> Nourished, guided by God's Spirit,
>   With which God will us endow.
>
> In these times confused and pressing,
>   In this troubled Zin-ful world,
> Here in our Canadian country
>   Zion's standard is unfurled. [Cheville notes]

At the close of a Center Stake Encampment, on July 16, 1966, Cheville gave a message he described as benedictory counsel. In that message was the call to realize that Zion is now in process. The message went on,

> I admonish my people to sense the essential spiritual nature of Zion. At the heart of Zionic living is love that is understanding and outreaching. This love inheres in your God, who is the Source of Zionic living. Let material wealth and the things that wealth can buy never become the ends of this community. Let these be desired and employed as means for bringing to pass true spirituality. Measure not Zion in terms of increase in numbers or in terms of recountable material possessions. Be not concerned with publicity citations which herald social approbation. Look rather to worthiness in saintly living. Be concerned with spiritual health and spiritual competency in this community of Zion. The increase will follow...
>
> My people, I call you to move forward with cheerful expectancy. Remember that I have many forces at work for good in this Universe, not known to you...

That message advised that many will cling to inadequate conceptions of what Zion is to be, but willing saints are to move ahead. "The day has come when those who will not advance are not to hold back those who want to be on the way. Go forth to build the blessed community. You will not be building alone."

On the evening of the day he was released as presiding patriarch Cheville addressed the World Conference assembly in a sermon. [D:1974A, B] He stated that he had given careful thought to what he would say on this occasion, and that he felt led to counsel the Saints. He warned the people, "Woe to those who are at ease in Zion!" This applied to those who would not face up to problems. It applied to those who would turn over their problems to God and expect him to work out everything for them. It applied to those who would leave decisions and interpretations to priesthood men in ascendant places.

The message continued with the warning, "Woe to those who are at odds in Zion!" This applied to those inclined to dwell on the negative and the unpleasant. It applied to those who sow seeds of discord, of despondency, of dissension. "These are they who neglect to note what is good, what expresses divine empowerment and guidance today." He said further,

> Go, my Saints, to bring to pass Zion in the circles of your home, of your congregations, and you shall be blessed with the empowerment, the endowment, the enthusiasm of my Spirit. [D:1974B]

To the Mormons

> I shall always have a deep concern for our work in Utah. It looked to me that for the first time we were beginning to take a wholesome approach to our work out there. Too long we have battled and argued. What is needed is an inspiring testimony and a wholesome fellowship, these can speak to the people of Utah. [Letter to Richard Hope, 1961]

> I look forward to meeting with you and shall be happy to continue the friendly relationship you established with President David O. McKay. With every good wish. Sincerely yours, Joseph Fielding Smith, President. [1970]

Roy Cheville had been concerned for a long time about animosity expressed by our church people toward the people of the Utah church and vice versa. He did something about it. He made friends with people who were leaders of the Mormon Church over a period of years. He also worked to develop within RLDS workers in Utah and other lands a friendly spirit which would aid communication with those who might be looking for an alternative to Mormonism.

In his "These are my people" article for May 30, 1960 he told about being in Utah for three days and being thrilled by what he saw. "During the recent two or three years women and men of excellent quality have affiliated with the Reorganization. They are inclined to testimony rather than to argument." One of these people was Richard Elmo (MO) Hope. Richard was pastor of the RLDS branch in Provo. He had grown up in Utah and had many Mormon friends, having been a Mormon himself in earlier years. His wife Norma came from an RLDS family, the Carters of Carterville, UT.

Strong bonds of friendship developed quickly between Cheville and Hope, and these bonds extended to the whole family. The Hope children were Richard, Faith, Carl,

Photo 17-1.
The Richard Elmo (MO) Hope family in 1974. Mo and Norma are in the front row. Roger is in the middle. On the back row are Rosemary, Faith, Richard, Carl, and Nancy.

Photo 17-2.
Cheville in travel mode in Utah in 1964. Cheville, Carl, Faith, and Richard Hope.

Nancy, Rosemary and Roger. Correspondence between Cheville and the Hope family was regular and frequent. They discussed ministry for people in Utah, and they regularly expressed personal sentiments and messages of uplift. As often as he could, Cheville arranged his schedule so he could visit in the Hope home. The letter of 1961, quoted in part above, also contained these encouraging words,

> In all of the pressing situations and annoyances may you never lose the vision of what can be done. .. I would like to sit down with you, Mo, and have a good heart to heart conversation. As I said before, I have a great big warm spot in my heart for you and shall always esteem you as my brother. I am relying on you and do not want anything to get in the way of your bringing to the fore the ministry you can give and the testimony you can express.

In 1963 Cheville wrote an article for the *Christian Century* with the title, "Mormonism on the Move." [D:1963O] An even handed status report of the Utah and the Independence Latter Day Saint churches, it described the movements and then identified seven basics the two groups have in common:

> (1) belief in the decline of Christianity through the centuries and the consequent necessity for "restoration" of the gospel and the spiritual dynamic of early Christianity;
> (2) the prophetic calling of Joseph Smith and others in effecting this "restoration";
> (3) the constant renewal of ministerial authority through continuing revelation;
> (4) the centrality of Jesus Christ in this revelatory experience;
> (5) re-establishment of the church of Jesus Christ pictured in the New Testament, with the polity and spiritual dynamic and the rites and sacraments described there;
> (6) the present-tense spiritual fellowship of saints, centering in a community known as Zion;
> (7) multiple canons of scripture, including the Bible of the Hebrews and the early Christians, the Book of Mormon and various contributions made in later and present times.

The article then described problems which each church would need to face. The Reorganized Church, he said, faces two major questions:

> (1) the relationship of administrative groups in conducting its affairs, together with the operation of hierarchical and democratic aspects of ecclesiastical government; and
> (2) identification of basic Latter Day Saint theology.

Cheville received a letter from President David O. McKay of the Utah church saying that it was kind and gracious of Cheville to write on September 7, 1964, extending thoughtful congratulations on his ninety-first birthday. "Your remembering me and your expressed sentiments of good will and friendship contributed much to the joy and satisfaction of the day. I especially appreciate your faith and prayers in my behalf." He said that Mrs. McKay joined in the expression of appreciation and in sending warm regards to him.

In June of 1966 Cheville wrote a letter to the pastor of the Provo, Utah branch. He said, "I find the argumentative, polemic spirit toward Mormons are diminishing." He commented on the need for evangelistic motivation and message to be constructive and contributive emphasizing common ground.

Cheville wrote President McKay in November of 1967 asking for an appointment to see him on December 6. Apparently they did meet, for McKay wrote him September 17, 1968 thanking Cheville for the letter sent on his ninety-fifth birthday saying, "I remember with appreciation our meeting last December, and the prayer offered on that occasion. Thank you again for your thoughtfulness in remembering me on my Birthday anniversary and for your expressions of friendship and goodwill."

On May 24, 1969 Cheville attended the ground breaking or dedication of the Mormon Visitor Center in Nauvoo. The next day Cheville wrote to the Honorable David M. Kennedy, Secretary of the Treasury of the United States who presented one of the dedicatory speeches, "Yesterday I listened to you and joined with you with sense of uplift. It was so wonderful to catch the spiritual tone of your message, the deep concern about the spiritual condition of our nation." Some time later Cheville said in a private conversation that he would like to baptize David Kennedy into our church and ordain him a patriarch.

Cheville received a letter dated May 30, 1969 from J. LeRoy Kimball, M. D., President of Nauvoo Restoration, Inc.,

> It was a great pleasure to meet you in Nauvoo and have you participate with us in the ground breaking for our Information Center. We feel we are on common ground with you here in this historic city of Nauvoo, where our Prophet, yours and ours, lived, spent one of the most productive periods of his life, and died a martyr for the Cause of Truth. I am grateful that you honored us with your presence and look forward to seeing you again.

On February 3, 1970 Cheville wrote to the new president of the Utah Church Joseph Fielding Smith, introducing himself and giving his church position. Then he noted that he had met George Albert Smith while he was the church president and they continued as friends until he died. He noted that during their last conversation he made this parting comment,

> President Smith, you and I are going to be differing, and differing very much in matters of theology, in matters of church administration, in matter of temple theory and practice. The question is, can we differ as Christian gentlemen?

He went on to say that next he met David O. McKay and respected the genuine spirituality of this good man. They met three times in his apartment in Hotel Utah. The last time was in early September of 1970. He was writing these things to indicate that he had endeavored to be friendly and had been satisfied with the outcome,

> So now I am writing to you as you come to the place of responsibility in leading your people. May you be blessed by the Good Spirit in enlisting them and in directing them! This letter is simply the greeting of a man who wants to replace hostility with friendship, misunderstanding with communication.

Cheville wrote again on April 22, 1970 to Joseph Fielding Smith, President of the Utah Church. He referred to his previous letter and noted that President Smith had responded with a friendly letter. Cheville said he would be passing through Salt Lake City on Monday, May 25 and would like to meet him. He said,

"I have no requests to make, no issues to discuss. Rather do I wish to greet you and meet you in gospel good will." Smith responded, "I want to assure you that I will be most pleased to see you once again and visit during your brief stop over." He offered to make arrangements to have someone pick Cheville up at the airport and bring him to his office. He said he looked forward to meeting with him again and "shall be happy to continue the friendly relationship you established with President David O. McKay."

That meeting took place on schedule and Cheville went on to the Richard Hope home that afternoon. He made a presentation that same evening at the Provo-Orem RLDS congregation on the good news of the gospel in Latin America.

On June 3, 1970 Cheville wrote to President and Mrs. Joseph Fielding Smith to express appreciation of their arranging to meet him as he came through Salt Lake City Monday, May 25. "I was so happy that I could meet both of you together. Twice when I met David O. McKay, his wife was with him."

Smith responded on June 8, 1970 saying, "It was a great pleasure to have you visit with Sister Smith and me during your brief stopover in Salt Lake City Monday, May 25, 1970." He went on,

> During the course of our conversation you expressed the hope that a book would be written about my grandfather, Hyrum Smith, the first patriarch to the Church. I mentioned then that one already had been prepared, but unfortunately I did not have a copy of "Hyrum Smith—Patriarch" by Pearson H. Corbett. Brother Corbett is a great-grandson of Hyrum Smith.
>
> I think you will find this book very interesting reading. It tells a great deal about a man whom we both love and respect and who stood at the side of his brother, the prophet Joseph, as they both sealed their testimonies with their blood. Sincerely yours, Joseph Fielding Smith, President.

Cheville responded to Smith on June 18, 1970, thanking him for sending him the copy of *Hyrum Smith, Patriarch* by Pearson H. Corbett. He waited three days to reply until he could finish reading the book. Cheville had observed that his idea had been that such a book might be called "The Man Who Stood by His Brother." And he said that quality stands out so clearly in the story and the interpretation given by P. H. Corbett. He went on,

> I have always said that I would like to have met Joseph Smith, Jr. with the warmth, the friendliness of his personhood. I can add to this now the comment that I would like to have been with Hyrum

who was gifted in his caring for others and in his amicable and reconciling nature.

As I read this story again, particularly the story of Nauvoo, how much I wish that some things might have happened otherwise. In the long run, however, there was a fitness that Joseph and Hyrum depart together as they had ever walked side by side.

Again, thanks so much for sending the book. This is the first story with continuity that I have had concerning Hyrum Smith, your grandfather.

I trust that you are being blessed with strength, stamina, and spiritual sight for the calling you are carrying on.

And give my regards, my greetings to your wife, Sister Jessie Smith. Sincerely, Roy A. Cheville.

In early September of 1970 Cheville had space between two obligations in Colorado. Traveling with Wayne and Ruth Zion, he used that time for a trip to the Hope home in Orem, Utah and a visit in Salt Lake City.

On November 17, 1970, Cheville again wrote to the First Presidency of the Mormon Church in Salt Lake City. He had been to the historic properties at Carthage, Illinois and was complimenting the Utah church on the way the properties were being maintained and the way he had been informed while there. On December 4, 1970 all three members of the First Presidency of the LDS church, Joseph Fielding Smith, Darroll McGee, and N. Eldon Farmer signed a letter to Cheville. They expressed appreciation for Cheville's letter to them.

In January of 1971 Cheville, traveling with Wayne Zion and Roger Bendorf, had spent New Year's with Ivan Vallier in Santa Cruz, CA. Detouring in their trip to spend two nights with the Richard Hope family, Cheville met with members of the Utah First Presidency in Salt Lake City. Then, at Richard Hope's arrangement, he met with a fundamentalist Mormon family who practiced polygamy.

On August 5, 1971 Cheville wrote to Joseph Fielding Smith, President of the Utah Church as follows:

Dear Brother Smith:

In last evening's paper I noted the news item that your wife Jessie Evans Smith had died in the outcome of a heart attack. I reread the article to be certain that I had read it aright. The last time I saw her she seemed in such good health.

The first time I heard her sing was several years ago in Oakland, California. The Tabernacle Choir was singing and she was a soloist. Then I noted and appreciated the deep rich quality of her voice. The last time I met her and heard her sing was at the dedication of the Visitors' Center here in Independence. That evening she sang "Bless This House, O Lord, we Pray." Her singing stood out that evening.

When I met her in your office in Salt Lake City in May 1970 she greeted me with such friendliness, with such cordiality. Then I sensed that she was considering living with you, caring for you as a foremost stewardship. She was considering your needs and your health with love, with an unusual consideration and sincerity.

When I read the item in the paper last evening I resolved to express my condolence, my remembrance in a letter to you. Yes, you will be missing her very much. It should be so. Friends do not remove the loneliness and the apartness that comes, but they can ease the feelings of a friend by letting this friend know that another cares and would like to help.

My own wife died some ten years ago. I missed her, but I did not want her to live on and suffer. I devoted myself in an extra way to the cause of God to which both of us were devoted. In this faith, in this cause, may you find surcease and may you find hope.

I shall say this simple prayer in benediction, "God be with you!" Sincerely Yours, Roy A. Cheville, Patriarch.

Cheville wrote to Richard Hope August 9, 1972 saying that he and Bill Bendorf were coming their way. "The Lord willing and the Hopes assenting," they would arrive Monday afternoon September 4 and he was applying for bunking quarters. Then on Tuesday he and Bill would be in Salt Lake City. "Perhaps I shall try to call on Harold B. Lee. He wrote me a friendly letter in response to the one that I sent him when he was made the president of the church." They would be back to meet with the Orem-Provo Saints on Saturday night in a meeting of "good newsing" in the church today.

In June of 1974 Cheville wrote to Arthur Haycock of the Mormon Church to ask when their October conference would be held and if he could be assured of getting in. He also wrote Richard Hope to say Wayne Zion would be with him and to ask if they could stay.

Arthur Haycock, Secretary to President Spencer W. Kimball of the Utah Church wrote Cheville on July 12, 1974,

> Dear Brother Cheville: Thank your for your kind letter advising that you plan to attend our General Conference in October. Sessions will be held at 10:00 a.m. and 2:00 p.m. each day, Friday, Saturday, and Sunday, October 4, 5, and 6. When we get closer to the date, I will obtain and forward to you reserved seat tickets for yourself and your friend who will be accompanying you.
>
> I assure you that you will be most welcome and that no advance notice will be given of your coming so that you can relax and enjoy the services. The fact that you are coming not out of curiosity but in the spirit of understanding and friendship does not surprise me. I have long appreciated your friendship and know of your great interest in the work of the Lord. Anything we can do to add to the pleasure and success of your visit will be a privilege.
>
> I had learned something regarding your retirement but did not know the actual status of your relationship as Presiding Patriarch Emeritus.
>
> Anything you and I can do to help our people understand one another better will be a contribution, I am sure, that in the final analysis will be appreciated not only by them but by the prophet Joseph whom we all love and revere.

Cheville did attend the conference without fanfare and without notice, though that took a bit of doing. "Mo" Hope explains that everybody in the Utah conference votes in favor of whatever the hierarchy proposes. Cheville told Mo that he voted on a lot of Utah stuff. He would have been noticed if he had not voted. He had to do so to keep his seat in the conference.

On July 30, 1974 an invitation was sent to Cheville from the Washington, D.C. area inviting him to a special preview tour of the LDS Washington Temple Friday September 13, 1974. After completion of the structure but before the dedication, the temple was open for inspection by non-Mormons. The letter was signed by Spencer Kimball, Weldon Tanner, and Marion Romney. Cheville made the preview tour in the company of Jack Gernhardt. Gernhardt reports that Cheville was very interested, but after getting a personal feeling of the place, they left before the visiting time was up—Cheville did not wish to remain longer. He felt that he had the measure of a building which would function primarily for things in the hereafter. One of the functions of the temple would be baptisms for the dead. Of this function Cheville had said, "Think what that implies about the nature of God."

On February 14, 1975 the Saints in Orem sent a letter to the branch in Oxford, England. This branch was composed essentially of converts from the Utah LDS Church. The letter noted that most of their members were converts from the Mormon faith, including the Pastor. Along with the letter they sent a copy of the *Doctrine and Covenants*. The Oxford Saints replied with "heart felt appreciation for the love and friendship in which your letter and gift expressed your welcome to us into Christ's Church." They noted that their branch was organized March 17, 1974.

The former LDS pastor of the Oxford group, Graham Stott, had gone to Brigham Young University to earn a doctoral degree in English Literature. He happened to attend the RLDS church in Orem only to discover through the letter from Oxford that his whole branch had joined the RLDS church. He joined also.

In his contacts with Utah Mormons, Cheville's sense of humor often broke the ice. In 1979 when he was on the campus of Wright State University in Dayton, Ohio, he was introduced to the Dean of Science and Engineering. The introduction included describing Cheville's office and the fact that the Dean was a member of the Mormon

Church. Cheville immediately asked with a smile, "And is your tithing paid up?" Without hesitation and with a matching smile the Dean responded, "As a matter of fact it is."

History Is Useful

> Robert E. Lee is credited with saying, "History teaches us hope." A one-minute squint at the human story will not suffice; it cannot put things together and disclose trends and relationships. [A:1975A]

For Roy Cheville history was an important tool. When he addressed a problem he wanted to know the background of that problem. It was not long after he was named to the Presidency of Lamoni Stake that he wrote (with or for a committee) a pamphlet on the history of Lamoni. [C:1929E] Not long after he began teaching at Graceland College he wrote a pamphlet on the history of education in the church. [C:1930J] A few years after being ordained a High Priest he wrote a review of High Priests in History. [D:1933B] Shortly after he became presiding patriarch he wrote an essay on the history of patriarchs in the church. [pBull Nov 58] He maintained that pattern of studying the history of his current activities, and the issues he was concerned with. To explore these the reader can consult 1934A, 1936I, 1937A, 1939B, 1942B, 1946A, 1955A, 1960A, 1062A, 1963Q, 1970A, 1977A.

Whenever he visited a country that was new to him he studied the history of that country. He wanted to know the background to better appreciate the values and the outlook to be expected of the people. For example, that study allowed him to understand that he would be perceived as a "gringo" by Mexicans, an insight that helped him to achieve the status of brother. Similar study sensitized him for ministry to black Africans.

Cheville wrote in his notes some observations about developments in Tahiti:

> Early in 1971 I was in the Society Islands. In earlier years as I had come to see and appreciate the Polynesian ways of living, I questioned picking these Saints up and transporting them to Jackson County, Missouri. I came to believe that there should be a colony or

colonies, Zionic and evangelistic in nature there in the Pacific. Such ministry was needed there. And something of high merit has happened...

Commercialism, tourism and the like brought break-up of traditional ways. The old large Polynesian family was disintegrating. With this came social confusion and social disintegration... The inherited educational system with its lycee left those who did not pass examinations to get into lycee stranded without further opportunity...

A few alert missionaries saw this. They consulted with French authorities. Out of all this came provision of a school with applied emphases for those who would not be attending the lycee. The French government gave and gives our church annual subsidy for this school. Jean Bouissou, who came from Paris some years ago, is director. We have more applications than we can handle. Everett Graffeo led the way in studying what was taking place in the family. Classes and counseling services were supplied... Here is colony in operation. [Cheville notes]

In 1971 he wrote about understanding Korea:

I was in South Korea to be with the members of our Restoration Church in that land. I had a week in Seoul where I got in touch with the story of Korea, of the present condition of things, and the story of our entry into this country. Then I went out into the more open area, about seventy miles from the capital city. Out there was where our health center was located. There I met and appreciated the unusual pioneer health work of Esme Smith, who had come from Australia. I walked out into the country areas and saw and greeted the native Koreans in their own setting.

I did not explore to find problems in order to construct a negative picture. I studied to picture rightly the Korean Mission Field. First I saw how Japan and China had had a long period of influence, sometimes of domination. I saw now the break up of the people into North Korea and South Korea with harsh antagonism and significant differences. I came to see the complexity in religions, which included Buddhism, Taoism, Confucianism, Shintoism, and Christianity of diverse church backgrounds. I saw the endeavors and the complications in trying to get an effective government. And there were many more problematical situations in health matters, in education, in family life, in agricultural operations. Here was a country in World III. I looked at all this with exploratory spirit and evangelistic intent. This picture is requisite for sensing of this benedictory song" (God Be With You Til We Meet Again). [Cheville notes]

Cheville understood the Bible, the *Book of Mormon*, and the *Doctrine and Covenants* in their historical setting. He attempted to see the events described in terms of what was going on in the culture at the time. Prophetic utterances he saw as always being related to specifics in the culture, though the intent would include principles of eternal quality. He was looking at the Scriptures as a historian.

He said that in his continuing quest to understand God he came to see the Scriptures as "selected writings of those who had lived before me, of those who had in their times sought to understand God." He saw the ones that were selected as scripture as being worthy because they were written by "prophetic pioneers" who saw beyond the practices of their day. They thus had an unusual quality in them. He described some of the results of this kind of historical inquiry of the Scriptures:

> At my best I caught the spirit of prophetic searching in these spiritual adventures. I sensed how they phrased their insights in the thought world and the language patterns of their times. They phrased what they saw of the eternal and the universal in the most advanced forms they knew. I caught something of their spiritual genius as I lived with them. This genius always has impelled me to go on in the quest they were advancing. [Cheville notes]

From Our Group to Yours

Roy Cheville was convinced that letter writing was an important ministry. He set one objective of letter writing to help church members everywhere appreciate that they were a part of a worldwide fellowship. One way he accomplished this was to have a group to which he was ministering sign a letter to some other group of church members. Cheville would write the message out, usually typed. He would have space for signatures. During the service he would explain the contents of the letter and ask everybody to sign it. Usually the letter would be signed by nearly everybody present at the service. When it was signed, Cheville would see that it was mailed.

It is difficult to tell how many letters were written by Cheville and sent from one group of Saints to another. The letters were sent wherever Cheville went. He chose the Saints to receive the letters based on his understanding of the need for a lift and the need for all groups to feel remembered and included as Saints of Jesus Christ.

The letters that follow are among those that happened to survive.

On October 9, 1968 Cheville invited members of the Stone Church Congregation in Independence to sign a letter to the Saints in Zwaagwesteinde, the Netherlands. It was a letter of greeting of good will and support. In that week the Stone Church group was meeting around the theme, *Good News and Good Hope in Zion.* They were thinking of their congregation as a unit in a worldwide fellowship. It was appropriate to select this congregation in the Netherlands because the Stone Church congregation understood how long the Dutch Saints had worked to procure funds for their church house, which was now open. "May you be strong and dependable in your witnessing of the Restoration gospel!," they wrote.

They reported singing a stanza of "The Old, Old Path" in Dutch.

On May 28, 1969 Cheville had the Saints in Slover Park Congregation in Independence sign a letter to four Saints in Cordoba, Argentina: Tolstoi Gimbatti, Oscar R. Parodi, Nieves Pitarch, and Juan Althabe. Cheville had told them about a letter from Gimbatti and Parodi to Apostle Earl T. Higdon, followed by the visit of Higdon and Darrell Mink to Cordoba, and of the recent baptism of the four addressed. The Slover Park letter said in part, "We greet you as brothers and sisters in the great Restoration Church. . This evening we are remembering you in our prayers. We are praying that the Holy Spirit will strengthen you and assure you."

Another letter to Cordoba had been sent from Rich Hill. Higdon wrote Cheville on December 17, 1969, saying that Robert Turner read the letter to the congregation at a baptismal service on November 29. The Saints in Cordoba appreciated the letter very much. Higdon thanked Cheville for his "warm, supporting ministry of the past year."

On December 23, 1969 Bob Turner wrote Cheville from Lima, Peru:

> I have been behind in my correspondence and have thought many times of writing to you, as you have been so wonderful in writing to me and to the Saints here in various parts of South America... I now have before me a letter that you sent in fellowship with two other brethren: Bro. Wayne M. Zion and Bro. Jim Nisley. At that time you were in the New Mallery Monastery, Iowa. I was very happy to hear from you and also happy to know that Bro. Higdon had shared with others the marvelous experience that the Lord afforded us as we have ministered, or tried to minister in Lima and Cordoba. I am happy in the thought that such experiences are being shared with others so that they may know and be assured again and again that the Lord does work in the hearts and minds of all people, everywhere.

On November 11, 1970 the Springfield, MO, branch sent a letter to Springe, Germany, "Bruder Roy Cheville, der

Patriarch des Kirche mit uns ist. Er in Springe in 1949 wart. This evening we are thinking of our youth around the world, carrying on "zusammen with Gott." From the youth in Springfield, Missouri, USA.

On May 22, 1971 Cheville wrote a letter of greetings signed by an encampment of the priesthood of the Arizona District to "our brothers and sisters who will be meeting in the reunion in Norway, July 10-18, 1971."

> You would be at home in our camp grounds. We are on mountain highland with pine trees in abundance. So our grounds are called Whispering Pines Camp.
>
> While we are concentrating on what we are going to be doing in our own congregations, in our own families, we are wanting to see that what we do is part of the outreach of our total church. We want to express our worldwide mission and message and experience fellowship with our Saints elsewhere. So we have chosen to send our greetings to you, in the reunion of the Scandinavian mission in our church.
>
> Our teaching minister in this camp school is Roy Cheville, presiding patriarch of our church. He carries a deep interest and a warm love for Saints in Denmark, in Norway, in Sweden. We join him in wanting so much that you will be richly blessed in your reunion this year.

On August 4, the Zioneer Youth sent from Camp Doniphan a letter to Ririfatu Mariterangi and the Saints in New Caledonia. The Zioneers had learned that many of the New Caledonia group had come from Tahiti and they presumed they would be singing their songs in Tahitian. To get the atmosphere of Tahitian culture Cheville sang for them a stanza of "Tei ia tatou to parau ha na ha na" in Tahitian.

> They also had heard anew the words of the hymn that we sing when we join with brothers and sisters of many lands. We dedicate these words to you.
>
> In Christ there is no East or West,
> In him no South or North,
> But one great fellowship of love,
> Throughout the whole, wide earth.

A letter was sent from the RLDS Saints in the Utah Missionary District in September 1974 to the Saints in Oxford, England. The letter noted that most of the Oxford Saints had been Mormons of the Utah variety,

> We rejoiced at your wanting to make covenant anew and hold true to the basics of the Restoration movement. Yes, this was a gift of good news to us.
>
> Under separate cover we are sending you a copy of the Doctrine and Covenants in the most recent edition. We think that this will express our belief that this book is not to be closed as long as we will incline to God so he will respond to us in revelation. This is so characteristic of the "Reorganized" Church in these present days. The canon of the Mormon Church is closed...
>
> We hope and pray that your Oxford group may bring fresh spirit and witness in the Church of Jesus Christ in the British Isles Mission...
>
> Our hearts reach across the many miles of land and water with the sense of spiritual fellowship. We sing with you, "In Christ there is no East or West!"
>
> Join hands now, Saints in Utah land,
> With friends across the sea;
> Be one with those in Oxford town,
> In God's great family.

The Bluff Springs, FL, camp sent a letter on 1 July, 1975 to the Saints in the International Youth Camp in Germany. The Bluff Springs Saints stated they were thrilled at the picture of bringing together Restoration youth from several lands and several languages. "May the language of love, the voice of inspiration be shared by you in joint fellowship."

> We are singing one song that pictures us singing together as in a worldwide symphony chorus, in many languages. While we do this, we feel one with you. With German youth we are saying, "Ein grosses and wunderbares Werk!" We sing with all of you. We would like you to sing a song and feel that you are joining with us.

On 16 September 1975 Cheville wrote a letter signed by the priesthood of Lamoni Stake, including the Stake President, Bishop, Pastor of Lamoni Congregation and six associate pastors, and pastors of the ten pastoral groups in Lamoni congregation. The letter was sent to S.C. Akpan, President of the Nigeria Mission and to his brothers and sisters there. The letter included a one-page history of Lamoni. It noted that Cheville had told them about the beginnings of our Restoration Church there in Nigeria; about their anniversary conference last November; about Akpan's being named mission president by the voice of the Saints; and about his energetic devotion and evangelistic enthusiasm in ministry. The letter ended with,

> We pray that God will bless you through his Spirit with discernment, with enlightenment, with assurance, with brotherly love as you minister as president of the Nigeria Mission. We are saying, "God bless Brother Akpan and his fellow Saints." In gospel fellowship, Your brother ministers in the Church of Jesus Christ.

Another letter to the Saints in Nigeria was sent October 18, 1975 signed by the Saints of the Central Washington District meeting in Wenatchee, Washington. During his four weeks stay with them, Cheville described what had been happening in Nigeria in these recent years,

> The story of what has been happening in Nigeria these recent years makes a wonderful testimonial story. The Spirit of God prompted some of you who dwell in Southeast Nigeria to seek the living gospel of Jesus Christ. Doors opened. Many individuals responded. This makes a wonderful story. Brother Cheville calls this a thrilling chapter in "Today's Book of Acts."

The letter sent greetings to the Nigerian mission conference. It saluted Brother Akpan and Brother Neff, apostle to Africa. It continued with a reference to Cheville's hymn, "Let Us Sing a Worldwide Anthem," which expressed their conviction and hope about bringing to pass a worldwide fellowship, the Church of Jesus Christ on mission.

Cheville not only had groups of Saints write to other groups of Saints, he also had groups of Saints write to individuals who had special needs. These needs might be due to special church missions in which they were carrying burdens alone, or the needs might be more personal. For example, Tony Onumajuru and his family had just been through the Biafran war when their very lives were at stake.

Tony had written a letter to Cheville on January 25, 1971 expressing his pleasure in receiving a letter from his brothers and sisters in Christ who were with Cheville on the cruise ship Hanseatic in the Caribbean when Cheville served as chaplain in December, 1970. Tony said, "Yes, I am happy that through your ministry a good number of people have heard about me. It is wonderful." The group of Saints who signed the letter to Tony would have been those in the tour group sponsored by Carpentours of Independence, MO.

Another letter to Tony Onumajuru was signed October 15, 1972 by the Saints in Slover Park Congregation. It said,

> We are reaching across miles and miles of land and water to your native Nigeria in Africa.
>
> We have become acquainted with you this evening through Brother Cheville who loves you as a son in the gospel.
>
> We have learned that you would like to construct a house for your family home, in which you would be able to invite your friends and share with them the Restoration gospel. This evening we are making a gift [of money] to you to further this purpose.

On 28 April 1973 Cheville wrote a letter that was signed by a group from the St. Louis District. It was addressed to Sam Agwanda and Richard Mbeche in Kisumu, Kenya, East Africa.

> Roy Cheville, patriarch of our church is with us. He has been telling us of his going to Kenya, in East Africa. He tells how he went at the direction of God. He tells us how ways opened to meet with you two men. We lived with him the experience of your baptism in a bay of historic Lake Victoria by Kisumu and of the confirmation meeting in the hotel room. A wonderful story.

On 20 April 1974 Cheville wrote a letter signed by the RLDS Girls in Kansas City Stake, meeting at Camp Doniphan. The letter was sent to Helen Pamela Agwanda in Kenya, East Africa. Roy Cheville had told them about Kenya and how he had baptized her father and her uncle Richard Mbeche in Lake Victoria in 1972, and had given her father the first patriarchal blessing given in Africa. They learned that Helen was baptized in Lake Victoria last October 23. "We shall be remembering you as our friend and fellow member in the Church of Christ."

A letter was signed on August 25, 1974 by the Saints of the Southern Hills Congregation in Topeka, Kansas addressed Wang Chung-Chang, in Taiwan, Chinese National Republic. It said in part,

> In his portrayal of "Today's Book of Acts of the Saints" Dr. Cheville brought us some happenings out of the life of our Church today. He told us of the beginnings of the Restoration Church in Taiwan, of your part in all this. He told us of the translation of the Book of Mormon into the Chinese language through your sustained and devoted endeavors. You have made a significant contribution. You and God have been working together. We want you to know that we appreciate this so very much. Brother Cheville brought the copy of this publication, the copy that you sent to him. He prizes this very much. So do we in the Southern Hills Congregation.

A letter to Tony Onumajuru was signed by the Saints of Greeley Colorado October 9, 1974. The letter noted that Wayne Zion and Roy Cheville were meeting with them. Cheville was conducting the meeting on the theme, "Friends in World Mission." "This is more than an ordinary letter. This is a message of good will and of good hope. We send this letter to you, Brother Tony, who is one of the most 'isolated' members in our church."

A letter signed on March 30, 1975 by the Goodland, Kansas Branch, went to Richard O. Mbeche, Standard Bank, Ltd., Box 354, Kisumu, Kenya, East Africa. They had learned from Cheville the good news of the gospel in Kenya, and he has helped us to feel that you and your people are our fellow Saints. Yes, it was Brother Cheville who baptized you in November 1972. He has a warm love for you and a high regard and expectation of you.

We learn that during the recent visit of Charles Neff you were called and ordained to be a priest in the Church of Jesus Christ. This is good news to all of us. Dr. Cheville testifies that he has expected this and so he brings his confirming testimony. May the Holy Spirit guide you and sustain you that you may be a witnessing minister for sharing the Restoration gospel with your people.

On May 26, 1975 a letter was sent to the Wycliffe Ochieng' family in Nairobi, Kenya, East Africa from the Temple Grove Camp Grounds in Pennsylvania. "Dear Friends in the Gospel, Brother Wycliffe, Sister Mary, Lavender, Elwyn, Maureen and Dawn." The letter noted that Roy Cheville

has told us of the letter that you first wrote him, a letter of inquiry and request. He has told us of the baptism of Brother Wycliffe and Sister Mary in Lake Victoria by Kisumu in West Kenya. Then he told us of the baptisms of Lavender and Elwyn in Nairobi. How we wish that you might be here to tell us your testimony in person. Brother Cheville feels very close to you in spiritual fellowship, even if he has not yet met you face to face.

We want so much for the four of you, including Lavender and Elwyn to feel that you are living members in the Restoration Church. We are thrilled to hear in your letter your testimony that you desire to have part in bringing the gospel, the Church of Jesus Christ to your city Nairobi and to your country Kenya.

Now fellow campers let's extend
Our hands across the sea
We greet in love in Kenya land
The Ochieng family.

Not all the letters went to other countries. On 21 June 1974 a letter signed by members of the Thirty-ninth Street Congregation in Independence went to the Saints in Bonners Ferry in Northern Idaho. A member of the Independence congregation was moving into the Idaho area and "we are hoping that they find a place among you."

On 1 July 1975 Cheville wrote a letter signed by the Saints in Bluff Springs Campgrounds, McDavid, Florida. It was addressed to the Saints in reunion at Eden, Utah,

> We think of you in the Utah Missionary District with friendly concern and with good hope. Few of us have been there. We are remembering you in our fellowship, in our prayer. We want so much that you will have a reunion that will increase your discernment, your devotion, your charity, your confidence as you move among the "others" who live in Utah. May you be blessed as you will be conversing about the living gospel to those affiliated with the Mormon Church. May you express the vision, the vitality of the living Church of Jesus Christ.

On February 12, 1970 Cheville sent a letter to Bob Turner signed by several members of the class in Sociology of Religion of the School of the Restoration, "The story of what has taken place in Cordoba sounds like a story out of the New Testament. This time the call was, 'Come over into Cordoba and help us!' And God guided those who were seeking and you who were responding that these searchers might find the light."

On January 11, 1969 a group of seven people, Dan and Sarah Allinson, Del and Jean Arduser from Osceola, Missouri, Wayne and Ruth Zion of Independence, and Roy Cheville, sent a letter to the W. E. Connells (Gene and Ruby) in India. (Gene was doing agricultural research work there for his U.S. university.) The seven were meeting in the Allinson home near Rockville, Missouri. "We have had our evening meal together and now we are in an evening circle. We are extending the radius of our circle and are including you with us." The letter noted the Connells' longtime association with the story of our church in India, and about their going there by way of the Philippine Islands. It cited their interest in bringing more hymns into the worship services in their part of India, where the Saints spoke Tamil but the larger part understand some

English. This group of seven was sending a copy of the *Saints' Hymnal* for them.

Cheville wrote a letter which was signed on September 29, 1974 by the Saints in conference in Denver Stake. It was sent to the Weldons—Clair, Jessie, and Kim in Cordoba, Argentina. That evening the Denver Saints had sung "Redeemer of Israel" in English and in Spanish. "We pray in this hymn that the light of God will guide you and assure you in your pioneering endeavors. Our signatures express our personal benedictions."

A letter to Everett Graffeo in Honolulu was signed October 13, 1974 by the Saints in Liberty, Missouri. Cheville had told them of Graffeo's ministry in the Society Islands and now in Hawaii. On November 1 he would be going to New Caledonia, where Ririfatu was ministering, and to Fiji, where Brother Das was the national minister.

> What pioneering for you!
>
> We write this letter to express our interest, our concern. We also write it to express our prayerful remembrance of you as you go.
>
> Brother Cheville looks forward to being with you in Hawaii, after you have been in Fiji and in New Caledonia. He has such a high regard for you and loves you as a brother and fellow saint.

Responses to these letters illustrated how much they were valued by those who received them.

A letter from Tony Onumajuru indicated that Tony had received a letter from the Saints in Kalihi, Hawaii. Cheville preached a sermon there February 14, 1971.

> I am very grateful to you for speaking to the congregation of our church at Kalihi. The congregation wrote me a wonderful letter greeting me and my family. Through your ministry people in many parts of the world have heard about me. I wish I could attend the next World Conference so that I can meet personally some of the people who have written to me and prayed for me.
>
> I shall soon reply to the letter to the Congregation Kalihi Branch to express my gratitude to them.
>
> More grease to your elbows for the wonderful work you are doing. Yours Sincerely, Tony Onumajuru, Ubulu-Ihejiofo, Via Orlu, East Central State, Nigeria [28 Mar 71]

Appointees expressed appreciation for supportive letters:

> We appreciate the letters very much... We want to thank you again for your constant remembering of us and of the work here. We will try to do our best to live up to the expectations of you and of the Lord in his work in this part of the world. [Letter from Everett Graffeo in Tahiti to Roy Cheville, 11 Sep 69]

Velma Ruch, Acting President of Graceland College wrote Cheville February 19, 1975,

> The letter I received from our Seijo congregation in Tokyo and from you gave me much blessing and joy. When Clara brought it in she said, "This is just what you need today." It was, too. The week had been filled with various stresses and strains with important decisions to be made. The letter gave me assurance and trust. Thank you for one more example of thoughtfulness and blessing.

A letter to Edward and Marjorie Barlow, of the British Isles Mission, was sent July 1, 1975 from the Bluff Springs Camp in Florida. "As we close our camp you will be leaving for England, for your work in the British Isles Mission. We are thinking of you and have chosen to write you so a letter would be there in England for you as you arrive." The letter expressed appreciation for their work of outreach during recent years. The Bluff Springs group was praying that the endowments of discernment, of brotherly and sisterly friendship, of courageous faith, of radiant inspiration may be their blessings.

BOOK XII

Macro Religion—People

People Gain Eternal Life

> A classic statement of God's eternal purpose and process is stated in Doctrine and Covenants 22:23. First of all, the extensiveness of the creation and the continuing nature of God's creative expression are set forth. Then comes this zenith statement, "This is my work and my glory, to bring to pass the immortality and eternal life of man." We might paraphrase it this way, "This is what I set out to do and in this is my crowning satisfaction; the development of persons with eternal quality in them." [Cheville notes]

> The gospel speaks to the person. God is concerned with the person. [A:1962C]

Roy Cheville had a lot to say about Zion, about Peace, and about World Fellowship. He also had a lot to say about people. And people are the concrete reality. The reason to promote the causes of Zion, Peace, and World Fellowship is that they are instrumental in developing personhoods of eternal quality. Salvation is the development of eternal quality in person's lives. Immortality of the personhood comes out of that. In 1951 Cheville wrote,

> We cannot get saved without getting saved from something.
>
> Many of the things from which we need to be saved are in us and in the world of which we are a part. In other words we have to save ourselves from ourselves.
>
> Jesus kept teaching this aspect of salvation. He talked of immersing oneself unreservedly in the work of God. He that would do this intelligently would find salvation. But he who set himself up as the center of things would be lost. Christianity says that the person who lines up with Christ in an outreach of concern for others will be saved. [A:1951B]

Cheville saw that Jesus of Nazareth spent a great deal of his time working with individuals in small groups. He knew each of his disciples well, and he had an inner circle of them he knew very well indeed. They were his close friends as well as his co-laborers. It was they who came to know him through association to the degree that they could detect his divinity. He worked with each to develop eternal qualities within them.

Cheville frequently made the distinction between living *among* and living *with*. Jesus could have lived *among* the people who followed his message without getting very close to any of them individually. Instead he lived *with* them. He was in daily interaction. He knew them as individuals, as persons. He was sensitive to their state of development. He took an active part in their growth as individuals. He was their friend and they were his friends.

From his high school days Cheville was regarded as a person who made friends easily. He could be described as a "powerful listener." He paid close attention to individuals and came to understand much about them as a result. As he grew in broad learning and in spiritual development, his capacity to listen and to understand individuals only increased (at least until he was nearing 80 years of age). He used that understanding to minister to individuals.

Though he was teaching principles in his ministry, he always paid attention to the role of these principles in the lives of individuals. In his writings and in his public speaking he frequently described individuals, particularly to cite their experience to illustrate principles. Sometimes he mentioned individuals in order to bring fellowship into the context of his presentation. Particularly in his later years, this public attention made some of those who were objects of this personal description uncomfortable.

One technique he used to bring focus on individuals was the columns he wrote in the *Saints' Herald* with the title, "These Are My People." He frequently talked about experiences in various congregations, but he also described things about and actions of individuals. This was a part of his overall program to focus attention on the person as the object of the gospel.

Cheville told a story he attributed to a 19th Century champion of liberal causes, William Jennings Bryan. The story goes that Bryan received a call from a friend asking for his company while they went to visit a mutual friend who was in poor spirits. Bryan's response that he was so busy with causes and organizations that he no longer had time for individuals. Whereupon the caller said, "Then you have become bigger than God." Cheville himself always took time for individuals.

Growing Up In Religion

> My theology affects every phase of my living. I can have a conception of God that makes me lazy or ignorant or superstitious or self-centered or provincial. Or I can believe in a God who stimulates me to be industrious, intelligent, and outreaching. The kind of theology I subscribe to conditions what my life is going to be. [D:1963A]

Cheville believed that as children we could believe that God was a super being who gave us gifts and did things for us when all we had to do was ask. As adults we understand that there is more to God than that. As people develop in understanding of the physical world, they should also develop in understanding of the nature of God and their relationship with him. Over a period of many years Cheville called this "growing up in religion." He used this phrase as the title of an article [D:1930H] and of a book [A:1951B].

To Cheville growing up in religion takes more than study, though study is important. One cannot become a good golfer solely by reading books and discussing the merits of one technique versus another. At some point one must get in the game and start learning to hit the ball with the club. When one does that the book learning takes on new meaning. Furthermore there are elements to the play that are hard to describe in words. As one's own experience develops there may come a time when one can write a book enlarging upon the things that were said in the older books.

This principle was a key one in Cheville's writing about religion. He said that one cannot understand religion without immersing one's self in religious practice. Only then can one understand what is in the books. Only then can the principles come to life. And, only in religious practice is one in a religious laboratory in which theological concepts can be tested.

As extensive as it was, Cheville's theology was no finished product. He said it never could be. His view was that he would go as far as he could in concepts and in validation by experience. Then, others could build upon what he had learned. He saw no limit to what was yet to be understood about divinity.

Though there is no conceivable limit to the yet-to-be-understood about divinity, he taught that it is critically important for each person to go as far as possible in increasing understanding by study and by practice. In that way each of us can grow up in religion and develop eternal qualities in our living. We need to keep in mind that our understanding is partial. Once he said it in this way,

> Dr. Harry Wieman used to say that the main obstacle to our experiencing the fullness of God is our partial conceptions of him. We build these up and hold to them rigidly. Then we tend to make God fit into our picture of him. Often we insist that others bow to our partial views. In time we set out to defend our portrayal of God. Thus we shut off further insight into God's nature and work. [D:1963A]

Growing up in religion is an individual matter. The church and friends can help but they cannot do it for us. Each person must first decide to grow up in this way. Then, after that decision is made, discipline must be exerted. Discipline is required to study the useful materials and join in with those who can help in the development. Then each individual must come clean before God. One does that by dropping pretenses, recognizing problems and tendencies, evaluating motivations, etc., so the real person stands before God. Alone in prayer and contemplation, the aspiring Saint seeks to see the present situation as God would see it, seeks to see what action can be taken to be in alignment with the purposes of God.

In this divine communion, the quest should not be for God to reveal the mysteries of the universe. Instead, the aspiring Saint should look to immediate decisions that need to be made. The lofty divine principles are applied in specific situations—the guidance to be sought is this specific. The response may carry with it principles in more general terms.

An example of the mature Cheville's use of this approach as presiding patriarch occurred in 1970. The general conference represented a situation that Cheville felt could have dire consequences for the Saints. In the months after April 1970 he sought guidance. He sensed the hungers, the confusions, the anxieties of the people. He sensed, too, that members were taking sides and classifying ministers. He prayed, "God, what do you want me to do?" In an early evening walk, he writes,

> As I was pondering on the conditions of the church, on the needs of the Saints, I sensed the close, uplifting presence of the Spirit of God. Clear in my soul stood out this directive, as clear as if this had been written on the wall before me. This was the directive, *Converse with my people, honestly and hopefully!* This was all.
>
> The directive pointed me to be *with* the Saints. I was not to preach *at* them. I was not to stand *above* them. The preposition was *with*. [pBull Jan 71]

This communication was a direct response to the question Cheville had posed. It did not solve the problems of the church in the immediate sense. It did give direction to Cheville's own actions, and he used all the avenues available to him to converse with the Saints on the issues as he saw them. With regard to the larger problems, Cheville stated repeatedly that God always takes the long view.

It was through the RLDS church that Cheville learned that the Holy Spirit is active in the lives of the people as they, through discipline, qualify for its presence in their lives. He said,

> The preaching about the Holy Spirit arrested my attention when I first came in contact with the Restoration movement. It meant more than a concept, more than a dogma, more than an abstraction. Here was vital spiritual reality. Here God was at work. Today this Spirit lies at the heart of my witness. The Holy Spirit is validated as the

enlivening and enlightening empowerment that Jesus promised. This Spirit has prompted me to make something worthy of my life, to expand and refine my love and understanding, to reach out to others and to be at home with God. I have developed Godward through the benign yet dynamic Spirit of God. I have witnessed the manifestations of the Spirit enumerated by Paul in his letter to the Corinthians. I anticipate richer endowment and edification. [D:1960H]

Friendship

In the Book of James is a significant phrase about a good man of ancient times—Abraham. Here is the statement, "Abraham was called the friend of God." (2:23) Then the writing goes on to say that Abraham was so considered because of what he did—-with God—for God. Then this statement follows, "You see that a man is right with God by what he does." [Cheville, Friends of God, 1971, Appendix H]

This is basic: Friendship requires that the *real stuff* of the people meet, the *wholeness* of the people meet. There has to be something inside... worth getting hold of. And what is in this person has to hang together... That word *integrity*—a oneness to this person. A symphony of harmony with variety. [Cheville notes]

Just before Cheville made his decision to join this church at age 16, a friend advised him against it. She said she hoped Roy would not get connected with this little church because it would change the course of his life. She said he got along very well with others and might be called a popular fellow. But if he were baptized by these Latter Day Saints he would lose all his friends and not have the friends he was capable of having.

The first part of the warning was accurate—his membership in the church did change the course of his life. However, the second part did not prove true. First, his friends and neighbors did not turn against him. As his patriarchal blessing affirmed, he made friends even among those who opposed the church but came to respect the church because of his integrity. And not once in his fifty plus years of membership did he recall one statement of a disparaging nature about his faith or his church.

Second, there has come to me in this Church of Jesus Christ a company of friends of precious quality. This circle reaches around the world. It includes those of every continent, of every race, of many languages. What a wealth of spiritual friendship has come to me. Once in a prophetic message I was told that an outstanding blessing of my life would be the friendship of the Saints, a friendship that would carry the love of brothers and sisters in Christ. I never expect to be rich in material goods, although I expect to have the things that will be essential for adequate living. But I shall be rich in spiritual friendship. [Friends of God, 1971, Appendix H]

Friendship was an important matter to Roy Cheville in several ways. One way was personal. He developed many personal friendships and these were very important to the way he lived. Another way was conceptual. He taught that friendships were important to lives of eternal quality. Another way was historical. He saw that Jesus accomplished his mission through the friends with whom he lived. It was they who sensed his divinity and carried on the work when he left.

Cheville talked about friendship at length in a 1971 presentation to a group of church workers in Korea with the title "We Are Called To Be Friends of God." The text of that presentation is found in Appendix H. He urged his coworkers to picture our God as a Father who wants all to love him as he loves them. Then he described the way Jesus, representing divinity in human form, related to his twelve disciples. At his farewell meal he was getting them ready to carry on the work after his departure. He discovered from their questions that they understood neither why he was leaving nor what he wanted them to be doing afterward. He could have given vent to his frustration.

> Rather did he speak with confidence and say to his men, "Let not your hearts be troubled!" and "Be of good cheer!" What a courageous faith! What a confident hope!

Jesus pointed out weakness in some of his men, but he did not reject them. Rather he told them that he was relying on them and was turning his work over to them to carry on. He told them he wanted them to love one another as he loved them, and that his greatest expression of love was to lay down his life for them. "Then he said this, which is worthy to be engraved in gold and held before us all,"

> You are my friends as you do as I have directed you.
> Henceforth I am not going to call you servants; I am calling you friends.
> A servant does not know what his master is doing.
> I call you friends, because I have told you everything I have heard from my Father.
> I have chosen you and ordained you that you might go out and bear forth the kind of fruit that endures.
> Yes, I call you friends. (John 15)

Then Cheville said, as Jesus had told his coworkers in Jerusalem, "'You are my friends,' he would say to us here today in Korea, 'You are my friends.'" He would express confidence in men of Japan and Korea as he did to men of Judea and Galilee. "As the circle of Jesus' apostles in those days included people of such diversity, so would his circle of Saints today include individuals of all temperaments, of all backgrounds, of all races, of all lands. And as then they would be one in Jesus Christ."

Cheville observed that friends do not merely sit and look at each other. Friends will not merely eat rice together; they will produce rice and provide means for purchasing rice. Abraham was God's friend because he and God were working together. God wanted him to develop a people who will reveal him to the world. He was saying, "I will bless you that through you others will be blessed." Abraham could be called the friend of God because he ventured with God, worked with God.

Cheville said that a mark of friendship is the giving out of one's very self to others. Jesus Christ came to earth because he wanted to help people. A friend always shares himself and what he has with others. Jesus was the outstanding friend because he had so much to share. Today it is urgent that we develop a wealth of what we can share with others. Joining in a great and

Photo 22-1.
Cheville among friends in the Avatoru congregation in Tahiti. Left to right are Davida Ami, Roonui, Roonui, Jr., Cheville, Timi Bennett, Davida Vahine, Mahina Bennett, Aberahama Fauura. *[Photo: Ruth Zion]*

marvelous work can produce great friendships that will continue and expand.

He once said that whenever he asked a person how they came into the church the response usually started with these words, "I had a friend. ." That was one way to describe the power of friends in shaping our lives. The statement also gives a clue to the importance of the values that are shared in the friendship. At another time Cheville said that a friend is a person who knows all about us and still likes us. In an unpublished manuscript, *Sayings* [see Appendix A], he included this one, "When I met him I was looking down; When I left him I was looking up." [unknown]

Among Roy Cheville's notes is a paper with the title "Field For Friendship," dated September 11, 1971, and apparently prepared for delivery at the Lansing (Kansas) Prison. In that presentation he was explaining to the prison inmates what friendship was about and how to go about being a friend. Cheville was no stranger to the prison. He carried on correspondence with the warden and some of the prisoners. He even helped some find their way in the outside world after they had served their terms.

In this 1971 presentation he told them that friendship does not come by salesmanship, but is fruit that comes through cultivation. He stated his conviction that

> God designs men to live together in mutuality, in mutual relationship, for a life of eternal quality... God designs us with what it takes to learn how to live together in this mutually helpful way. Much of the time we flub this job and live in disregard of the other fellow...

He said the friend is one who knows about you and sticks with you—one who draws out of you the good stuff on the inside. The worthy friend exerts "kindling influence." You are stimulated to want to make something out of yourself, to some good end. He talked to them about Jesus of Nazareth who lived with his men and taught them through association. At the Last Supper he told them he was going to call them friends. He also told them that "prayer is friendly conversation, talking things over with God, when God and I are doing things together... Praying is more than trying to get God to come across with some favor." He closed by saying,

> This morning I would like you to meet my friend, Jesus of Nazareth, who says to me, "Henceforth, I am calling you friend!" He knows what kind of a fellow Roy Cheville is. He sees potentials in me yet to be tapped for worthy purpose. He says to me, "Come, let's work together for reaching out in friendship to my other men. Men, let's do some cultivating in this field of friendship."

An exchange of letters reveals some elements of Cheville's friendship. Villy Lundin wrote from Odense, Denmark on April 16, 1970,

Dear Roy Cheville,

Just a few words, If I may let you know a few of my problems and wishes?—Since we met in Copenhagen, I've been married and have two children and are [sic.] expecting a third, we are all happy most of the time. I've got a good job and the family and I live in a new flat, but in spite of all good fortune I need some close contact with the reorganized church!

My biggest wish is that if you again came to Europe, would you baptize me, and bless my wife and children with understanding of the gospel?

If you don't mind, I should like to continue writing to you. Sincerely, Villy Lundin

Cheville replied by return mail:

My Dear Friend Villy:

Your letter has just come to me and I am going to reply at once. When I saw the letter and the name, I took a second look at it to assure me that it was from Denmark, from you.

Yes, I remember well how we met in Copenhagen in a very unusual way, at the Tivoli [in June 1961]. Fred Banta and Richard Andersen had been wanting to make contact with you. Someone in Australia had written about you. As I recall you had come in contact with the Reorganized Church while you were hunting for the meeting place of the Mormons.

Then you went with us out to the home of Brother Blume, a few miles from Copenhagen, where we had the evening meal together and then had a circle meeting, the six of us.

Then somehow the correspondence broke down. I believe that you were ill for a while. Now you write that you are married and have two children and are expecting a third. And you have a good job.

It is good to hear you say that you are hungry for something more. Yes, we have spiritual hungers, just as essential as our biological hungers. And I felt when I was with you that you had capacity for such spiritual hungers. I wanted to have more time with you, in spiritual fellowship.

I am sending a copy of your letter to Brother Kasper Anholt who has just gone to our Scandinavian mission field. He will be living in Oslo. There we have a mission house. I do not know the program and the arrangements for his work. I do know that he will reach out to you in a friendly way. He does speak Norwegian. I understand that the Danish people understand Norwegian fairly well. Then, too, you speak English. Since he has just arrived in Norway, it may take a while for him to get in touch with you, but you will not be forgotten.

During recent years Aleah Koury has been and is the apostle assigned to our European mission field. I do not know what his schedule is about coming to Scandinavian lands. You will find him a warmhearted, outreaching person.

Yes, Villy, I would like to be with you again. I would like to stand by your side as a brother in the gospel of Jesus Christ. Be assured that I shall not forget you. And I shall be expecting that someone will reach out to you and to your family.

So Villy, if there is anything more that I can do I want to do it. Yes, I would like to see you again. Meanwhile I shall say, "God be with you!" Fraternally Yours, Roy A. Cheville, Presiding Patriarch, The Reorganized Church of Jesus Christ of Latter Day Saints.

On the morning of August 17, 1970 a letter was sent by the Auditorium staff during morning devotions to Villy Lundin of Odense, Denmark. Villy responded on September 2, "I am glad each time I receive a letter, but it was a joy to get your last letter with all the signatures of the staff of the Auditorium."

The story of Villy Lundin's becoming acquainted with the church and becoming a friend of Roy Cheville is told in an article by Cheville in the *Saints' Herald* of March 1981 entitled "A Trilogy of Memories." It is reproduced in Appendix J. In that article are also accounts of his friendship with George Ventura of Spain and Mariko Saito of Japan.

George (Jordi in Spanish) Ventura is a native of Barcelona, Spain (the old capital of Catalonia). He speaks Catalan as well as Castilian Spanish, French, and English. He had joined the Mormon Church and was sent by them to Utah to translate temple rite materials. He had been converted to the basics of the movement, and he became disenchanted as he discovered the nature of these secret rites and the theology associated with them. He came into contact with our church in Utah and later joined.

Ventura and Cheville met in Utah in 1955. In 1961 they shared a room at the British Isles reunion and there

Cheville gave Jordi his patriarchal blessing. They were together several times when Jordi came to Graceland College to give a Winter Term course on "Contemporary Spain." In 1975 Cheville and Wayne Zion detoured on a trip from Africa to England to spend an evening with Jordi in the Hotel Colon in Barcelona. Jordi is now Professor of Economics in the University of Barcelona. In 1976 Cheville wrote to him,

> This letter is written to you as a good will, good news epistle. So often I wonder how you are getting along in your Barcelona setting. How often I would like to be with you as a friend, as a brother in Christ, if only for a short while.
>
> I could write a book in six chapters, each one narrating our meetings in diverse places, in diverse situations. Chapter I would be laid in Salt Lake City, Utah. There Houston Hobart told me about you. After we had conversed a while, he said to me, "You are so interested—would you like to meet Jordi?" So we met. You told me of your breaking with the Mormon Church and of your leaving Utah.
>
> Chapter II would be laid in Hanover, Germany. After you left Utah, I mailed 3 letters to you at your Barcelona address. No reply. After about two years I met Houston Hobart in Independence. I inquired about you. I thought he might possess news from your brother in Salt Lake City. The next day he brought the letter you had sent to Charles Hield. In this you indicated your desire to unite with the "Reorg. Church." Out of this came your journey to Hanover, Germany. There you were baptized by Vern Webb, confirmed by A. Ash and Enghohrs and ordained a priest by Ash Cr. and Dulshn. That very day you wrote me a letter. I was happy and appreciative at your thoughtfulness.
>
> Chapter III would be laid in England, in the reunion camp and at the Darcy home. At my request it was arranged that you and I room together at the reunion. I recall how much you wanted to have conversational friendship. At Nuneaten you received your patriarchal blessing.
>
> Chapter IV would be in the United States, in Independence, in Lamoni. This was when you came to Graceland College for the winter term to teach a course on Contemporary Spain. Outstanding was the evening in the Engle home in Lamoni when eight of us sat in a circle for the Lord's supper. You and I knelt. I offered the prayer of blessing in the English language, you in Spanish. We sang the

hymn, Redeemer of Israel in Spanish. Then Wayne Zion, you and I went to Lancaster, Wisconsin to the Bendorfs.

Chapter V will be in Barcelona, Spain in early December 1975. I had written two or three letters and received no reply. Then I made a courageous endeavor. I arranged that Wayne and I would come from Nairobi Kenya by way of Barcelona. I wrote that we would be at Colon Hotel on a specific Thursday evening. After we had arrived in our hotel room, you telephoned. You would come to the hotel room after you had completed your teaching. I went out and purchased a bread roll and some orange juice for the sacrament of covenanting and communing. I was thrilled to have spiritual fellowship with you again.

Today, Jordi, we are needing and wanting to move out into the Spanish speaking world. Maybe I should say into the Latin-language world. This world includes Brazil, that speaks Portuguese...

Yes, Jordi, this is a day of possibilities, of promises. We wish the inspiring, sustaining ministry of the Holy Spirit to enable all of us to "bring to pass a marvelous work."

I think of Spain. What a story during the centuries. The Spanish genius can bring so much to our Restoration Church of Jesus Christ. And Spain needs the living, restoring gospel.

I write this letter in benediction, in spiritual fellowship. I am saying this,

God, be with my brother Jordi,
In his loved Cordoba land
How I'd like to be close to him
With the covenanting hand.

In Christian fellowship, Roy A. Cheville, in Our Restoration Church of Jesus Christ of Latter Day Saints.

Cheville was introduced to Mariko Saito in Tokyo in 1971. She had been baptized in 1965. Though her husband had not joined the church he supported her in aiding the development of the church in many ways. During that 1971 visit, Cheville spent two nights in the Saito home and he gave Mariko her patriarchal blessing, which was translated later into Japanese. She said that during the blessing, "I did not understand all the words as they were spoken in English, but I sensed the wonderful Spirit." Cheville wrote a letter to her March 18, 1978 that was signed by her sisters in the Southeast Texas District. They included a check for her Tokyo church activities. Mariko answered the letter August 22,

> I have no word to explain your wonderful works, with thanks... I have many Sisters and brothers. Thank you very much. Please come to Japan to see new building. I get new experience, that is the Spirit of God guide us in our planning, in our business. We have enjoy working together. I want to show you our church.

Cheville wrote another letter in December of 1979 that was signed by members of the Laurel Club in Independence. Mariko came to Independence and participated in two world conferences. In the Conference of 1980 she was awarded the International Youth Service Award for her outstanding ministry to youth. Early in 1980 she learned she had cancer. Three months before her death in June 1980 she wrote Cheville, "When I was with you in conference ministry, we sang about Christ in both East and West. I sang with you. I have never forgotten." In her final paragraph she said she thinks of him and others who have helped her so much. "You have brought great purpose, great satisfaction, great joy in my life. You have helped me to live with God."

Roy Cheville as a friend helped individuals to live with God.

These Are My People

Many still ask me if there is any special significance to the words, "These are my people." Yes, they come from a rare happening. They are not original with me. In those years when times were hard for the young Reorganization in Canada, a baptismal service was held rather late one night at the Thames River near London, Ontario. A man remained at one side to scoff. As a light shone down on the small company, this onlooker heard these words with the admonition to refrain from ridicule: "These are my people!"

These are the testimonial words of God. I am eligible to use this phrase as with the ministering of the Holy Spirit I sense oneness with the Saints of God. I reserve the words to designate spiritual comradeship. [D:1970D]

Even before Roy Cheville became presiding patriarch he had a legendary ability to remember people. He could not only recognize the face and call the name, he could also recall the family and the church branch the family was associated with. It was as if he had a mental map of all the branches in the church with the names of the families and the individuals listed in their appropriate places. That ability became more pronounced after he moved to church headquarters. As he visited even more branches than before, his "people" map became even more detailed.

It has been said that a good teacher must be first and foremost interested in the development of each of his students. Cheville was that. As he moved to headquarters, every person in the church became his student in that respect. He wanted to meet them all, to size up each one, and to keep track of their development. He wanted to be a friend to each one. Above all, he wanted to see each one of them as a person. And he wanted them to know he looked upon each as a personal friend. He would no doubt have said that it was the effect of the Good Spirit working with him over the years that produced this expansive outlook.

Soon after he became presiding patriarch he wrote the first of a series of articles in the *Saints' Herald* with the title, "These are my people." The first of these was 1959E and the forty-third and last was 1973E. In that first article he told of a good woman who felt some strains in the church and began to turn away from it. She felt that the members were no longer friendly and the Spirit of God was gone from the body at large. One night she dreamed that she was standing near the entrance to the Stone Church and was inclined to turn away as many were entering. Then she was prompted to turn toward them and said to herself, "These are my people. My place is with them!" In this restored fellowship, she found a flood of light and peace filling her soul. Then Cheville spoke for himself,

> Thirty years have passed since this happened. Today in the processions of people hurrying thither and yon I single out the company of the Saints, and I say as I walk with them, "These are my people!" In these living days I am finding good fellowship with them.

He went on in that article to tell of being in a meeting in June with elders of Michigan and Ontario at the Blue Water Reunion grounds by Lake Huron. He was teaching about the vital way we believe in Jesus Christ and the contemporary way we commune with him. "We sensed together the presence of the everlasting Christ." Then he said, "These were my brothers in ministry."

In that same article he told of being with 140 boys and girls at Camp Liahona near Sanford, Michigan. They sang together and he walked and ran with them on a woodland hike. In the evening chats he told them about good things happening in the church today—-in India, in Japan, in Pakistan, in Brazil. They responded with enthusiasm and he noted that "These junior members became my people also."

Some of these 43 "These are my people" articles were intended to help priesthood broaden their understanding of the types of ministry that might be accomplished. Other articles were intended to introduce individuals to the church at large. Others were intended to publicize activities of merit in the various branches. Others emphasized to all members the value to each individual of making and keeping the commitment to be with "my people."

In one of these columns he told of preaching the funeral service for Congressman Steven Carter in the filled-to-capacity high school gymnasium at Leon, Iowa. Carter's body had been brought back from Washington, D. C. for burial. He had lost the fight with cancer but had gained a victory in his own soul. Cheville sensed the dignity of the occasion with congressmen and the governor present. He wanted them to feel the sustaining faith of his people.

> There was an inner peace as I rose to speak. I talked of "mountains of Faith," a testimonial expression of my own life and thinking.
>
> Moses, I recalled, went up to see the overview of the Promised Land. He was not to enter the country with his people for whom he had given his life. Great souls give themselves to causes that go beyond their lifetime. Then Moses charged Joshua and his people to "be strong and of good courage."
>
> In his closing days—with the ministry of E. J. Gleazer, Jr., in Washington—my friend "Steve" had ascended this mountain of faith. [D:1959N]

A memorial service for Congressman Carter was held in Washington, D.C. when Congress resumed in January of 1960. That service was conducted by Edmund J. Gleazer, Jr. Some of the congressmen who attended the funeral service in Iowa were so impressed with the sermon by Cheville that they had it printed in its entirety in the proceedings of the memorial service. [D:1960C]

In the same article with the story about Steven Carter's funeral was a statement of a friend of Cheville's who told him "You have so many who are your people." Cheville said he was right. "One of the glorious things about the gospel is that we keep on taking others into our circle of brotherhood without needing to give up any who have been there. The way of Christian fellowship is the way of the expanding heart." [D:1961N]

In another article [D:1959F] he told of 90-year-old Hattie Clark asking him to stop in after a service and give a prayer of benediction on her and her daughter. She was a stalwart who had been a member of the Rhodes congregation when Cheville was baptized in 1914. In that same article he told of a freckle-faced boy of twelve grasping his hand after a service and saying, "Brother Cheville, come back as soon as you can." He commented that we benefit from having such food-consuming, ball-playing genuine youth in the church fellowship today.

Cheville recalled [D:1960Q] Roscoe Faunce, whose funeral he had just preached. In talking about Roscoe he had recalled a phrase from Paul's second letter to Timothy, "I call to remembrance your unfeigned faith." He said that Roscoe was no pretender. He never put on acts to further himself. He did not talk behind any person's back. His faith was simple and "unfeigned." Those remarks reflect an important friendship between Cheville and Faunce. Richard Cheville said that his father was "easy" with Roscoe.

Cheville tells [D:1965Q] the story of a young man from Texas who came to Graceland and registered without being aware of the church that sponsored the college. He attended a year and a half, married a young woman in the church, and was called into two years of military service. Then he returned for his fourth semester. As the four-year curriculum was beginning, he wanted to apply. Cheville asked him directly why? His answer was ready, "These are the kind of people I want to be with. I want these to be my people." The youth was Barney Parker.

In the article 1965R, he tells about a large, well-built young black man, James Ivy, who had migrated from Mississippi to Chicago. There he found the restored church and was baptized. In time, Cheville gave him his patriarchal blessing, and Ivy invited Cheville to come to his home. After some time, Cheville learned that Ivy had been in the Veterans Hospital with a serious malignancy and the doctors offered no hope for recovery. Cheville went to see him on a weekend when he was allowed to go home.

> When ready to go I said, "Brother Jim, I'm going to offer a prayer of benediction." With my left hand in his hand and my right hand on his head I commended him to God. There was no prompting to pray for recovery. I should pray for peace, ease, and assurance—so I commended my brother to God. As we parted he said with deep feeling, "You can never know what it means to me to have you come into my home and visit me." With fervency I said, "Good-bye, Brother Jim"

Wherever he went, Roy Cheville could truly say of the Saints, "These are my people."

In identifying with his people, Cheville had a role model. This role model is revealed in a series of six meetings he prepared for both the Lamoni and the Spring Branch Congregation in Independence with the overall theme of "Meet Jesus Christ in His Friends." He gave both sets of meetings in December of 1976. Here are the six meetings in Lamoni and the Friends of Jesus:

> 5 December 1976 Sunday evening; Meet His Friends in Ancient America: King Benjamin, Ammon, Helamon, Nephi III.
>
> 6 December 1976 Monday Evening; Meet His Friends in Classic Judea; Peter, Matthew, Judas Iscariot, Paul of Tarsus.
>
> 7 December Tuesday Evening; Meet His Friends in Frontier United States: Joseph Smith II, Oliver Cowdery, Emma Smith, David Whitmer.
>
> 8 December Wednesday Evening; Meet His Friends in Mid-West Lands of Our Country: Jason Briggs, Zenas Gurley, Joseph Smith III, Emma Smith.
>
> 9 December Thursday evening; Meet His Friends in Other Lands Today: Jean Bouissou, Wycliffe Ochieng, Esme Smith, Kisuke Sekine.
>
> 12 December 1976 Sunday Morning; Meet His Friends in Contemporary America: Foundation Meeting for the Venture, Our Evangelistic Enterprise Today.

Photo 23-1.
Cheville ministering to women's gathering at Tarona congregation, Papeete, Tahiti. *[Photo: Ruth Zion]*

Patriarchal Blessings

> My hands were laid in patriarchal blessing on the head of a young man in his later twenties. There were only three of us in the worship room in the patriarchal office in the Auditorium. His wife, of another faith, was there. When we conversed for a while after sacrament of blessing, he said his mother had told him he might well expect a "good spanking." Then I asked if he had been taking a recess. "More than a recess" was his reply. It had not been a rebuke, not a censure, that had come during the blessing, but a warm invitation to a son to return to his Father who was wanting him and needing him. And he will respond. In such times there is a brotherly bond and a deep concern for my people. [D:1961D]

Shortly after Roy Cheville became presiding patriarch, he stated that he did not plan to give very many patriarchal blessings himself, preferring that the patriarchs in the field give blessings to those close to them. He did slow down his pace to some extent. In the eight years between becoming a patriarch and becoming presiding patriarch he gave 592 blessings for an average of 74 per year. In the 15 and one half years he was presiding patriarch he gave 1,060 blessings for an average of 68 of per year. He gave 1,979 blessings in all.

During Roy Cheville's life patriarchal blessings were written down. One copy was given to the recipient and a file copy was stored in the offices of the presiding patriarch. They were retained in file so a substitute copy could be provided in case the recipient's copy was lost. These copies were handled as private and confidential material.

Patriarchal blessings have a personal and private element to them. For this reason they are usually given with only the patriarch and the recipient present, though a spouse may be included. Sometimes there is a translator present or perhaps a local church minister. The objective of the blessing is to provide spiritual guidance to the recipient. To meet that objective required, according to

Cheville, serious preparation on the part of the patriarch and of the recipient. Preparation for the recipient was addressed this way,

> What is the soundest preparation a person can make for a patriarchal blessing?
>
> The foremost essential is that the person be concerned about what he wants to do with his life. This has to do with the total program and the total span of living. It carries the presumption that a person wants to line up his life with God. His powers and potentials are to be conceived as part of his stewardship. [D:1971E]

Cheville described preparation on the part of the patriarch as exacting. The blessing is to be conditioned by the Holy Spirit. Therefore, the patriarch must qualify for the presence of the Spirit:

> How does a patriarch make ready for giving a blessing?
>
> The major preparation is in his total way of living. For most of us who are patriarchs giving a blessing is an exacting experience. Here are some essentials:
>
> (1) The patriarch seeks to live with a clean pattern so his integrity affords a good framework for inspiration.
>
> (2) He cultivates spiritual sensitivity that provides several channels of communication with God and multiple expressions for God to his people.
>
> (3) He develops in understanding human nature and human needs and human problems. He is where the people are.
>
> (4) He endeavors to express himself clearly and consistently. He wants his message to be free from misunderstanding, to be uplifting in style and spirit.
>
> (5) He sees the candidate as a child of God, who is to be understood and guided into an uplifting relationship with God.
>
> (6) He sees God working through him. He does not tie a person's loyalty to him but through him to God.
>
> Inspiration quickens the capacities of a person. It does not dehumanize. It never reduces to mechanism. The patriarch wants, therefore, to develop his powers of mind and heart and hand so that God will have more through which to express himself. [D:1971E]

Cheville had developed his own procedures of making ready for the blessing to qualify for the illumination of his mind by the Holy Spirit. He described his own preparation for giving the patriarchal blessing to Anthony Jude Chindi Onumajuru on New Year's Day in 1966;

> In making ready for this blessing I came to sense that Tony would face some hard, dangerous times ahead for him and his family on his return to his homeland. I sensed, too, that he would need foundational assurance and guidance. This man had more than ordinary potentials for leading out, for reaching out, in gospel mission. I planned to stand by him in God-directed companionship. [D:1981C]

Cheville said that "The blessing expressed approval of Tony's integrity, of his honest motivation. It pointed with assurance to happenings that he would be facing and to the commission that should be his in the evangelistic mission of the church." It was Tony's later testimony that the blessing did just that in the years during the Biafran war when he lost his home and all other possessions and was fully involved in just keeping his family alive.

For Patriarch Cheville, the process of giving the patriarchal blessing combined his love of people with his friendship with Jesus Christ, whose spirit was involved in the exacting process of giving the blessing.

Dear Saint:

The writing of letters—a hundred of them, to brothers around the world. I am sensing even more the universal spiritual fraternity possible in the Church of Jesus Christ. [Cheville notes written at Christmas 1964]

At the opening of the New Year I am writing letters to one hundred and fifty fellow saints in the Church of Jesus Christ. This circle of fellow saints stretches around the world, in all continents, in many islands. These brothers are coworkers in the cause of Christ. You are ambassadors with the good news of God. You are men with whom I make common covenant with Jesus Christ, our Friend.

I write because I rely on you, because God is needing you and relying on you these important days.

This year 1971 is calling us to achieve enlightened consensus that will emerge out of the creative fellowship of those who seek humbly and honestly together. We are needing divine direction. [Cheville letter to M. Ritchie in 1971]

As we have seen, Cheville's leadership in motivating congregations to write to individuals and groups offered an important ministry. Another facet of his ministerial use of letters was his person-to-person effort.

In these days of word processors it is difficult to comprehend what he managed to do with a fountain pen and paper. In the quotations above he was writing 100 letters at one Christmas time and 150 at another. Joe Bayless said that when he was with Roy during busy ministry weeks in Germany, Roy still found time to write something like 15 to 20 letters a week.

His letters were thoughtful and substantive. For example, when Velma Ruch was named Acting President of Graceland College in 1974 she wrote Cheville a letter which revealed periodic meaningful contacts. She began with "You have been involved in many important moments in my life, and I was deeply moved and appreciative of your beautiful letter."

Cheville wrote from time to time to Les and Ava Gardner. In December of 1964 he wrote to them in Korea,

> Dear Les and Ava,
>
> How many times during the year I have thought of you! I have endeavored to keep in touch with the happenings in the Korean Mission... I think of you working away with intent to bring good news to the people of Korea... Sometimes you will feel that we are far away and not in contact with you in the Orient. I assure you that I remember you... As I write, my heart turns to you in benedictory prayer... What a time to be living in the Church! May the Good Spirit direct as you explore and bond you and the Saints in fellowship.
>
> Fraternally Yours, Roy A. Cheville

In December of 1965 Cheville wrote again to Les and Ava Gardner,

> Months have passed since you wrote me. In your letter I was transported to the Orient and in imagination lived there. Since then you have gone to the land down under and returned to your field.
>
> And now as I remember the salutation at Bethlehem—"Which shall be to all people." You could stay in Korea, you could return to Australia, to New Zealand, you could go to Nigeria, to many places. The field is so great. The needs are so many. The calls are to urgent. The demands for effective interpretation and expression of the gospel are so insistent. What a day to be living, to be ministering!

Two months later Cheville again wrote to Les and Ava Gardner. This time they were in Honolulu. Les planned to attend the University of Hawaii for a time, then return to Korea. Cheville expressed pleasure at that prospect and noted that the result would enable Les to bring a more comprehensive and more competent contribution:

> I am sure that in Korea you face the need of developing and indigenous expression of the Restoration gospel together with the need to identify and cultivate the universals, the basics that are essential to this gospel. What a discriminating, discerning job is involved. I am glad you can get away for a while in order to see the situation panoramically and incisively.

In December of 1966 Cheville wrote again to the Gardners in Honolulu. In the letter was this observation,

> I do not know where your studies and subsequent years will bring. I am confident that these can open up a field of ministry richer than you have supposed. It might take you into university areas. Just now we are needing men and women of competence who will keep exploring as they keep living in the ongoing stream of the church. My legalistic friends do not want a stream—they want a placid pool. My "rebel" friends do not get into the stream—they sit on the bank and criticize the course of the stream. We need you, Les, as explorer, as participant.

Cheville continued to write to Les and Ava regularly while they were serving abroad, and from time to time after they returned to the continental U.S.

Glenn E. Hands, with his wife Margaret and son Roger, was in Lahore, West Pakistan as an employee of the Parsons Corporation. They had contact with other church members and considered themselves an "outpost of Zion." He wrote Cheville on September 12, 1965, saying, "I know you of the Center Place must be concerned... At times I can almost feel your prayers." They were caught up in the war between India and Pakistan, and Margaret and Roger were required to return to the U.S. "But," he said, "it is wonderful to know that God is watching over us. We are all perfectly safe."

Hands wrote Cheville again on September 30, 1965, saying,

> Your welcomed letter came today, one of the first since the cease-fire... It is so reassuring to have your message of encouragement and hope. Thank you for your prayers.

Cheville wrote to Mo Hope January 25, 1971 in response to a letter from Mo about a person he was counseling. Cheville wrote,

> ____'s case is so complex, yet so typical. I have been exposed to some of these cases. This week I am writing to a young man from

Buffalo, New York who is now in Grand Rapids, Michigan. He is on the way to healthiness.

Thanks for your picture of ____'s earlier life. It looks as if he had never learned the way of achieving through continuing application to a well-formulated purpose. Lonely and confused, he turned to find uplift and satisfaction in "quickie" methods. Today so many are needing meaning and motivation and they are looking to drugs and related measures to find something to bring "glow" to their living.

Keep writing to him. These fellows need companionship. Do not argue with him. Do not dwell on his experiences. I would be inclined to get him to write you the great things he thinks he has seen.

His staring at the head of lettuce or at the ceiling was typical. He really was staring without meaning, without insight, without commitment.

The use of drugs is widespread. Youth are rejecting the values and the methods of our contemporary society. They do not know how to go about changing things, so they escape in drug "elevations."

Write to ____ as a friend. Maybe you can draw him to go with you in the living of a disciple of Jesus Christ. Ordinarily Jesus rates well with them. Write of expanding, satisfying experience that reaches out to lift people.

I would say that you and I are about the only men with whom he feels free to write. Don't break the link. He needs you.

It was so good to be in your home. And Mo, it is always good to be with you. I feel a genuine spiritual fraternity with you. Sincerely, Roy."

In 1975 Cheville wrote a letter to Mrs. Dessa Hampton of Baxter, Iowa in honor of her birthday. She wrote him on February 26,

It was so nice to get a letter from you and I thank you for your verse about me. Ha Ha. I had a most wonderful 97th Birthday as many friends called and I received 86 Birthday cards. Not so bad to grow old when you are so well remembered.

I have kept tab on you thru the "Herald." I saw you baptized and felt at the time that God had need of clean young men like you and that He would make good use of you. He has done so and you have been faithful to his trust. May He continue to bless you all thru your days is my Prayer for you.

In November of 1980 Cheville wrote a letter to E. J. Gleazer, Jr. which had special significance to Ed. It was mostly about Ed's father, who had passed away in September 1980,

> I presume that your mother portrayed to you the happenings of the closing day. While I was at the lunch table in the dining room, a nurse said your mother requested that I come to their room on the third floor. Again I went alone. At her request I administered. A peaceful experience. I prayed for ease of body and of soul. In my inner praying I was looking to his peaceful departure, that it was time for him to move on.
>
> Your mother was sitting near by. I placed my hand on her shoulder and spoke a benedictory prayer.
>
> Later your mother told me that a half hour after I left, she stood by his bed, felt his hands, kissed them and she realized that he had just died—she responded with assurance that "the good thing" had taken place.
>
> During the memorial meeting at the Stone Church, I found myself thinking it would have been fitting for me to say a few testimonial words about my contacts and consociation with him during these closing days...
>
> It was your father who ordained me a high priest during a Lamoni reunion. I came from the University of Chicago summer session for the ordination. In the ordination prayer he spoke to me with prophetic counsel...
>
> Once in a high priests conference in Kirtland Temple he spoke significantly. He did not designate it as prophetic, but it was.

In early January of 1974, Cheville summarized his correspondence and other contacts in a letter to Duane Couey, of the First Presidency,

> My correspondence and my other contacts, such as by telephone reaches far, through the United States, to Canada, to other lands. I do not herald this. Publicity could weaken the ministry and distort the purpose. This is a phase of my ministry that does not go "through channels." Some of these reachings to me are for confession, some for soul-outpouring, some for counsel, some for benediction, and so on. Some of this entails going to where these people live. This ministry is in a worldwide field. [letter to Couey 1 Jan 74]

On April 19, 1974, Clifford A. Cole wrote to Cheville in reply to a letter of April 9.

> I appreciate very much your kindness in taking time to write. Of course, this has been true for most of the time you have served as presiding patriarch. I have quite a folder of letters you have written to me at various times and these have and still do mean a lot to me… Your affirmative attitude, your faith in God, your warm support of others and your wholesome view of life are so important. Your hope and faith in the future is catching.

Letters Received

> "Such as we are in word by letters when we are absent, such will be also in deed when we are present." II Cor. 10:11

> So wrote Paul of Tarsus to the Corinthian branch. He was pointing out that in his letters he reflected what he was. His epistles were an extension of him. When he could not go, he wrote. He sent counsel, encouragement, rebuke, instruction, testimony and personal greetings. The Christian movement was helped to get on its feet through the letters Paul wrote to people and to congregations. [pBull July 1960]

With these words, Cheville began a section entitled, "The Ministry of Letter Writing" in his *Bulletin to the Patriarchs* of July 1960. He went on to say that some are more comfortable in writing than others. Yet all can minister through simple messages sent at the right time and in the right spirit. Sometimes there is less danger of misunderstanding when the word is written. The simplest message sincerely written can speak to the heart.

He gave one example of a brief note he wrote to a man who had lost his wife. In his reply the man reminded Cheville, "You know how a man feels when he loses his companion. Things like your letter makes things a little easier." Cheville said that he regretted that he does not do more, for he believes in that ministry.

> I believe we can minister in this way when we cannot be present in body. Always we can be sincere and understanding. Always we can encourage to rightness and fidelity. Always we can keep the spirit of the benediction of Paul.

One measure of Cheville's spiritual stature coupled with his approachability lies in the number of letters he received from people who were encountering serious problems in their lives. A number of these had marital problems. Others had engaged in unwise behavior and were trying to find their way to personal reintegration.

Some had reached the point at which they wanted to have a better relationship with God.

Not every marriage was saved. Not every correspondent found his way to personal wholeness. And not every seeker found a new level of relating to divinity. But Cheville's deep understanding of people exerted a powerful influence for good. One letter he received from Topeka in September 1979 began, "Do you realize the changes you made in two people's lives? At one time...one day would drag along and then change into the next day... NOW we wish the days would not go so fast. ."

One young man who had been Cheville's Graceland student wrote him a letter in verse in 1963 about his searching and longing. He was looking to Cheville as a father but did not want to burden him too much with his problems. Over a number of years this young man wrote from time to time and came to visit Cheville occasionally. He felt that Cheville was the only person in the world to whom he could bare the inner feelings of his soul.

Another young man wrote in some despair about things going wrong for him in his job. He was ready to leave it. Cheville's response to that was rather direct,

> If you are leaving because a small group opposed you, I would not want you to go. On this basis I would have left Graceland several times. A man who stands for something in a significant way cannot want to be a hail-fellow-well-met with everyone liking him. Such a man, wanting like him, becomes weak as rainwater.

To a couple who were experiencing difficulty in their marriage he wrote in 1968,

> Dear _____ and _____,
>
> When I was in ___ I wanted to see you. This was no "official" call. I am well aware that when there is family tension no half-hour call is going to straighten things out. I never meant to do this.
>
> On my desk now is a letter from [your child] in _____. I met him first in _____ and then in _____. He told me of his reactions. And then he said he had written you. This was so promising. He said he felt at home with me.

I wish we had time to sit down together and confer. By now you need very much an understanding person to be with you in your conversing. By now you have developed some allergies toward one another. You need a third somebody to help resolve the strains.

Now your situation is strained but not impossible. One thing I suggest. When you converse, never try to find out whose "fault" it has been that things are as they are. Children seek to name whose "fault" it is. Mature individuals seek for "factors." They ask what factors entered in to bring about what emerged.

____, I see that the death of the baby came at a time when you were not developed and fortified for such an experience. Now you need not censure yourself because you blamed God. Use this experience to understand how others feel. God does not send specific germs to specific people. My wife died ten years ago of complicated malignancy. Some wanted me to call an all-church fast. I would not do so. I would not claim any priority. I was lonesome but never belligerent. I learned something about how people may react in bereavement. My personhood was mellowed. So can yours be.

____, when I was there I wanted to put my arm around you as a brother, in fraternal love. Yes, you have had frustrations in your achievements and setbacks in your idealism. God has not given up with you. Nor have I. As you master your way through present circumstances you can qualify for counseling ministry. I left that day with a sense of incompleteness.

You need so much to develop the art of conversing, of conversing without whacking away at problems, the art of putting things out on the table to discern the wholeness of the situation. You need to work out programs of procedures and principles with your children independent of specific tensions.

You will do well to include God as working with you in the solving of your problems, not giving easy, ready-made answers. You can do a wonderful exploration in searching for this insight.

So, _____, I read your letter through very carefully on my return to the office. I would say that I sense your perplexities. _____ is facing confusion, too, so do not pressure him now. Ask concerning specific problems without trying to force response or reply.

And _____, I suggest you listen as best you can, so you can catch moods and hungers. May it help you to realize I'd like to stand by you as a brother.

Don't give up now! The growing period can come.

Sincerely, Roy C. Roy Cheville

To another couple he wrote in 1969 that his heart had gone out to both of them when he had been in their home for a short while. To the husband he discussed his difficulty in the teaching profession especially in classroom discipline. Cheville surmised this was connected with his own inner confusion and turmoil, and he advised the man not to surrender to his problems. Cheville felt that the family turmoil was of long standing, and he wondered if they had ever been able to sit at a conference table and plan together so as to achieve common consent with mutuality.

In 1970 Cheville received a letter from another person giving a progress report after counseling,

> Sure was nice to hear from you and as you said it really is great to have a friend… During the months and years when I was abusing the proper use of drugs so much I fell into many vain and foolish trains of thought and I guess I was pretty ill in my attitudes. I frightened my parents excessively with the wild doctrines and philosophies I came up with. After about three years of fairly heavy drug abuse I came to be a rather deteriorated soul. In fact there were days that I just screamed out in agony saying things like, "God, I wish I were dead."… I'd like to tell you of my conversion to Christ. It was a very dynamic experience… Well, as I've rebuilt my life, that marvelous vision has come to be a daily part of my life… I told you that day in your office I want to be a missionary and a musician. You asked my why I couldn't do both. I never forgot that and that's what I'm doing." All my love,

In 1974 Cheville received a letter which admitted, "I sat down many times to write you, but I could not overcome my shame and self-pity." The writer had been divorced and said he had tried to find his way in the world without the Lord's help. He had not held a steady job, and had met old friends following the ways of the world and fell into the same old rut. But now he was working for some fine people of the church. He was reading and studying again and said, "I shall *never* fall away again. God be with you. Thank you for being my friend. Love, Peace, Happiness."

Cheville was on the receiving end of the group letter process in 1973. On July 24 Kasper and Anna Anholt wrote from Oslo, Norway,

> Enclosed herewith you will find a letter addressed to you from the Saints of Norway, Sweden and Denmark, plus Brother and Sister Gordon Schofield and their family from England.
>
> I believe that we got the signatures of all who were present—43. The largest reunion we have ever had since we were assigned to this mission.
>
> It was an outstanding reunion. All the services were exceptionally good.
>
> We ended with baptizing 4. This included Kirsten Lundin, Villy's wife and their oldest son Jens; and two children from Porsgrunn…
>
> We want to close this letter with our personal gratitude for your interest in us, in what we are endeavoring to accomplish. Thank you for the kind words you mentioned about us in the Tennessee-Kentucky reunion. May you remain in good health. May God bless you! Sincerely, Kasper and Anna Anholt.

On June 29, 1974 R. L. Booker wrote Cheville after hearing of his release as presiding patriarch. His letter included these thoughts,

> Somehow your life has been so full; you have given so much; your vitality seemed never to tire and like the three Nephite I just thought you would go on and on.
>
> However, regardless of not being the presiding patriarch, I know that *you will go on and on* and as long as there is a church, the impact of your versatility; you will be in the hearts and minds of people.
>
> In some ways, you have been like the hero of my boyhood story books—the Horatio Alger series. You have given so much but although you may have had encouragement from many, you worked and climbed to the top in just about everything that I know about you.

Ted Medler wrote Cheville July 21, 1976 to thank him for Cheville's letter to him. He said "It is very nice to know that there are those good friends who are always concerned about our welfare… The other way, Roy, I want you to know that we are always concerned about you and have a great deal of affection for you and your ministry and the things you have done for so many people. You are a challenge and an example for a great amount of good."

The letters Cheville received had a powerful effect on him. He was always energized by his contact with other people:

> Between all people there is some personal force. In great souls it is almost magnetic, stimulating and inspiring us when we meet them... In a similar manner God's presence should inspire men, if they are in tune with him. His infinite personality—his Holy Spirit—can touch our limited personalities and warm, inspire, and lead us. [C:1933D]

When he received letters from his church friends, he was stimulated in the area of his lifetime covenant. He gained some insights into current issues affecting the people to whom he was committed. He frequently learned from their responses that the ministry which was his life work was indeed being effective. Frequently his response was to create some new written expression to incorporate a new interpretation of the spiritual world about him. For example the comprehensive letter in Appendix K about the nature of the church was written in January of 1977 in response to an inquiry by Washington Bot Otiene, of Nairobi, Kenya.

Cheville made a somewhat similar response when Wilson Ritchie wrote him from Southern California in October of 1984 asking for guidance on putting together a meeting on evangelism. Cheville wrote an eight page response in long hand on October 27. [Appendix L]

Cheville's response to the request of Wilson Ritchie was typical. Many letters addressed to Cheville clearly energized him to thought and to action. Even though he was extraordinarily generous with his ministerial energy, this exchange clearly shows the synergistic reciprocal force which activated his creativity.

W. Wallace Smith wrote Cheville November 16, 1984 in response to a Cheville letter which was signed by a number of friends of Wallace. Smith expressed appreciation for Cheville's group letter and for Cheville's letters over the years:

> Dear Roy: This holographic communication answer to you, two days before my 84th birthday anniversary, with deep appreciation for your friendship and support of my ministry for lo these many years.
>
> Your birthday communications thru the years has created quite an extensive file in my office. Each one has been *unique* and *meaningful*. This one with the accompanying list of signatures holds a special place for me, coming as it does 6 days after Rosamond and I celebrated our 60th wedding anniversary. I will share it with our son and daughter.
>
> I will not try to respond to each person on the list of "signing friends" but I will appreciate having you express my heartfelt thanks to each and every one of my well wishers when you are next together. Yours in the bonds of the Gospel. W. Wallace Smith, President Emeritus

Prison Ministry

> I happen to be inclined toward those who need some brothering. Recently I have gone out to Lansing Prison, Lansing, Kansas, in the Seven Steps Program which looks to helping prisoners to get ready for release, for taking their place in society. I figure that this is part of my ministry. Some weeks or so ago I made acquaintance with a young man, now twenty nine years of age. A fine appearing fellow. When I talked to him, he opened up and said, "I've been in four federal and state institutions—this is the first time any man has ever expressed any interest or compassion in me. I shall never forget this as long as I live." [Cheville letter to Ned Lysinger 16 Sept 1970]

The first written references to Roy Cheville's ministry to people in prison dates from 1970. His son Richard states that such ministry to prison inmates began while Cheville lived in Iowa, before 1960. Richard remembers that his father visited the Iowa state prison at Fort Madison. Wayne Zion said that he drove Cheville several times to Lansing, Kansas to the state prison there after Cheville's ordination to presiding patriarch. Ruth Zion says that many trips were made to prisons, including some when she went along.

A letter to Cheville from a man we will call I.Y., whom Cheville met on one of these trips, responded in July of 1970 to a letter written by Cheville,

> I was deeply moved when I read your letter. I am not used to receiving letters from people that are really concerned about my welfare, from people who expect very much out of my future. It gives me a good feeling inside of me, to be able to call you a true friend. It helps so much to know that someone thinks you are worth something. I have been wondering how you and I did develop a friendship. You come from an environment so different from what I have known... Roy, I wish that someday we could just sit down and talk for a few hours.

(In 1973 Cheville offered to sponsor I.Y. when he was to be released.)

Another prisoner connection is revealed in a letter to Cheville from John P. Davenport, Chaplain of the Florida State Prison, written December 30, 1970. He said that Cheville's letter was referred to him and he had given the letter to F. He said F. deeply appreciated it. "If you would like to visit F. please write me and give me a tentative day and time you plan to be in the area on two weeks notice. We will be glad to arrange a meeting for you." It is not clear whether a meeting with F ever took place.

In Cheville's notes there is a paper with the title "Field for Friendship," dated September 11, 1971. It was apparently prepared for delivery at the Lansing State Prison. One paragraph from that paper is,

> This morning I would like you to meet my friend, Jesus of Nazareth, who says to me, "Henceforth, I am calling you friend!" He knows what kind of a fellow Roy Cheville is. He sees potentials in me yet to be tapped for worthy purpose. He says to me, "Come, let's work together for reaching out in friendship to my other men. Men, let's do some cultivating in this field of friendship." [notes found in 1986]

A letter to Cheville dated June 28, 1973 implies that he had written to H.G., an inmate, in the prison in Raiford, Florida. H.G. wrote,

> I received your letter and enclosed pamphlets. Thank you. It was very nice to hear from you and I really appreciate your kindness and help. I wrote a letter to Mr. Ronald Yager. You mentioned in your letter that you would be interested in learning more of my nature and my situations that brought me to Raiford. So here it goes pertaining to my background. I was born in... New York. I moved to Florida when I was thirteen. This is the time when I started getting in trouble. Things like skipping school and such. I was sent to a home for this. Later on I progressed to more serious things like stealing by breaking and entering houses and businesses.
>
> I am in here for the crime of buying and concealing stolen property. I have finally reached the end of the line and this type of life as it is not for me. I received a seven year sentence for this crime. I never have been up on religion and I read some articles about your Church and I know it holds something for me and I know I can be a good useful person to myself others and the church. So this is why

I wrote you. I am looking very much to hear from Mr. Ronald Yager in the near future.

I am very grateful to you as a man in your position showing attention to me. As I never have received this from anyone as my parents were all ways to busy for me, business first me next. As I came from what you would call a secure well off family. Well thank you for taking time out of your busy schedule to read this letter. Please excuse the writing instrument I used but this is all I had at present and wanted to answer your letter as soon as I could. Well, I'll bring this letter to a close. Hope to hear from you soon. That you again. I remain most, Respectfully yours, H.G.

H.G. sent Cheville a Christmas card in 1973 from the prison in Raiford, and he wrote another letter in December of 1973,

Received your most welcomed letter tonight at Mail Call. Glad to hear you enjoyed your trip. It sure must have been a most interesting one as it was a little extensive. Yes, I was most glad of the visit by Mr. Ron Yager and Company. I never was aware of Mr. Yager's background as he has sure traveled much abroad.

I must truthfully say that your involvement with Mr. I. Y. is one that I'm very much proud of you for as many people are unaware that prisoners are people like everyone else and just that they have made the mistake of going astray shouldn't be cut off or no concern shown.

This has been a short coming in regards to many people on their outlook on prisoners for some reason. I will take your advice on asking Mr. Yager to counsel with me in regards of my personal situation. I have found two things that I never had since I came here to Prison, God and you. You just don't know what a part you have played. Your talks just give off a fellowship and concern that is incomparable to describe. I really look forward to your letters greatly.

I'm eligible for parole at anytime under the Florida laws. The Chaplain here (James Tompkins) has been a great light unto my feet as he sure has shown patience, kindness, and understanding. I really enjoy working with him at the Chapel very much.

The weather here has been most mild and nice and sunny the last few days. Really more like Spring than winter. Well, Christmas is right around the corner. May my prayers and best wishes be with you and your family at this Season of Greetings.

I guess I better close this letter for now as it is about lights out—bedtime. So until later, take care and write soon as I'll be waiting for your letter. Respectfully Yours, H.G.

H.G. wrote Cheville again in July of 1974 from the prison in Raiford, Florida

> Just received your letter, which was as always joy sent my way... I would appreciate any material you may furnish me on pertaining to the church, as I wish to know more. You have never push [sic] any material on me and now I believe is the time for me to learn more, as I feel that the Church is for me and I wish to get it all together. I would like to let you know that you are the greatest person I have ever known in any way. You never cease to amaze me! It would be a great privilege to me if we ever get the opportunity to meet each other in person. We have already met in the Spirit, which is truly beautiful...

It is not clear how long the prison ministry of Roy Cheville continued.

BOOK XIII

Evolving Theology

Perception of Divinity

> He was the Messiah they had been looking for: only they had been mistaken about his mission, about what made him divine. They had to look for a different kind of sign—not what happened before their eyes but what took place inside them. [A:1951B]

> Jesus did not spend time arguing that he was divine. Never did he debate about it. Never did he parade it...
>
> His method was to select men to be with him, to live with him, to work with him, that out of his association they would detect his divinity...
>
> Jesus meant for his disciples to sense the divine qualities that were expressed in his personhood. They had to be able to detect these. This required spiritual development in them. These were the qualities of divinity that were in his Father. [pBull Feb 66]

In our age, it is difficult to carry on a discussion about the reality of divinity. Many individuals deny its very existence. In the United States we have laws restricting the places where religious symbols and practices can be seen and heard. On the other hand we have a large percentage of the population who declare themselves to be religious and demonstrate that declaration by attending religious services.

A recent study has put a new slant on the reality of divinity. This study reported that the overwhelming majority of the surgeons questioned said that prayer affects the physical healing process in their patients, thus reporting on the results of their own observations. This is not about what they believe; it is about what they have seen—evidence of something at work in their field which is the result of religious practice.

How does one perceive divinity? In the New Testament accounts it is clear that most of the people who saw and heard Jesus did not perceive his divinity. Those among his own people who insisted that he be put to death could not see that he was divine. Even when their wish was carried out they no idea that they had been wrong. They were looking for evidence that would appear before their eyes. Roy Cheville said they were using the wrong sensors.

Cheville talked and wrote many times about the way to perceive divinity. He believed that people should look not at what appears before their eyes, but that they should pay attention to what happens inside them. There lies the effect of their interaction with divinity. Do they feel the power of uplift? Is there definitive assurance? Do they understand with enlarged perspective? Such questions as these can direct attention to the presence of divinity. People may be alone in prayer, in a meeting, with a friend, with a teacher, or with a witness. Divinity may be present in many situations. The ability to detect divinity is a matter of developing the ability to sense and to identify the spiritual qualities.

Cheville once told the story of an old fisherman who was asked how he knew the Christ is risen. He answered,

> Do you see those cottages on the shore near the cliff? Sometimes when I am far out at sea, I know that the sun is risen by the reflection on those windows. In the same way I know that Christ is risen because I see the light of eternal life reflected from the faces of my friends and neighbors. I see the life of Christ in them. [pBull Mar 59]

The point of divinity working within the person was present in Cheville's description of an event that occurred at a meeting of High Priests in Kirtland Temple in 1960. An air of expectancy prevailed. Some hoped for the extraordinary to happen as was recorded in that Temple in 1836. One morning E.J. Gleazer, Sr. spoke in the testimony meeting with what Cheville described as great spiritual clarity and insight:

> You have longed for the expression of my Spirit. You have wanted marvelous manifestations. Were you to return to your congregations and your communities and tell them that here you had heard

> the voice of angels, the words of prophecy, the gift of tongues, men could discount and deny your testimony... If, however, you return with lives changed because here you have been with God and have heard his voice, men will not deny this testimony. [pBull Aug 66]

People tend to look for evidences of the action of divinity in faith healing and other events described in the New Testament as "miracles." They are looking for things which can be seen by the eye. Cheville notes that Jesus did not draw attention to these happenings. He told those who were healed not to tell about their experience. He did not repeat the feeding of the multitude with the five loaves and fishes. These acts of compassion on his part did not carry the essential message he was working to transmit.

Cheville believed that the great miracle is to happen within us. He said,

> The genuine testimony has to do with what happens in a person's life as God's transforming power functions in his whole personhood. Then as Paul says in the fifth chapter of II Corinthians this person becomes "a new creation." The "quiet miracle" takes place on the *inside*. It is expressed on the *outside*... Such qualities as love and faith and hope cannot be put on the stage and paraded. They have to be lived with in order to be discerned. [pBull Aug 66]

Cheville taught that if Jesus had based his program on repetitions of such acts as healing and feeding the multitude, he would have had increasing numbers of followers. But, in the end his movement would not have survived. It would not have had the dynamic in it to make permanent changes in the lives of the followers.

Instead, Jesus selected a small number of men who became his disciples. He lived with them and he taught them. He did not live *among* them, he lived *with* them. They were in close association so they could come to understand how he worked, how he thought, and how he prayed. In this process they finally came to understand what divinity was like within Jesus and to recognize it. What was happening was a change within themselves that would allow this understanding. This growing action of the good Spirit within them allowed them to perceive the Christ within Jesus. The survival of Christianity depended on these changes which had taken place *within* these few disciples.

Cheville advised the patriarchs to nourish and detect the effects of divinity by living with the church people for whom they were called. They were to reinforce each other in developing spiritual qualities. They were to learn increasingly more about recognizing those spiritual qualities in each other. And, they were to live with the Spirit of the ever living Jesus Christ. They were to maintain their communion with him as the single most important person with whom they could interact. Perceiving the actions of divinity was to be a matter of developing and recognizing those significant things that took place *inside* them. He said, "The Holy Spirit comes to man by living for inspiration rather than by begging for spiritual favor." [D:1961G]

Cheville wrote further,

> Jesus never indulged in processions except once. He went apart with his chosen disciples that they might get to know him and catch the dynamic qualities of his personality. Only those who have spiritual qualities in their own natures would be able to detect divine attributes within him. So he told his followers, "Blessed are the pure in heart, for they shall see God." The crowds shouted "Hosannah!" and strewed the road with palm branches as Jesus rode into Jerusalem in his one triumphal procession. They were seeing the externals. They never saw what made him divine. [A:1951B]

Beyond Scriptural Monopoly

> The Restoration movement has contributed something invaluable to my theological explorations. The Book of Mormon and the Doctrine and Covenants have delivered me from reliance on some one scriptural source. Without diminishing in any way the contribution of the Bible, these Scriptures picture God at work on another continent in ancient times and in our modern age, enlightening exploring souls who tried to see him at work through history. They widen the witness and extend the inspiration of God. They break down the limitations that men have imposed on God. [D:1961R]

From his earliest days in the Church, Roy Cheville understood that God interacts with any person who achieves the right state of heart and mind in seeking contact with divinity. Some people who have done that are described in the Bible, but only some of them. That being the case, one can look for additional experiences to learn more about the relation of divinity to humans. The belief and practice of contemporary interaction with the Holy Spirit does not diminish the value of the Bible. Instead of replacing or diminishing, it supplements and validates the Bible. One can achieve additional evidence to support the experiences related in the Bible and to enrich one's understanding of them.

Cheville found additional evidence to illuminate God's work with humans in four places; 1) his own experiences, 2) experiences of his coworkers, 3) experiences related in the Book of Mormon, and 4) experiences recorded in the Doctrine and Covenants. Without these additional sources of evidence he would have found himself restricted to those accounts which are found in the Bible. That is what he meant by the phrase "scriptural monopoly." He used that phrase in referring to the writings of Karl Barth,

> I struggled through the writings of such as Barth and found a narrow monopoly of the Bible. Most of the "neo-s" take a course that is not dissimilar. I came to want something else that would give a world functioning of God. I came to say that if we did not have

> something like the Book of Mormon, we ought to have, that we might be delivered from this fencing-in Biblicism. I still think so. [Letter to Verne Sparks 11 Aug 69]

In an article entitled "Beyond Scriptural Monopoly" Cheville noted that Christianity has often been called "the religion of a book." The only other competitor for such a title is the Moslem faith with the Koran, but the Moslems have not quoted their book for proof as have Christians. Jews have looked to the Old Testament, but they also have the Talmud. "Christians have elevated their one book, the Bible, to a place of eminence and have accorded it high authority." This has been especially true of Protestant churches.

Further, Cheville wrote,

> In the early decades of the nineteenth century the Latter Day Saints came into this picture with a daring declaration. These pioneers struck right at the citadel of Bible monopoly. They said that a Bible had been produced in ancient times on the Western continent and that it had recently been published. This western Bible was scriptural, too. [D:1968F]

The Latter Day Saint belief and practice about scriptures was extended when the Doctrine and Covenants was published in 1835 and after. Now the young church was selecting what should go into the canon of scripture. Cheville wrote, "these pioneers were sure of this: God had never signed off in scripture producing. They affirmed a present-tense, communicating God."

Among the Latter Day Saints, the Bible is held in high repute as "the word of God," but it is not looked upon as "the only word" or as the "completed word." Jesus Christ is considered the core person, but he is not to be limited to one time and place. After one has consulted the Bible, one can learn more about divinity by reading the other two scriptures and by seeking direct inspiring guidance of the Spirit of the ever-present, ever-living Jesus Christ. Such spiritual experience can validate the results of those past spiritual experiences found in the Bible. Cheville wrote,

> As we mature in spiritual appreciation of scriptures we come to see that the true validation has to come through using what is in them. The testing is on the laboratory of living out the message of the writing. Supporters can bring in correlative materials and supports. If there is no inherent worth in the scriptural writing, it cannot be "proved." And this method of examination and validation applies to every scriptural writing.

Cheville continued with a list of contributions the Book of Mormon can make to stand alongside the Bible:

> (1) Needed: a universal Christ whose living, teaching, and revealing rise above any restricting cultural pattern in which they are expressed. The Book of Mormon makes the Christ of Judah and Galilee the Christ of the Western lands also. It makes him the "one shepherd" of all times and places.
>
> (2) Needed: a theology of history that portrays God in ongoing purpose, in all-peoples operation. The Book of Mormon pushes out the operation of God into all the world. God is ever creating, ever working everywhere, with his plans and processes rising above restricting notions of any one set of writings.
>
> (3) Needed: the functioning of a library of scriptures that express the divine outreach of God to man in multiple thought worlds and languages. The Book of Mormon brings scripture to this library from the Western continent...
>
> The Book of Mormon belongs in the world's library of scripture. [D:1968F]

Of Cheville's writings about the Book of Mormon, the most definitive is his book *The Book of Mormon Speaks for Itself.* [A:1971A] Here are two selections from a group he calls "passages of merit,"

> *Soliloquy on Evangelistic Ministry* [pp. 153, f]
>
> Alma is speaking out of a troubled situation. A disastrous war between the Nephites and the Lamanites has just come to a close. Casualties have been heavy. Anguish of mourning pervades the country. Alma is saying to himself, "Must there be war? Is there not a better way?" as he wonders, he sees two things in contrast: "sorrow because of death and destruction among men, and joy because

of the light of Christ unto life" (Alma 15:51). The longing to be a missionary with the gospel of transforming spiritual power prompts Alma to pour out his soul in reflection. There is nothing in scripture that stands above it. It rises to the height when he senses the satisfaction of affecting one life for good. Here is an affirmation of the worth of every person. Here is the expression of true evangelistic joy. There is no concern for "conversions." Here is expressed the satisfaction of finding brotherly consociation in Christ (see Doctrine and Covenants 16:2c-d). (What is given here is an abridged version of selected passages.)

O that I were an angel
and could have the wish of my heart,
that I might go forth
and speak with the trump of God,
and with a voice to shake the earth,
and cry repentance to this people!

Yea, I would declare unto every soul,
as with the voice of thunder,
repentance and the plan of salvation,
that they might repent, and come unto our God,
that there might be no more sorrow
upon all the face of the earth.

But behold, I am a man,
And I do sin in my wish!
I ought to be content
with the things which the Lord
has allotted to me.

I know that he allots unto men
according to their wills,
whether they be to salvation
or unto destruction.

Now, seeing these things,
why should I desire more
than to perform this work to which I have been called?

Why should I wish that I were an angel,
that I could speak
unto all the ends of the earth?
I know that the Lord has commanded me,
and I glory in it,
not of myself, but in the Lord.

And this is my glory,
that perhaps I may be an instrument
in the hands of God
to bring some soul to repentance.

And this is my joy!

The Functioning of Faith [pp. 156, ff]

The classic adapted for use here is rightly called a treatise, a testimony, on "the functioning of faith." Here Alma interprets faith as a growing experience, ever in process. Faith does not come all at once and does not "stay put" as a finished product. Alma likens faith experience to the growing of a fruit-bearing tree from a simple seed. He uses the words "experiment" and "exercise." Faith-nurturing and the fruit-bearing go together. And such a faith has roots; it is more than wishing and daydreaming. Planting and cultivating are involved.

Alma had just been among the Zoramites. He had noted their strange Rameumpton form of worship (see Alma 16:97ff). This required little of the worshipers and brought forth little from them. It caused a breach between the well-to-do and the less privileged and identified divine favor with material things. Against this background Alma poured out his reflections on dynamic, exacting, adventuring faith. He made faith operative in the laboratory of living.

This is a digest of his longer treatise. It brings together his key comments. The material begins with Alma 16:139.

If you have faith,
you hope for things which are not seen,
which are true.

There are many who say,
If you will show us a sign from heaven,
then we will know of a surety;
then we shall believe.

Now I ask you, Is this faith?
I say unto you that it is not.
Faith is hope for things not yet seen,
things which are true.

And this is so with my words.
Awake and arouse your faculties
and experiment upon my words.
Exercise a particle of faith.

Compare the word unto a seed.
If a seed is planted in your heart,
  a true seed, a good seed,
if you do not cast it out by your unbelief,
if you resist not the Spirit of the Lord,
it will begin to swell within you.

You will say to yourself,
This must be a good seed,
for it begins to enlighten my understanding.

Because you have tried the experiment,
when you planted the seed,
and because it swells, and sprouts and grows,
you will know that the seed is good.

As the seed grows into a tree, you will say,
Let us nourish the tree, with great care,
that it may grow and bring forth fruit.

The seed may be good, but your ground may be barren,
and you may not nourish the tree,
so you will not have fruit from it.

When I speak to you,
you do not know of the surety
of my words at first:
you must experiment upon them.

If you will nourish the seed that is planted,
and nourish the tree,
there will be a tree springing up into everlasting life.

Alma's words on the functioning of faith are very similar to Cheville's references to validating religion in the laboratory of living. Both imply that there should be an empiricism in religion. Both conclude that the way to learn more after having read the books is through one's own personal experiences.

Grace Versus Holy Spirit

Heretofore in this book one or two quotations have introduced a chapter. In this chapter four are used. Each captures an important statement by Cheville on his distinctive and controversial conclusions about grace, the Holy Spirit, and salvation. The first of these declares that "grace" and "salvation" do not carry meaning in today's thought world as they did in biblical days:

> An oft-spoken criticism of religion is that it frequently uses an archaic terminology and an outgrown thought pattern. Theologians and preachers are credited with tossing about in parrot-like repetition phrases that do not carry meaning to moderns. Words so listed are "atonement," "redemption," "sin," "salvation," "grace," "justification." When originally used these words spoke to their times. Men of today are telling theologians to drop them and find fresh, meaningful words or interpret them in terms that carry clear, functional meaning for now. These comments invite the exploring theologian to exacting study. [D:1961R]

The second quotation reports comments by Saints in 1971 that talk of grace did not serve their concern about matters of the Holy Spirit:

> Concern XII. Our theologians are weak in their interpretations and emphases of what is vital in our Restoration church. We hear a lot about grace and the like, but not much about the Holy Spirit. ["Let's Listen to and Learn From Our People!" [*pBull* April 1971]

The third quotation from Cheville's 1975 book about the Holy Spirit draws historical and functional differences between grace and the Holy Spirit:

> Not much has been written and published about the Holy Spirit. Books on theology have had little, if anything, to say. Sometimes it appears that the subject is avoided...
>
> 1. The Holy Ghost was considered something to be experienced, not examined. It was to speak for itself. Critical thinking was looked upon as hostile to and destructive of the expected experience...

5. Other words could be used that would be safer—words that would take care of the matter with less confusion and speculation. Such a word was *grace*...

8. When administrators wanted to develop and maintain a centralized operation of a church, both in thinking and in operation, they could do so more effectively when they disregarded the "life of the Spirit." The person who advocated guidance by the Spirit tended to look directly to God rather than to church administrators. People "led by the Spirit" got in the way with their individualistic interpretations and expressions. [A:1975A]

The fourth quotation is a short treatise on Cheville's conception of the functional work of the Holy Spirit:

> *Holy Spirit*. The Holy Spirit is the personal spiritual power that emanates from God, for enabling the person to live the saintly life. Jesus promised to his disciples that this Spirit would minister to them, after he would be away from them in bodily presence. As the sunlight enables plants and trees to grow, this Spirit enables people to live, to grow spiritually. This Spirit is designed to develop spiritual *fruits* in people (Galatians 5:22). God endows certain people with additional expressions that are called spiritual *gifts* (I Corinthians 12). Jesus advised that this Holy Spirit is to comfort (strengthen) his disciples for good works, to enlighten, to achieve harmony and peace in the person, with God, with the Saints. [Appendix K, 1977]

The concept of grace occupies an important position in the New Testament. It originated with the Apostle Paul, who wrote about it in many of his letters. From that origin it developed into a key theological principle in the Roman Catholic Church and then in Protestant churches. That position continues.

Paul was one of Roy Cheville's favorite biblical individuals. He quoted him more often than any other in the New Testament except Jesus. He was impressed with Paul's vigor and intellectual honesty. He saw Paul as having honest intent and enthusiasm as he persecuted Christians. He said that Paul was the kind of person God wanted and all God had to do was change Paul's direction. Cheville saw his own experiences reflected in Paul's description of being influenced by the Holy Spirit. He agreed that one becomes a new being under the influence of the Spirit.

However, Cheville came to the conclusion that Paul did a lot of damage to Christianity with his theory of grace, particularly in the connection with salvation. In his statements opposing grace and works he created an enduring, exhausting, but fruitless controversy.

Cheville noted that Jesus did not talk about grace. The message to the young Joseph Smith, "This is my beloved son, hear him," Cheville regarded in part as an invitation to pay prime attention to original sources.

The Restoration began with that direct spiritual experience initiated by the young Joseph Smith. The movement continued with a central emphasis on direct contact with the Holy Spirit. Church procedures were set up to institutionalize the recognition and confirmation of spiritual guidance to the church. These were called revelations, the result of seeking spiritual guidance by the prophet on behalf of all the church. All members were taught to seek spiritual guidance to enlighten their own development. Over the years members shared their testimony of spiritual guidance to the church and to individual members.

Roy Cheville identified these spiritual experiences as the basic substance of religion. He noted that such experiences were the essence of much of the Bible. A particularly dramatic example lay in the description of the events on the day of Pentecost, in confirmation of the teachings of Jesus. Further, Cheville noted that the Spirit seemed to work with people in biblical days in much the same way as it worked with him and with his friends in the church.

When Cheville went to the University of Chicago, he learned a great deal about the history and substance of theology. He learned particularly how theologies had developed. He proceeded to develop over the years a theology which would explain systematically the religious experiences and practices of his own people. He continued refining that theology until the day he died. He hoped others would carry on that effort, building on what he had accomplished. The basic element in his theology was that of the direct contact between individuals and divinity. He symbolized that defining principle above the baptismal font in the Lamoni church as people reaching up and God reaching down to make direct contact with the words "This is my beloved son, hear him." For Cheville himself he said he had made contact.

In the World Conference of 1966 a resolution was passed laying out six objectives for the church. One of these was "to clarify the theology of the church." The Committee on Basic Beliefs took the lead in implementing this objective. The committee reified the term *theology*; e.g., they started with the assumption that it existed. Having reified it, they went looking for it. They identified it to their satisfaction in Protestant seminaries where they found a rich and flourishing theological culture. They studied the work of many theologians, but they did not find the work of Roy Cheville among them. They did find *grace,* and they proceeded over the years to articulate a theology of grace.

The committee's emphasis on grace in part grew from their feeling that grace had been neglected or even ignored in the thought of the church. When they issued a book in 1970, *Exploring The Faith*, four of their nineteen paragraphs were about the Holy Spirit, but there was one about grace and salvation:

> We believe that man cannot be saved in the Kingdom of God except by the grace of the Lord Jesus Christ, who loves us while we are yet in our sins, and who gave his life to reconcile us unto God. Through this atonement of the Lord Jesus Christ and by the gift of the Holy Spirit, men receive power to choose God and to commit their lives to him; thus they are turned from rebellion, healed from sin, renewed in spirit, and transformed after the image of God in righteousness and holiness.

If Cheville had been on that committee he would have explained that there is nothing functional in the idea of grace that cannot be handled better with a refined understanding of the Holy Spirit. He believed that abundant evidence of the Holy Spirit existed in personal experiences, and thus it was a reality to be explored. Grace, on the other hand, is an idea about the nature of God, which Cheville thought to be untestable, and therefore without useful meaning.

These were the reasons he rejected Paul's concept of grace and its connection to salvation. Salvation, he said, is the process by which people work with the Holy Spirit to develop eternal qualities in their lives. He specifically rejected the notion that we gain eternal life because Jesus paid a price for us in his crucifixion. For him, the symbol of spiritual power in the relation between God and human is not the cross but the image of human reaching up to God and God reaching down to human. He believed that Jesus Christ is that part of divinity which is involved in human development and reached down by taking human form. He believed that the Holy Spirit is the Spirit of Jesus Christ.

Members of the Church found it difficult to reconcile the theology of grace with the role of the Holy Spirit in the Church's history; to reconcile grace with the operation of revelation by the prophet in leading the Church; and to relate their own experiences with the Holy Spirit to this theology of grace. But the work of "clarifying the theology of the Church" went on, now being defined and implemented as a theology of grace.

Finally, in 1995 Gregory Prymak could report [*Authority in the RLDS Theological Tradition,* Independence, Mo. Graceland/Park Press 1995] that the defined theology for the Church was in place. But the problem, as he saw it, was that the members of the Church did not believe it. Their views and their experiences were somewhere else.

In short, the work to clarify the theology of the Church was an intellectual triumph and an operational failure. It was a brilliant work in internal consistency, but it did not explain, nor did it further the religious experiences of the Saints. A great many Saints have voted with their feet against the theology of grace by leaving the church.

Presiding Patriarch Cheville faced up to the ferment about theology as it was developing. He could not lobby his way onto the Committee on Basic Beliefs. He could not charm his way to an invitation to sit in on the meetings of the Joint Council. He could not engage members of those groups in conversation in an attempt to influence their outlook. He could preach to church congregations. He could write books and articles to be read by church members. He could use his monthly *Bulletins to the Patriarchs* to refine the thinking of the patriarchs, and to communicate with members of the committee and the Council. He proceeded to do all these. After he became presiding patriarch, he wrote 16 books, 171 articles and 184 *Bulletins to the Patriarchs*. But the leaders of the Church chose a different emphasis.

Cheville's extraordinary power as teacher and minister came from the integrating force of his belief in the availability of the Holy Spirit. It was operational in his life and many people responded to his theological message. They found in it a functional religious practice based on the life-enlarging actions of the Holy Spirit, the Spirit of the ever-living Jesus Christ. They found in it something to which they could dedicate their lives.

BOOK XIV

Life Style

On the Other Hand

> As I read of your experiences in the March issue of the Herald, I am reminded that you were my first real minister. And you continue to Minister! I know of no other people who has had as much influence over as many people as you. I sometimes wonder if Christ is in our midst, and we just really are unaware of it. With admiration and love. [Letter from Phil Briggs, Graceland 1943, to Cheville, 17 Mar 80]

> The last time I saw him socially he was quite a bore. He kept turning the group conversation to stories he wanted to tell. [1926 Graceland graduate referring to an event in the 1980s]

When Roy Cheville arrived at church headquarters in 1958 as presiding patriarch he was widely loved, respected, and honored. At the time of his death in 1986 there was a good deal of ambivalence toward him. Some administrators were opposed to his theological stance; others felt threatened by his vigorous and effective ministry in their territory. Some church people were offended by his self-confidence, which they interpreted, rightly or wrongly, as arrogance; others felt that he singled out people he wanted to be with and ignored many others.

One question that arises is whether he could have alleviated this ambivalence if he had done some things differently. That question has several parts. Could he have spent time in discussions with administrators to defuse negative attitudes? Could he have made it a point to have frequent personal contacts with people in administrative positions? Could he have been more of a team player?

He had established his concepts and his ministry at Graceland College in the context of colleagues and of administrators who were not always in agreement with his approaches. Many of them could see in a few short years how effective his service was. In time he won many of them over, though some colleagues never accepted his ministry. His underlying theology had the support of Frederick M. Smith, then President of the RLDS Church, for the first 23 years of his faculty service at Graceland.

When Cheville became presiding patriarch the major opponent to his ideas was F. Henry Edwards. Edwards had sparked the move to rival Cheville's program in religion at Graceland by starting the School of the Restoration. Edwards was also the chairman of the Committee on Basic Beliefs, which took the lead in defining theology for the church. And Edwards was designated to be the member of the First Presidency responsible for relations with the presiding patriarch. Among the first actions of the First Presidency affecting Cheville were the decision not to invite him to attend meetings of the Joint Council and the decision not to invite him to become a member of the Committee on Basic Beliefs.

Cheville would have understood that these actions were not oversights. He knew they were not based on a lack of information. He would have interpreted any direct action on his own part to get these decisions reversed to be a matter of playing politics. That was something he could not bring himself to do. It was apparently eleven years before he even mentioned either action. What he did was constructive; he set about to perform his job functions to the best of his ability within the conditions which were laid down.

He could not bring himself to initiate direct conversations about theology with members of the Committee on Basic Beliefs. In his view that would have been politicking, and therefore against his principles. However, his door was always open and he would have welcomed such discussion initiated by others. He continued to make his own ideas clear in writing for each of the church publication series in addition to his books.

When Cheville was asked in 1978 if a chapel at Graceland could bear his name he hesitated because the building would stand apart from the academic buildings associated with the arts and sciences. He felt that he had emphasized the intimate association of religion and theology with the arts and sciences through his whole career. That is true, but he could have done more to make that clear, particularly with the four-year program in religion which he created at Graceland. He could have designed the program to incorporate some of the steps toward the synthesis he achieved in his own studies.

Cheville hardly ever described his formal qualifications in academic degrees; never mentioning them in print or in public. He did that in part out of basic modesty, but more importantly because he did not want the degrees to define him. That could get in the way of his relations with some people. Some might think that the degrees meant that he considered himself better than other saints.

His decision to downplay his academic degrees may have had a down side for him. When church headquarters began its push toward theology in the 1960s. some of his colleagues may have been unaware of Cheville's formal qualifications in that area. For example, Don Landon stated that Dick Lancaster was "the only professionally trained theologian in the headquarters environment at the time." [Oral History Memoirs, p. 89]

Some saints complained that Cheville the patriarch was intellectually arrogant. That complaint, too, had been heard during his Graceland faculty days. He felt that he was always ready to listen to the ideas of others, even when they challenged his own. His own conclusions were invariably based on a great deal of thought, research and analysis. He also tested his religious practices for their effect on the lives of people. Thus, he had a great deal of confidence in his positions and his practices. When confronted with ideas that were different he was ready to listen but not easily convinced.

Many of Cheville's patterns were formed during the many years he was teaching primarily freshmen and sophomores. He was thus far advanced in his thinking patterns and had to select material to be taught. Some who knew him thought he held that outlook also when interacting with individuals nearer to his own intellectual level. That idea could be supported by the fact that he never had a coauthor, writing all his materials himself.

It was said of Cheville that over the years he was increasingly the hero of the stories he told. That seems true to a large extent. He saw himself in the position of teaching and educating in a church environment growing increasingly hostile to his approach to theology and to religion. He related many stories about other people and their experiences, but also told many stories from his own experiences and observations. In a sense he was bearing his testimony in many ways. He maintained that when anyone bears his testimony he is talking about things for which he is the world's prime expert. As he grew older he had more difficulty in discriminating which accounts would be well received.

The last years of Cheville's life should be studied with charity. The aging process was not very kind to him. From the middle 1970s. Cheville became somewhat less careful about personal hygiene. He could hear well but he missed some things because he could not see well. In later years he relaxed in the company of those who would listen to him at length. He still had interesting things to talk about, for those who were interested in him and his ideas.

Cheville's writing style declined in this period. His early works were models of clear and forceful writing. In later years he frequently used words and grammatical structures for which he had a logic, but for which ordinary words and structures might have served as well. The result was distracting to some readers. These issues, however, are not dominant in his last major books: the two volume edition on spiritual resources. [A:1975A,B] (Perhaps the editors of the Herald House persuaded him to use more straightforward language.) His 1979 book-length manuscript "74 Key Happenings in the Story of Our Restoration Church" has many odd words and odd sentence structures. The content, however, is substantial.

In this period he continued his practice of speaking in counsel when he felt the Spirit was leading him. In his Graceland days he often said that one does not need to use the words, "Thus saith the spirit," but the message should stand on its own. He made a deliberate decision to change this practice when he became presiding patriarch. That practice seems to have had a down side in his later years. In many of these messages he conveyed counsel to individuals who were present. This practice made some of his friends quite uncomfortable, even though the messages were usually complimentary and usually provided useful guidance. Some friends reported apprehension about agreeing to appear with him lest they be embarrassed by being singled out and talked to and about in the public service.

For several years Duane Couey was coordinator in the First Presidency of Roy Cheville's activities. He has given this summary of Cheville's ministerial career:

> If someone were to ask me, I would say that Roy had been a very effective person in reaching two and a half generations of church members. I am thinking now in terms of a fifty-year span. I would also say that few would do as well as he did. That effectiveness will come to others to some extent through his writings as well as the writings of others such as you are producing. But the fire and the passion will not be as great and will not be understood as deeply among the generations of this present time. This is why it is important for people such as you to convey as much of this understanding as possible for the present and oncoming future...
>
> As you would know, Roy always saw himself as a minister to young people, and especially at the college his distinguished service in this role is familiar to everyone. However, as another generation began

to come along, he was less effective in working with them. I know that this was hard for him to accept because of his deep love for the young, but this is a process which anyone who has played such a role will experience. [Couey letter to M. Ritchie 3 Apr 96]

Personal Life

> Jesus never paraded his spiritual qualities and counseled his men against doing so. In New Testament times problems arose when a man gifted by the Holy Spirit would go among the people and move them by his endowment. Sometimes Paul would cry out that he was no god, and Ammon had to do this in King Lamoni's court. Sometimes the person people see as inspired of God will assume an imperial role. Such a leader will seem to be saying, "I have spoken. Did you not hear God speaking through me?" And those who do not receive his "inspiration" are labeled as "unspiritual" by him. A major question centers on the placement of devotion. Is it to God, to Christ Jesus, or to some man or woman? A prophet truly inspired by the Holy Spirit is concerned about helping individuals to get with God in refined and regenerated living. God uses people through increasing their vision. [A:1975A]

Roy Cheville lived the life of a prophet. As such he needed to spend a certain amount of time alone. Alone with God he would reflect on the situation of his people and the church. He would address his communication with God in the direction of seeing the choices before him as God would see them. He understood that the kind of spiritual guidance he sought depended in part on the quality of the questions he would pose. That is reflected in a statement that he made once about people who ask for God to speak to them without preparation on their part. He said that he could imagine God responding, "All right. I will speak to you. What do you want me to talk about?"

In his experience the action of the Holy Spirit was intensely personal. Though he could talk about some of the results of the experiences, much of the experience itself went deep into the makeup of his personhood. One does not share one's innermost thoughts, and that is where the Spirit worked with him. It sometimes took exacting discipline to discriminate the illuminating influence of the Spirit from tentative conclusions he had already reached and from positions that were personal preferences. He described that as "coming clean" before God. And he said that God knows the kind of person Roy Cheville really is. That took the kind of intellectual honesty he looked for in those people he would keep as close friends.

Cheville was better educated than most of the Saints with whom he worked. That was true beginning in 1916 when he finished a year at Drake University and became a country school teacher. He used his educational achievement as an aid to his association with them and not as a barrier. He did not criticize and he did not look down on those who knew less. Instead he used his knowledge to understand better those with whom he lived and worked. His genuine interest in knowing people well and understanding how they looked at things can help explain his remarkable ability to remember people. He managed to find some traits to admire in almost everybody. Those were the things he liked to emphasize in his association with them.

He was at ease in meeting anybody—presidents of the Mormon Church, senators, and professors. He made friends quickly among accomplished individuals. However, not many of these became close friends. Dick Cheville says that his father had more close friends before World War II than after. He had an "ease and closeness" with several who had been fellow faculty members in the 1920s. and 1930s] Roscoe Faunce, Bill Gould, Gus Platz, Tess Morgan, Earl Higdon, Evan Walden, and Mabel Carlile Hyde. Dick says further,

> He accepted them and shared with them in an open easy way that did not apply to his post 1945 faculty colleagues. He changed, had greater vistas, felt surer of his positions, was busy with his own agenda and either felt no need or could not open up to the new people.

Cheville went out of his way to make friends with people of all economic levels, especially those from other countries and those from disadvantaged backgrounds in the U.S. Friendships with those he called "my people" were very important to him. He counseled the patriarchs to spend some time regularly with those of the lower economic and educational levels.

When Roy Cheville became presiding patriarch-evangelist he had been a widower for nearly a year. He was adjusting to living alone and to being without the support of Nelle. He had given up the home in which he and Nelle had raised their family, and he had moved to smaller quarters near the Graceland campus. He moved to Independence in December of 1959, into an apartment one short block from church headquarters in the Auditorium. His was a small apartment above the Speaks Funeral Home at the corner of Walnut and Lexington. This was his home until he completed his tenure as presiding patriarch in 1974.

In Independence as presiding patriarch he was free to travel and his assignment was worldwide. Most of the places he went are listed in Appendix E. Before 1960 he went beyond the Lamoni and Independence regions mostly in the summers. In February of 1960 he began a five week trip to Hawaii and in subsequent years ministered in Europe, South America, Asia, Africa, and Tahiti, as well as Canada and Alaska.

His overseas trips were made by air, as were some domestic trips. He sometimes made trips by rail, but most of his domestic travel was by automobile. He never owned or drove a car himself. He made his automobile trips by arranging for willing friends to drive him to places where he had ministerial engagements. Roger Bendorf and his father William, of Lancaster, Wisconsin, drove Cheville to many places all over the U.S. and Canada for many years. Then Wayne Zion began to be his regular resource for transportation and companionship. In Roy's later years Wayne accompanied him on some overseas trips.

Photo 32-1. Wayne and Ruth Zion. *[Photo: Ruth Zion]*

On most of these trips the only excitement in travel was an occasional speeding ticket for Wayne. But there was one accident in August of 1969 as Wayne, his wife, his daughter, and Roy were leaving Chicago and driving toward Lancaster, Wisconsin. Roy described the experience in a letter:

> Thursday morning we started for Lancaster, Wisconsin. A few miles east of Elgin, Illinois, it happened. A woman crossed the road at an intersection. She must have struck some moisture on the pavement. She swung around and came immediately in front of us. Bang! Whomp! It is quite a sensation to see a car a few feet in front of us. With the woman who was driving were her son of eight years or so and her daughter about two years older. The boy was unconscious. Later in the hospital he recovered consciousness and except for a few broken bones seemed to be recovering.
>
> Wayne Zion was driving. No injuries. Elaine, the daughter was in the rear seat. No injuries. Ruth Zion was in the rear seat. I think that she was mostly unnerved. In my front seat location I was jarred. For a little while I was a little retarded in consciousness. When my jammed door was opened, I was bloodied on the shirt and generally messed up. The patrolman looked at my mouth and said I had a deep inner gash and that I should go to the hospital. He said one thing encouraging; he said I clotted unusually well. So at the hospital I took a preventive shot or more. And they took

stitches on the inside of my mouth. It is noteworthy that the first stitches I have ever had were to sew up my mouth.

I looked on the oral regions like a cross between overeating of blueberries and getting a punch in the mouth with intense swelling effects. For a day or so articulation was not easy. On Sunday I was in Des Moines and speaking came through all right. Things are on the mend. All of us are grateful for the way things turned out. If I had not been buttoned in the seat, I would have punctured the windshield with entailed puncturing of me.

Cheville visited friends whenever he traveled. Ivan Vallier's home was a frequent stop. A Graceland graduate, Ivan became Professor of Sociology at the University of California in Santa Cruz. When he wrote a scholarly book he dedicated it to Roy Cheville, friend and patriarch. Ivan died prematurely of Hodgkin's disease.

Another regular visiting place was the home of Richard E. (Mo) Hope in Orem, Utah. Cheville became a part of the family. After a visit in September 1970 (in company with Wayne and Ruth Zion), Roy wrote a letter to Mo commemorating two incidents during the visit. When Roy and the Zions arrived Mrs. Hope laid out a picnic dinner. When Mo arrived from work he reached across the table to greet Roy and spilled fruit drink all over Roy's clothing. During the night rain water collected in the ceiling from a leak, then broke through onto Roy's bed, hitting him in the face. After the visit, Roy wrote the following inquiries:

TEN BASIC INQUIRIES CONCERNING BAPTISM

These questions are prompted by the partial baptisms of Roy Arthur Cheville in the early days of September 1970 while he was sojourning for a few days in Camp Hope.

1. May baptism by immersion be conducted piecemeal, a section at a time, or may it be done with a single covering of the body? Are there any factors that determine which parts of the body are to be immersed first? Is there any prescribed sequence?

2. Must water be used for this immersing or are there liquids of color and flavor that would serve with meaningful symbolism? Or is pure rainwater preferred? Would red Kool-Aid express something more than ordinary water would express?

3. Would there be more holiness involved when the water comes down from heaven on the recipient? When the water drips down from heaven, even if through the roof, is there some advantage when it is not touched by human hands?

4. Does the motivation of the person instigating the baptism have anything to do with the effectiveness of the baptism? May there be some uncertain, unexplainable motivations?

5. Does the place where the baptism is performed have any influence upon the tone and the taking hold of the baptism?

For instance, may the baptizing take place at a dinner table, outdoors? Or in a bed in a living room?

6. Does posture of the recipient in any way condition the effectiveness of the baptizing? May the person be sitting at a table or reclining in bed?

7. Need words of salutation or phrases of authorization be spoken? May the performer merely think with concentration upon the rite, leaving the recipient in doubt as to the motivation?

8. Is this baptism by sections to be applied to the most needing, most problematical parts of the recipient? There is one case in which the fluid was spilled upon the portion of the body where the legs come together, and the drops of water descended upon the head.

9. Is the baptism more effective if performed in unusual places and unconventional times?

10. Baptism is intended to engender hope. Will it be more effective if it is conducted by Hope?

These ten questions are submitted for consideration and evaluation. If considered of sufficient consequence, it might be advisable to ask church administrators to appoint a commission to study them and formulate appropriate resolutions to be presented to the general conference. This is no imagined matter. Conditions similar to those suggested here have prompted the asking of these matters. There is little or nothing in the standard books of the church that throws light on these situations.

Submitted to Richard Elmo Hope and his family for consideration in their domestic parliament, by Roy Arthur Cheville, A.A., Ph.B., A.M., Ph.D., D.D., who admits that the academic training indicated in the fore listed degrees throw little if any light on these questions.

On July 27, 1966 Cheville wrote Mo Hope in preparation for an article he wanted to write in his series "These are My People." He wanted to verify the names of the two

Hope children with whom he had conversed on a particular occasion. He wrote, "I remember my stay with you, with happy memories. I was so thrilled at the way you did things together with all participating. There will always be a spot in my heart for the Mo Hope family."

About the matter, Mo wrote,

> He was asking about our youngest daughter Rosemary 9, and adopted son Roger 8. Bro. Cheville helped them get our steer back into the pasture. Then he sat with the two children ages 9 and 8 on a pole fence while they explained in length to him what a steer was versus a cow and why a gelding horse differed from a mare or stallion. He was very impressed and mentioned it several times later.

Most of Roy's activities were with members of his own church. As one exception, he spent 12 days at Christmas time in 1970 as chaplain of a cruise ship in the Caribbean. He taught some classes on family living. Of the trip he commented, "I returned restless as I noted how so many people, so many couples of good potential had such thinness in their life purpose and plan."

Maintaining close relations with his people was one reason Cheville was very careful about his association with women. He knew of a number of ministers who lost acceptance as ministers among the people as a result of gossip about their relation to women. For some this took the form of a reputation for "having an eye for the ladies." Cheville's daughter Charlotte has said he was very careful indeed lest this kind of thing happen to him. He was intense in his friendships and that intensity could easily have been interpreted as improper behavior. He knew these were silent judgments and one was never given a chance to respond to them. The only defense was prevention.

Roy Cheville had gone into a period of depression after the death of his wife Nelle in 1957. That depression had lasted for about a year, according to his son Richard. That opinion is supported by Eugene Painter, who was Roy's assistant at Graceland during that year. It was then and is now difficult to detect the signs of depression in Cheville because of his determination to be positive at all times, and because of his driving will and work habits.

In late 1973 he suffered another blow to his emotional well-being that, in its effects on him, might be compared with the loss of Nelle. The First Presidency sent him a directive letter which Cheville described as setting forth "the policy of church administrators concerning my procedures and patterns of action, particularly in fields outside the United States." [See the chapter "The Bureaucracy" for details] He felt a sense of frustration and said he felt hemmed in with respect to what he considered his field of ministry. These limitations he felt would affect the fulfillment of the covenant he had made at age 16, and which he felt he had been serving with all there was of him to give.

When he was released as presiding patriarch in 1974 Wayne and Ruth Zion offered Cheville an apartment on the second floor of their home at 1510 North Main Street in Independence. There they provided many kinds of loyal support for him. They believed him to be a great man and they aimed to do whatever would maximize his ministry and preserve it for future generations. That included their role as close friends. They were intelligent and straightforward people. Wayne held the priesthood office of elder and he participated in many services. He had been a heavy equipment operator and Ruth had been a nurse.

Wayne and Ruth were important to Cheville's emotional balance in this period. Cheville was carrying on his objectives in the face of complex difficulties in the church that affected him deeply. With Wayne and Ruth he could be completely at ease and relaxed. Spending days at a time in the car with Wayne helped him gain a balanced perspective on his tasks.

In August of 1974 the offices of the presiding patriarch were moved from the Auditorium to Room 300 in the Central Professional Building, near the center of Independence. Roy Cheville was given a small office in the suite.

On November 9, 1977 Cheville wrote to the Hope family about being with them for Christmas in company with Wayne Zion. He said, "I confess that I am thinking of coming to the Hope Hope-tel because I want to be with you. You Hopes mean ever so much to me. I am ever wanting Mo' hope." He closed with these lines,

> Here's to the Hopes who live in Provo,
> Ever inclined to things "de novo."
> After I've been called to roam,
> It's great to get in their friendly home.
> Here's to Norma and here's to Mo!
> I count on them to make things go.
> I hope things shape this Christmas time well
> To permit me to get into their Hope-tel.

In 1980 he moved into an assisted living unit in the church-supported retirement home Resthaven. About the change his daughter Charlotte wrote him from Maryland, "I have quite mixed feelings—I'm glad you're getting good care—food, medical services—but I'm sure you're feeling confined and unprivate. I wish we weren't so far away." He lived at Resthaven until his death April 6, 1986.

His bouts with depression seem to have deepened in 1980 after another letter from the presidency further limited his ministry to the area around Independence. Before he moved to Resthaven he brought a car trunk full of books and papers to Dayton to add to the Ritchie collection. In Independence he had Wayne Zion drive him to the dump, where he discarded many of his books and collected papers. He tore the covers from some of the books and tore some of the pages apart. Among the books thus torn were his sister Mildred's Graceland textbooks and Cheville's copy of the Official Zion's League Handbook [A:1941E], which contained several of his hymns, including "Open My Eyes That I May See."

Photo 32-2.
Cheville playing the pump organ in the home of Mo Hope in Utah. *[Photo: R. E. Hope]*

Photo 32-3.
Cheville and Wayne Zion in the home of Mo Hope at Christmas in 1977. *[Photo: R. E. Hope]*

Wayne and Dick Cheville drove back to the dump later and rescued a great many of the papers and books. Cheville's son Dick and daughter Charlotte gave all his collected papers to the RLDS Church Archives.

In the 1980s he tried once to deliver a message to the World Conference in song. He was confused but the presiding officer allowed him to continue out of respect. It was an embarrassing moment in the conference.

Cheville's eyes were always something of a problem for him. He said that they had never been rated by doctors as of good quality. Late in 1970 Wallace B. Smith, in his professional capacity, advised him after examination that he had a cataract condition which was slowly developing and did not call for immediate attention. His eyes did get worse and he did have cataract surgery. His eyes were the main reason he moved in 1980 from his apartment in Wayne Zion's home to an assisted living unit in Resthaven. In 1980 he could see well enough to write letters for a few hours in the mornings, but he did not try to do much in the afternoons. At that time he could heat soup for himself if it had been poured into a pan, but he did not trust himself to use a can opener.

In 1984 Cheville finally planned cataract surgery on one eye. His daughter Charlotte wrote supporting the plan and noted that there was now little risk to the surgery. Bob and Alice Fredenberg sent him a card with a note that they had heard of his eye surgery. They said, "We were praying for you and had you in our thoughts. David Smith was telling me this was the first time you've been in a hospital for an operation." Dick Cheville wrote from Panama, "We are anxious to have some word about your recent eye surgery. Our prayers are that all went well."

On October 1, 1983 a birthday party for Cheville was held at Beacon Heights Church in Independence. Seventy-six people signed the guest register, including Wayne and Ruth Zion, Charles and Nita Hield, Olive Mortimore,

Jack and Jane Wight, Ed and Joy Browne, R. Elaine (Zion) Clements, Ammon and Bernice Andes, and Daisy and Neal Deaver.

Mary Morris wrote Cheville on March 12, 1984 from Springfield, IL noting that she and her husband Ed shed tears as they read Cheville's letter to them, remembering the good times shared in their home. Ed was hospitalized and paralyzed from the waist down. She closed the letter with "Please continue to remember him when you talk to our Friend."

Cheville attended the Graceland College Homecoming in 1985. He missed a dental plate after he returned to Independence and wrote Clara Morell to ask if she could find it. The search turned up empty, but Clara wrote, "We were so glad you and Wayne were here for Homecoming. It is such a busy time that those of us on campus don't get to spend time with some of our 'special' people. Hope you get to visit the campus soon again and we can have time to 'chew the fat.'"

Both of Cheville's children kept in close contact with him and he shared his personal concerns with them. He had his bank set up his accounts to be jointly owned with them. Both Dick and Charlotte followed Roy's physical condition by correspondence and telephone. Dick, the physician, was his interpreter and advisor. During Roy's final illness, his daughter Charlotte went to Independence to supervise his care during his last three weeks.

Roy Cheville died April 6, 1986 on the 156th anniversary of the founding of the church. Some of his friends said they thought, given Cheville's appreciation of drama, it was no accident that he departed this life on such a momentous day.

By prearrangement his body was sent to the University of Iowa Medical School. A memorial service was held in the Stone Church in Independence April 13, 1986. Apostle William T. Higdon presided. Jack Ergo played the organ for singing hymns of Roy Cheville. President Wallace B. Smith gave the opening prayer. Presentations on the contributions of Roy Cheville were given by Barbara Higdon (on his contributions at Graceland), Malcolm Ritchie (on his contributions in thought and theology), Kisuke Sekine (on his contributions as mentor and in outreach), and Duane Couey (on his contributions as minister and evangelist).

Among the papers found in his room was a note about singing with God. He recalled the hymn he had written nearly 50 years earlier, Open My Eyes That I May See. In these notes he wrote,

> Today I would involve exercise and exploration on my part as I would line up with God. Today my song would run this way in lining up with God:
>
> Help me have vision, Lord, that I may see
> Whatever glimpse of truth you have for me.
> New frontiers beckon me, known but to you:
> And as I go, I'll pray, God, lead me through.
>
> As I sing this to God, I shall expect him to respond in his chosen way. These lines indicate what God might be singing along with me with these words:
>
> New frontiers beckon you, known but to me,
> And as you go, my light will help you see.
>
> God and I will be singing together, each in his own world of perception.

Photo 33-1.
Roy Cheville with his mother and sister Cora Shimel in 1964.
[Photo: Ruth Zion]

Roy Cheville's Family

> Will you be free for four or five days the latter part of May? I plan to be in Independence at that time to visit you and attend some health matters for Lyle and Ruth [Lila's parents]… I would like to travel to Lamoni, Nauvoo and perhaps a few intermediate places at that time. I can rent a car in Kansas City to provide transportation. [Letter to Cheville from Dick Cheville in Panama 14 Mar 83]

> Dad, with all the years of our being scattered over the world, I very much appreciate your support, your saying, "go for it!" and not laying any guilt on us for reaching out to new things. I'll try to pass this onto our boys. We do love you. [Letter to Cheville from Charlotte Cheville Farrand 5 Aug 85]

Roy Cheville's biological family was very important to him and he never forgot about them. He visited his parents in Rhodes as long as they lived. His father died in Rhodes in 1951 at age 84. Cheville visited his mother four or five times every year until she died in 1966 at age 94, and he wrote a book chapter in 1970 describing her. [A:1970E]

Roy had three sisters and one brother. His younger sister Mildred died in 1925. The others, Mabel Atkinson, Cora Shimel, and Fred Cheville, stayed in or near Rhodes and they lived to old age. Roy visited and corresponded with them and their children.

Roy always had a good relationship with his wife's family. Two of them stayed at the Cheville home during their first year at Graceland: Chester, Nelle's youngest brother (in 1937), and Dennis, the son of Nelle's brother L. D. (in 1951). The Christmas following Nelle's death in 1957, Roy, Charlotte, Dick and Nelle's sister Rae, drove to Tucson, AZ to share the Holidays with her brother L. D. and his family. Roy maintained contact with several members of the Weldon family. Nelle's oldest brother, Roy, was noted in church circles for his historical and archeological inter-

Photo 33-2.
Roy Cheville and his siblings in 1980. Roy is on the left, then Cora Shimel, Mabel Atkinson, and Fred Cheville.
[Photo: Farrand]

Photo 33-3.
Roy Cheville with members of the Weldon family shortly after the death of Nelle in 1957. Seated on the ground is Lila Cheville. Left to right behind her are Dennis Weldon, L. D. Weldon, Roy, Dick Cheville, Frances (Mrs. L. D.), Rae Weldon, and Charlotte Cheville Farrand. [Photo: Dick Cheville]

est in the Book of Mormon, and was a member of the order of patriarchs during the time Cheville was presiding patriarch. Roy Weldon's son Clair was a Spanish-speaking missionary for the church to Middle and South American peoples during Cheville's tenure as presiding patriarch. Cheville and Clair ministered together on several occasions, providing significant memories for Cheville.

The family life of Roy and Nelle was described in Book IV in the volume *Roy Cheville: The Graceland College Years*. With their parents' whole lives now in perspective, Roy's children Dick and Charlotte share rich and unique memories of the home of Nell and Roy Cheville as they were growing up.

Music was always a special theme. An old upright piano, mostly in tune, was often in use although no one was an accomplished pianist. Many hours of individual plunking and singing and group harmonizing occurred. Musical fare ranged from opera and hymns to folk music, popular ballads and songs made up on the spot. Most of Roy's hymns were composed at this old upright. The family had a tradition of caroling at Christmas. The Chevilles would start out and collect the neighborhood, moving from house to house. The Faunces, Goodes, and Goulds were always among the first to be gathered. When Roy brought musical groups for Lamoni-Graceland concerts (such as the United States Marine Band, I Solisti di Zagreb, and the Fiske Jubilee Singers) the children not only listened but met the musicians. Music is still central to both their lives.

The house was often full of college "kids" as a Town Home for College Daughters, and for assemblings of campus groups where endless mounds of waffles and gallons of "bug juice" would be produced and devoured. Students in trouble or without funds came home with Roy and became family for a time. Dick remembers the sadness and tears of young women who had just become World War II widows. There were couples seeking guidance in the aftermath of careless love and young men whose faith had been shattered by new concepts. Honorary family members also included such campus visitors as RLDS Church President F. M. Smith, Ronald "Dutch" Reagan (when he was still with radio station WHO in Des Moines), Maya Deran, an experimental cinematographer, and sociologist Evelyn Mills Duvall. The young Chevilles assumed all homes were like this.

Nelle's kindness brought a different group of visitors to the Cheville home. During the depression years, two or three men out of work and traveling (hoboes) sat on the back steps to share whatever the family had for lunch. She required some yard work or an odd job, but never turned anyone away. Dick absorbed their tales of hard times. Her public health work brought the Cheville children early awareness of the world's pain and suffering. Dick still recalls going along on a home visit to a family of five who survived in one room on $20 a month. After Lamoni's only doctor went off to War, Nelle became what would today be called a nurse practitioner. The children remember watching their mother in her navy and white nurse's uniform ride off on her green, three speed English bicycle to make house calls.

Quite artistic, Nelle designed family Christmas cards and valentines, made *creches* of *paper mache* for relatives and family friends and repaired broken dolls. Charlotte recalls having to fight her way into the bathroom past the recently painted arms and legs that hung in every corner. Later Nelle build a kiln, dug and prepared clay, then molded and fired her own pottery. One of Dick's most prized possessions is a Madonna created by his mother shortly before her death.

The Chevilles always had a garden. During World War II, it was called a victory garden, but in the depression years it was a survival garden. Neat rows of corn, beans, spuds, radishes, tomatoes, beets, lettuce and cabbage testified to Roy's green thumb. Each summer the whole family pitched in to can the garden's abundance for winter. Dick and Charlotte remember picking potato bugs, weeding strawberries, hoeing corn and picking beans. Roy gardened skillfully because he grew up on a farm. Farm life shaped him. His prodigious work habits started from having to milk the cows, slop the pigs and toss hay down from the loft for the horses before getting ready for school in the morning. Dick believes his Dad always had an image of the rural Iowa friends and neighbors of his childhood in mind while teaching or speaking. If he could successfully present complex ideas to this internal home town audience, others would surely understand.

At least once a year the Cheville family returned to Roy's childhood home. They boarded a Jefferson bus in Lamoni and asked the driver to stop and let them off along the highway two miles from his father's farm in Rhodes, Iowa. Roy's Dad, George Cheville, met them with his horse and buggy or his old green Plymouth. Dick remembers an abundance of pigs, cows, chickens, horses, corn fields, cherry trees and gooseberry bushes. Charlotte relished rainy days in her grandmother Cheville's attic among china dolls dressed in 1890s. costumes, fifty year old Sears catalogs, family mementos from Yorkshire and turn-of-the-century fashion magazines. The tracks of the Milwaukee Railroad ran along the western edge of George Cheville's farm. When the afternoon passenger train whistled, Roy raced the children and their cousins to wave at the sleek orange-and-brown southbound Hiawatha. The train whistle still represented all that had waited for Roy beyond Rhodes and the family farm. Getting their Dad to hitch up the horses and go for a wagon ride was paradise for Charlotte and Dick. Freshly baked bread, Saturday night baths in the summer kitchen, hot cherry pie, chamber pots under the beds, and chicken with homemade noodles complete their memories of the farm.

In Charlotte and Dick's eyes, Grandmother Cheville was filled with magical sunshine. They were her "Little Miss Blue Eyes" and "Dicky Richard." Neither can remember her with a frown or an unkind word. They believe she is central to any understanding of their father. Memories of her contagious laughter, happy singing and smiling face convince them that Roy's optimism, ready smile, way of moving, choice of words, and manner of speaking were a direct legacy from their grandmother Cheville.

Nelle grew up in the sparsely settled, grass-covered hills east of Berkeley, CA. In this open environment the seven Weldon children were free spirits. Charlotte and Dick grew up listening to tall Weldon tales of rattlesnakes and wild bulls. Nelle attended Contra Costa County consolidated school, which had a truly multi-cultural student body. The minority Anglos mixed easily with Japanese, Chinese, Portuguese, a few Native Americans, and assorted Hispanics. Following high school she and her sister Rae took nurses' training at the Highland Alameda Hospital in Oakland. Dick believes that when she married and returned permanently to Lamoni, she found life in small town Iowa constricting. She knowingly traded horse back riding in the hills and the vibrant culture of San Francisco for life as a minister's wife, but retained a sense of loss the rest of her life. She felt called to assist Roy in his ministry, believed his work was uniquely important, and dedicated herself to supporting him. The success of her dedication was demonstrated by Roy's inconsolable sense of loss and the long period of mourning that followed her death in 1957. Dick thinks the loneliness of his Dad's move to Independence and frustration over the hierarchical difficulties encountered at RLDS World Headquarters would have been eased if Nelle had lived longer.

Dick and Charlotte learned from their mother early in life that their father had an important, God-given work and that the rest of the Chevilles were called to support him. As Roy became busier and busier with Lamoni Stake, Graceland, summer camps, priesthood retreats, reunions, youth emphasis weeks, writing books and Saturday-through-Sunday ministry somewhere else, there was less and less time for family. Summertime meant just Mom and the two kids. Any voiced resentment was silenced by Nelle's quiet admonition, "your father is about the Lord's work." The children resented this neglect and often wondered how to tell God's work from Roy's. They independently concluded that their father's concept of "quality time" was a poor apology for his absences. Even so there were wonderful times together. Charlotte cherishes the memory of a family trip to Des Moines with dinner at Yonker's Tea Room and fourth row seats for Sigmund Romberg's "The Student Prince." In reaction to their childhood, both have placed a high priority on family time and activities in their own marriages.

Richard Arthur Cheville was born to Roy and Nelle December 26, 1931. After graduation from Graceland College in 1952 he took a summer tour of Europe by bicycle, contacting at least two friends of his father, Franz Beil in Germany and Franklin Schofield in England. He earned an undergraduate degree in history and spent two years in military service in Japan before receiving his M.D. in 1961 from the University of Iowa. He fulfilled his Internship requirement at Gorgas Hospital in the Canal Zone and completed a residency in Internal Medicine and a fellowship in Metabolic Disease at Stanford University Hospital. He worked in community medicine with the Office of Economic Opportunity until 1970, when the Richard Chevilles returned to Panama. He worked in a variety of clinical and preventive medicine positions and was the Chief Medical Officer of the Panama Canal Commission at the time of his 1993 retirement. Recently he has worked in alcohol and drug abuse rehabilitation for Spanish speaking people in Washington, DC.

Dick experienced periods of depression as early as Junior High School. By his mid twenties these became severe enough to create problems in his pursuit of academic Internal Medicine. He changed to Public Health and Preventive Medicine, which allowed him to follow a productive medical career despite periods of depression. The same depressive illness has affected individuals in several generations of the Weldon family. Dick is convinced that his mother's periods of withdrawal, frequent migraines, loss of interest and "psychosomatic" symptoms, were manifestations of the same disease. During his mother's lifetime, there were no effective treatments for unipolar (depressive) illness. Guilt, which is an integral part of depression's clinical picture, must have been magnified for her by the attitude of most church members of that era toward depression and by self-condemnation because she could not work or pray her way out of the undiagnosed illness. Over the course of their marriage, Roy and Nelle tended to grow apart from each other. Part of the distance that developed between them can be attributed to her periods of depression.

Dick married Lila Davis in 1957. A Graceland graduate in 1951, Lila received her B.A. in Health and Physical Education from Central Missouri State College in 1953. She accepted a faculty position in Physical Education at Graceland College in the Autumn of 1953, where she taught until the 1956-57 academic year when she began postgraduate work in the Physical Education Department of the University of Iowa. She received her M.A. in 1958 and her Ph.D. in 1964. Her doctoral dissertation concerned folk dance in the Republic of Panama. She continues her studies of Hispanic American folklore. She also studied at the Instituto de Folklor in Caracas, Venezuela and spent

12 months in 1975-76 filming, taping and interviewing in a number of Central and South American countries. She is the author of two books and a number of papers about Panamanian dance and Hispanic folklore. Her tapes and films are archived in the Ethnomusicology Library at the University of Indiana. She is currently Coordinator of Science for the department of Defense Dependents Schools.

Dick and Lila made their home in Iowa City, IA until 1961, in Palo Alto, CA until 1970, in Balboa and Panama City, PA until 1994, and in Washington, DC to the present. They are building a permanent home in Charleston, SC. The patriarch visited their homes in Palo Alto and in Panama on a number of occasions. He enthusiastically joined in Lila's ethnomusicologic adventures and helped Dick cook pancakes on Cub Scout outings. Alan and Andrea remember running the ramps on the way to the patriarch's auditorium office and eating scalloped corn at his nearby apartment during family visits to Independence.

Alan Cheville is Roy's oldest grandchild. He was born to Dick and Lila in Palo Alto, CA February 17, 1964 and attended public schools in the Canal Zone. Following Roy's 1979 visit to Panama, Alan asked to join the church. The baptism took place in the Washington, DC RLDS church in June of that year with Granddad officiating and all the family present. He attended Rice University in Houston, TX from the Fall of 1982 until he received his Ph. D. In Electrical Engineering in 1994. He researches and teaches in the Department of Electrical Engineering at Oklahoma State University in Stillwater, Oklahoma. His main interest is lasers and he is currently evaluating wavelengths between radar and infra red. He bicycles competitively.

Andrea Cheville was born in Palo Alto, CA Mar. 20, 1965 and she attended public schools in the Canal Zone and in Panama. She was graduated from Swarthmore College with an undergraduate major of Art History. Following

Photo 33-4.
Roy and Dick Cheville. *[Photo: Farrand]*

Photo 33-5.
Lila Cheville in 1962 collecting data in Panama for her doctoral dissertation. *[Photo: Dick Cheville]*

graduation she was involved in breast cancer and simian immunosuppressive virus research at the National Institutes of Health and Georgetown University. She earned the M.D. from Harvard Medical College. Following a medicine internship she began a residency program in physical and rehabilitation medicine at the Kessler Institute in New Jersey. She will begin a clinical fellowship in pain management at the Sloan Kettering Institute in NY in July, 1997.

Charlotte Estelle Cheville was born to Roy and Nelle on January 11, 1937, graduating from Graceland in 1957. She has enjoyed being the only extrovert in the Roy Cheville family. She met Bob Farrand in 1963 while she was a member of the faculty at the University of Maryland in College Park, MD as an instructor in the College of Education and the Institute for Child Study. She had completed her Bachelor's Degree at Iowa State University in Ames, Iowa and was in the process of completing her Master's Degree. Bob had completed a tour in the Army assigned to the Pentagon, and was a civilian employee of the Department of Defense. they were married in 1965, often referring to the union as a "mixed marriage" combining Iowa and New York. Bob completed a Bachelor's Degree in Business at the University of Maryland. Charlotte moved on to work with the development of the Head Start programs in Maryland and then was named Director of Early Childhood programs for the new city of Columbia, MD.

Bob's work for the Department of Defense moved the family to the Far East for assignments in the mid 70s and again in the early 80s. When they returned to the States Charlotte began work also with the Department of Defense. Roy visited their home regularly when they lived in Maryland and he visited them twice in the Far East. Bob retired in 1995 after 40 years of service in the Department of Defense and currently works as a consultant with a corporation in the Washington, DC area. Charlotte plans to retire in 1999, but is now active in leading an organization focused on developing ways for employees to balance the demands of work and life within a major Department of Defense agency. They plan to move close to the Smoky Mountains near Asheville, NC when Charlotte retires.

Christopher and Gregory Farrand were born to Bob and Charlotte in 1970 and 1972 respectively. By the time they were 10 and 12 they had spent almost half of their lives in Asia. Both Chris and Greg developed a strong interest in the Christian missionary field. Greg was involved with the international campus Christian organization, InterVarsity, while attending the University of North Carolina at Greensboro. During his first year, he met Beth Rowe, who was also a freshman and they were married a week after they both graduated in 1994. Their work for Christ while at the University included summer in Africa with World Harvest Missions. Beth was in Kenya and Greg in Uganda. The couple then applied and were accepted by World Harvest for a two-year assignment in Uganda with a mission group in a remote village of Bundibugyo near the Zaire (now Congo) border. They spent the year following graduation raising funds to support their mission, and moved to Uganda in January 1995. Greg has focused on Church Planting and Beth has worked in bringing the Gospel to the women of the area. When they return from their mission in December 1997, Greg will attend Reformed Theological Seminary in Charlotte, NC, and work in campus ministries at Wake Forest University.

After attending the University of Maryland for two years, Chris joined Bob and Charlotte in England, where they were on a three-year assignment. Chris spent time working and touring in Britain, and met several people who had a profound impact on his life, leading him to ac-

Photo 33-6.
Roy Cheville with Alan and Andrea Cheville at Christmas 1965 in Palo Alto, CA. *[Photo: Dick Cheville]*

Photo 33-7.
Trudi Mahi, Kenneth Chun-Ming, Charlotte Cheville Farrand, and Roy Cheville in Japan in 1974. *[Photo: Ruth Zion]*

cept Christ. He moved to Greensboro, NC where he felt the call of God to support the work of missionaries, but in an unusual way—as a missionary aviation pilot. With the support of close friends and his church, Chris obtained his private pilot's license, and raised funds to attend Moody Bible Institute in Chicago. While conditionally enrolled in Moody's Aviation Technology Program, Chris had to undergo a rigorous evaluation at the Institute's aviation facility in Tennessee before acceptance into the program. He did indeed pass and was approved for the three-year aviation program for training as a missionary pilot (as well as an airplane mechanic, since there will be little other help if repairs are needed in the jungle).

Both Dick and Charlotte planned activities to keep their children in contact with their grandfather and with their families. Dick and Lila took their vacations regularly in the U.S., and the cousins spent time together in the summers. Andrea lived with the Farrands in Maryland while she worked at the National Institutes of Health in Bethesda before attending medical school.

From the time Chris and Greg were quite young, Charlotte had them communicating directly with Roy. They regularly sent "Grand Dad" cards to him on Father's Day, even when they had difficulty signing their own names. As they grew older Chris and Greg wrote "Dear Grand Dad" letters of their own. Their last Grand Dad card was sent in 1985, Roy's last Father's Day. They were 14 and 16 when he died. Both of them attended the memorial service in Independence.

Dick and Charlotte remember their father with love. With understanding softened by more years of living, they have a keen appreciation for the unique childhood he provided. They are certain that at his new address he is making sure the heavenly choir is on key and singing to his beat. They see him quite at home with bigger vistas and new challenges. And they say, "after all, heaven is no place to just sit around!"

Photo 33-8.
Roy Cheville with the Farrand family. Bob, Roy and Charlotte are in the back, with Christopher and Gregory in front.
[Photo: Farrand]

Photo 33-9.
The four grandchildren of Roy Cheville in 1997. Christopher Farrand, Andrea Cheville, Gregory Farrand, and Alan Cheville. [Photo: Farrand]

BOOK XV

Epilogue

Forward to the Bible

> The dreams that matter stir people to action. They are not castles in Spain, not escapes from reality, not wishful thinking. They combine knowledge of things as they are and have been with imagination of things as they can be. Sound dreaming starts from where we are and builds to where we are to go. Any dream that starts out yonder and divorces this out-yonder from the world in which we live is unsound... Edwin Markham has made this sage conclusion,
>
> Oh, great it is to believe the dream
> As we stand in youth by the starry stream,
> But a greater thing is to fight life through
> And say at the end, "The dream is true." [pBull Feb 59]

The work and thought of Roy Cheville have much to contribute to the life and future development of the RLDS Church. He believed that it is essential to put the experiences of religion in first place in the life of the individual and in the work of the church, and to put theology in second place. While the value of his work has not yet been generally recognized, it is not too late.

Sadly, the effort of the past 30 years to open the mind of the church theologically had the effect of closing it in critical ways. In effect, these theological changes imposed on the church a Protestant set of beliefs that do not reflect the special spiritual heritage of the Restoration experience. Ironically, in a good faith and necessary effort to counteract a narrow and stunted interpretation of that heritage held by many members, church leaders embraced existing Protestant theology which diverted church thought from the essence of the founding experiences of the Restoration. Although he would be the first to state that his own beliefs were not ultimate truth and that others must evaluate his insights, Cheville maintained that the origins of and contexts for religious experience must be the basic study of the Restoration. To that end, for example, he planned and led worship experiences to help individuals make genuine, personal contact with the Holy Spirit.

Cheville believed that religion begins for an individual when something causes a response deep within the person, resulting in a dedication to do that which is right and virtuous. This may be called repentance, and it may be described as an elementary spiritual experience. This experience can cause the person to look for companionship with others who have and are seeking righteousness and virtue. Thus, in order to be a dynamic, living spiritual force in the lives of people, in contrast to a social fellowship and in contrast to a cold intellectual construct, the church needs to nourish religious experiences at all levels.

Theologies are interpretations of the divinity that lies behind religious experiences. The church should encourage many interpretations, including those of the Apostle Paul, 2,000 years ago and of Roy Cheville 30 years ago. Unity within this diversity is provided by the common commitment to be guided by the spirit of the ever-living Jesus Christ.

The focal point for Cheville and for renewal within the Restoration movement is the phrase, "This is my beloved Son; hear Him." These words represent the defining experience of the restored Church of Jesus Christ. The young Joseph Smith realized that he lacked wisdom and asked God in sincere prayer to guide him. His subsequent experiences validated the statement of James that God would respond to all. In the words of Roy Cheville, "God responds to every person to the degree that this person will respond to him." [Appendix K]

Joseph Smith's continuing experiences with the Spirit of God resulted in founding the restored Church of Jesus Christ. Continuing contemporary contact between human beings and the person of Jesus Christ is what was restored and what remains the Church's vital core.

Restoration renewal defines the work of the Church as assisting the Holy Spirit in the development of people so that their living embodies eternal qualities. This is the process of salvation. In making progress toward salvation, people achieve growing spiritual health. As the sunlight enables plants and trees to grow, the Holy Spirit enables people to live and to grow spiritually. It is God's work and his glory to bring these achievements to pass. Peace is one by-product of radiant saintly living, immortality and eternal life its objective.

Compassionate service to humankind is also an important component of saintly living. It should not, however, distract individuals or the Church from the real objective. Healing the sick, for example, may not further the development of eternal qualities within people. Giving money to the poor may not result in increasing an individual's capability for quality living. The life and ministry of Jesus clearly showed that the work of the saints still remains to be done after compassion has been shown.

Our Church has a wealth of resources to use in our restoration renewal. It has a history of dealing with the Holy Spirit and with divine revelation. It has established procedures for evaluating and approving works of the Spirit. It has additional scriptures to help illuminate the work of the Spirit. It has established procedures for assembling together in pursuit of spiritual guidance. It has a program called Zion for recognizing that Saints do not live to themselves or by themselves, and that personal development is entwined with their social environment. It has a pattern of encouraging education in the development of spiritual health.

Divinity is not visible to the eye. The disciples of Jesus perceived his divinity only when they sensed changes within themselves after their period of living with him. Divinity enters into our lives when we are engaged together in doing the work of elevating the quality of living of our friends. We cannot stand on the sidelines as spectators and perceive the presence and operation of divinity. In the long view we need to learn how to describe the effects of divinity within us and better understand its operation. This is a need for an extended scientific method. It is an invitation for people who would dare great things for God.

Following the work of Roy Cheville we can understand that we should look to the Bible for principles of living with divinity. We do not go back to the Bible to live again with tribal kings or to live with first century theologies. Instead, we implement principles of spiritual living, the Spirit of the ever living Jesus Christ, in our day. Then we can understand the messages that have been in the Bible all along. With the guidance of Cheville, our rallying cry can be FORWARD TO THE BIBLE!

In Retrospect

> Your life has been an inspiration not only to hundreds but literally to thousands of people. [D. T. Williams Apr. 1974]

> Your life has enriched the lives of so many people in so many parts of the world. Your ministry to the church cannot be measured. [Madeline Ostertag Apr. 1974]

By about 1980 most of the work of Roy Cheville had been accomplished. He was then one of the most highly respected and best loved people in the RLDS Church. Professor Jordi Ventura of the University of Barcelona said in 1997, "He was the most wonderful person I have ever met." He personally was instrumental in shaping the lives of thousands of people. To influence for good the living of his people was his lifelong objective.

By 1980, he also had published much of the results of his spiritual explorations. His publications document his original, extensive, and coherent theoretical thought structure. His theology was validated from point to point by his own experiences and the experiences of others, including those in history. In these publications are the principles and the structure which may yet cause him to be judged a world-class theologian, as well as a great religious teacher. He himself made no effort toward recognition beyond his own church.

Crucial to his thought was the concept that some element of spirituality is inherent in all people, now and in the past. He said that most of the world's religions began with a genuine spiritual experience at some level. It is important to recognize that these experiences occur and to learn the criteria and the conditions under which spiritual power is exercised. And then, he said,

> ...what I see has to be interpreted and validated in the laboratory of living. This laboratory includes living with God, living with others, living with myself. [Cheville notes written in 1968]

At the end there was one group of people who did not have a high regard for Cheville's teachings. This group comprised the leaders in his own church headquarters. They neutralized and ignored his teachings, though most of them loved and respected him as a person.

An overview of the period in which this state of affairs came about is contained in a 1995 book by Gregory Prymak [*Authority in the RLDS Theological Tradition,* Independence, Mo. Graceland/Park Press]. A competent and thoughtful researcher, Prymak says that the concept of authority has undergone a 180 degree shift in the theology of the Church since 1967, as a part of a broad theological change. He says that change has not been an outgrowth of the experiences of the people, but has been imposed from the top. The result has been a loss of allegiance as many have felt the new principles do not reflect their deepest feelings about what is important in life. As he continues his exposition, Prymak says,

> We therefore appear to have a void at the core of our belief-structure: we do not really *believe* the incarnational (existential/ethical) theology that is now in place. [p. 86]

These statements represent accurately what Cheville had said would be the result of top-down determinations and neglect of the core belief in personal interaction with the Good Spirit. He said that theology should grow out of the experiences of the people, and be validated by their experiences. There should be a diversity of theological positions, with unity in seeking guidance by the Spirit.

At the end of his life, it appeared that Cheville had lost his battle to upgrade the theology of the Church. By the time of his death in 1986, it was hard to find references to his work in writings by Church scholars. In the Prymak book cited above, despite a list of references and 415 extensive notes, the name of Roy Cheville does not appear. By 1995, one could not find his books among those advertised for sale by Church units. Few young scholars in the Church knew much about his work.

Cheville had said that God always takes the "long view." Although Cheville died without having shaped the Church's theological mainstream, his story may not be over. His work has a quality that could yet survive and prosper.

Cheville was a Prophet of Good News. He demonstrated in his own life and ministry that the core of the good news is the Spirit of the ever-living Jesus Christ. That Spirit works to bind the Saints to each other worldwide in love and to elevate the level of their living toward eternal values.

Cheville was the "scientists' theologian." In his work he emphasized the unity of spiritual dynamic and material substance. He showed how to use the laboratory methods of experience and validation in spiritual development of personhood.

For the final word about Roy Cheville let us turn to a passage from the funeral sermon he gave for Steven V. Carter who died while a Congressional Representative from Iowa. This sermon was printed in the *Congressional Record, 86th Congress, Second Session*.

THE MOUNTAIN VIEW OF MOSES

And Moses went up from the plains of Moab, unto the mountains of Nebo, to the top of Pisgah... And the Lord showed him all the land of Gilead, unto Dan... And the Lord said unto him, "this is the land which I sware unto Abraham, and unto Jacob... I have caused thee to see it with thine eyes, but thou shalt not go thither."

Here was faith of the first order. Moses saw his place in an outgoing purpose that was to last beyond his day. A measure of a man is that to which he devotes his life, for which he gives all he has. Little souls want comforts and awards at the immediate moment. Great souls give themselves to things that may not be realized in their lifetime. They believe the worthful will come to pass. They are happy in moving forward toward the goodly land. [D:1960C]

Appendix A
Books by Roy A. Cheville

The author has assigned a coded designator to each publication of Roy Cheville. The code begins with four digits for the year of publication. Then follows one or more letters to indicate sequence within the year. Thus 1942A is his first publication in the year 1942. When there were more than 26 publications in a given year, two letters will appear after the year.

1939A. *The Bible in Everyday Living*, (Independence, Mo. Herald House, 1939), 343 pages. First printing 1939A. Reprinted 1944A, 1948A, 1951A, 1956A, 1961A. Utilizes material in 1934A, 1935B, 1935C, AND 1935D.

1941A. *The Branch of Today and Tomorrow*, (Independence, Mo. Herald House, 1941), 160 p. Library of Congress listing BX 8671.A1R4 1941.

1941E. *Official Zion's League Handbook*, (Independence, Mo. Herald House, 1941), 285 p. Written by a class in Religious Education under the direction of Roy A. Cheville, edited for publication by Floyd M. McDowell and C. B. Woodstock, 1941.

1942A. Dissertation: *The Role of Religious Education in the Accommodation of a Sect*. Cover title; Religious Education and Sectarian Accommodation. Thesis, University of Chicago, 1942. Library of Congress Number BX8672.C45, typescript, carbon copy. viii, 405 l. 32cm. Chicago, 1942. (University of Chicago Library call number BX 10999.)

1946A. *Through the West Door*, (Independence, Mo. Herald House, 1946), 327 p. A history of Graceland College.

1950G. *The Hymnal for Youth*, (Independence, Mo. Herald House, 1950). Cheville was a member of a committee including Anne Morgan, Aleta Runkle, and Chris B. Hartshorn, which developed the book. The entire hymnal was reprinted in 1951 and 1955.

1951B. *Growing Up in Religion*, (Independence, Mo. Herald House, 1951), 233 p. Library of Congress listing BV 4531.2.C45. Reprinted in 1953.

1954A. *When They Seek Counsel*, (Independence, Mo. Herald House, 1954), 133 p.

1955A. *They Sang of the Restoration*, (Independence, Mo. Herald House, 1955), 267 p. Library of Congress listing BV 420.A1C4.

1955P. *The Latter Day Saints and Family Life*, (Independence, Mo. Herald House, 1955), pp. 108. Reprinted in 1957.

1956B. *By What Authority?* (Independence, Mo. Herald House, 1956), 96 p. Reprinted in 1959. Library of Congress listing BX 8674.C48.

1958A. *Ten Considerations For Family Living*, (Independence, Mo. Herald House, 1958), 150 p. Library of Congress listing BX 8672.C47.

1959B. *The Field of Theology*, (Independence, Mo. Herald House, 1959), 144 p. Library of Congress listing BX 8674.C5. (Univ. of Chicago. listing BX 8671.C517.) Reprinted in 1960.

1960A. *Meet Them in the Scriptures*, (Independence, Mo. Herald House, 1960), 224 p. Library of Congress Listing BS 571.C485.

1962A. *Did the Light Go Out?* (Independence, Mo. Herald House, 1962), 261 p. Library of Congress listing BX 1765.2.C5. Library of Congress Catalog Card No. 62-21344. (University of Chicago Library listing BX 1765.C54.)

1962C. *Spirituality in the Space Age*, (Independence, Mo.

Herald House, 1962), 264 p. Library of Congress listing BL 254.C47.

1964A. *Scriptures From Ancient America*, (Independence, Mo. Herald House, 1964), 368 p. Library of Congress listing BX 8628.C5. (Univ. of Chicago Library listing BV 8628.C53)

1966A. *Spiritual Health*, (Independence, Mo. Herald House, 1966), 412 p. Library of Congress listing, BX 8656.C48. (Univ. of Chicago Library listing BV 8656.C52.)

1968A. *When Teen-Agers Talk Theology*, (Independence, Mo. Herald House, 1968), 445 p. Library of Congress listing BX 8643.Y6C5.

1970A. *They Made a Difference*, (Independence, Mo. Herald House, 1970), 350 p. Library of Congress listing BX 8678.A2.

1970E. Chapter, "Charlotte Cheville," pp. 75-80 in Emma M. Phillips, (Ed.), *Dedicated to Serve*. (Independence, Mo. Herald House, 1970), 211 p.

1971A. *The Book of Mormon Speaks For Itself*, (Independence, Mo. Herald House, 1971), 203 p. 21 cm. Library of Congress number BX 8627.C47.

1972A. *Expectations For Endowed Living*, (Independence, Mo. Herald House, 1961), 122 p. Library of Congress listing BX 8656.C47.

1975A. *Spiritual Resources Are Available Today*, (Independence, Mo. Herald House, 1975), 2 volumes. Library of Congress listing BX 8656.C49.

1977A. *Joseph and Emma Smith; Companions For Seventeen and a Half Years, 1827-1844*, (Independence, Mo. Herald House, 1977), 206 p. Library of Congress listing BX 8695.S6C53.

1978A. *Humor in Gospel Living*, (Independence, Mo. Herald House, 1978), 153 p. Library of Congress listing BR 115.H84C47.

Unpublished Book-length Manuscripts By Roy A. Cheville

1923. Master's Thesis, "The function of music in Religious Education." University of Chicago, Dept. of Practical Theology, University of Chicago Library call number ML 3999.C54.

1925. D.B. Thesis, "The Junior Church." University of Chicago, Dept. of Practical Theology. University of Chicago Library call number BV 9999 .C485.

1942A. Thesis: THE ROLE OF RELIGIOUS EDUCATION IN THE ACCOMMODATION OF A SECT. Cover title; RELIGIOUS EDUCATION AND SECTARIAN ACCOMMODATION. Thesis, University of Chicago. Library of Congress Number BX8672.C45, typescript, carbon copy. viii, 405 l. 32cm. Chicago, 1942. (University of Chicago Library call number BX 10999.)

1968I. Audio tape, "The Heart of Graceland." Recorded Sept. 12, 1968 at Graceland College. Graceland College Library call number AT113, side 2.

1979. Roy Cheville prepared a book-length manuscript with the title, "Renaissance in Our Restoration Church." Subtitle, "The Story of Three Decades in the Church of Jesus Christ—1843-1873." The typed manuscript has 397 pages double-spaced. He said of it, "I regret very much the administrative decision that denied publication... To me, the events in what we call 'the Reorganization' period are as spiritually rich and significant as the preceding happenings from 1820 through 1836."

1979. About 1979 Roy Cheville prepared a book-length manuscript with the title "74 Key Happenings in the Story of Our Restoration Church." It was edited posthumously by Malcolm L. Ritchie and resubmitted to the *Herald House* for publication, with the title modified to "75 Key Happenings" after a recount of the chapters. It has not been accepted for publication. It is available in computer disk form in the RLDS Archives.

1980. On July 5, 1980 Roy Cheville sent a book-length manuscript to the *Herald House* with the title, "Sayings That Keep Speaking." It had 178 double spaced typed pages. Subtitle; A selection of words of wisdom, wit and worth that have been speaking through seventy years. These sayings relate to God, to the universe, to others, to me. These sayings relate to the past, to the present, to the future. These sayings express guiding directives for managing my living. It has not been published.

1980? Roy Cheville prepared a book-length manuscript with the title, "Conversing For Co-Sights." It was submitted to *Herald House* for publication. It has not been published.

Appendix B
Published Hymns by Roy A. Cheville

1921A. Hymn, "Song of Entreaty." In Margaret Davis (Ed.) "A Hundred Years of Latter Day Saintism—A most effective pageant, especially adapted for production at Reunions." *Autumn Leaves*, 1921, Vol. 34, No. 5, pp 223,f.

1928D. Hymn, "Sons of Graceland—song" [The Alma Mater Hymn], in *Autumn Leaves*, vol. 41, #9:p. 386, Sept. 1928. Text set to music. First publication of the Graceland Alma Mater Hymn. Republished 1928D, 1933C, 1933J, 1950M, 1955B, 1956Y, 1960AG. Additional verse (humorous) in 1972F. For a description of its writing, see 1955B.

1933C. Hymn, "Alma Mater Hymn," No. 434 in *Saints' Hymnal*, Herald House, 1933. Text set to music.

1933J. Hymn, "Alma Mater Hymn," in *Graceland Tower*, March 19, 1933, in text form.

1950M. Hymn, "O Come Ye Sons of Graceland All," No. 395 in *The Hymnal For Youth,* Herald House 1950. Text set to music.

1955B. Hymn, "Sons of Graceland," [Alma Mater Hymn], in Cheville 1955A, *They Sang of The Restoration*, Herald House, 1955.

1956Y. Hymn, "O Come Ye Sons of Graceland," Number 523 in *The Hymnal*, Herald House, 1956. Text set to music.

1960AG. Hymn, "O come, ye sons of Graceland," Number 523 in *The Little Hymnal*, Herald House 1960, in poem form.

1972F. Additional verse to Graceland Alma

Mater Hymn. In Edwards, Paul, *The Hilltop Where*, The Venture Foundation, Lamoni, Iowa, 1972.

1930K. Camp song, "We're coming back to you, Dear Old Nauvoo, In article, "The Boys' and Girls' Camp at Nauvoo," *Saints' Herald*, Vol. 77, # 31, p. 859, July 30, 1930. Republished 1930K, 1934B.

1934B. Hymn, "Dear Old Nauvoo," in the *Lamoni Chronicle* of March 8, 1934, p. 1, article entitled "R. A. Cheville addresses audience on Nauvoo."

1932B. Prayer Hymn, "A Youth's Prayer of Thanksgiving." In Cheville 1932A, *What it Means to Be a Latter Day Saint*, p. 46, Herald House, 1932. In poem form. Republished 1938L, 1941I, 1944O, 1946G, 1947N, 1948T, 1949I, 1952F, 1954M, 1955N.

1933F. Hymn, "I Know That My Redeemer Lives," pp. 22f in Cheville 1933E, Quarterly, *Membership Qualifications*, Herald House, 1933. In poem form. Republished 1939O, 1942O, 1945H, 1947K, 1949L, 1956AB, 1959R.

1933G. Poem, "Speak of the Best," pp. 46 in Cheville 1933E, Quarterly, *Membership Qualifications*, Herald House, 1933.

1933I. Hymn, "God Send Us Men," pp. 10 in Cheville 1933H, Quarterly, *The Program of the Church*, Herald House, 1933. In poem form. Republished 1939N, 1942Q.

1939G. Hymn, "Are Ye Able." P. 33 in Pamphlet [1939F] *Youth Shares, A Manual of Review, The Youth Conference, June 10-18, 1939 At Graceland College*, edited by Roy Cheville, Herald House.

1939H. Hymn, "O Lord of Life, of Light and Inspiration." P. 46 in Pamphlet [1939F] *Youth Shares, A Manual of Review, The Youth Conference, June*

10-18, 1939 At Graceland College, edited by Roy Cheville, Herald House. (Written for the convention.)

1939I. Hymn, "Our Homes We Dedicate to Thee." P. 5 in Pamphlet [1939F] *Youth Shares, A Manual of Review, The Youth Conference, June 10-18, 1939 At Graceland College*, edited by Roy Cheville, Herald House.

1941F. Hymn, "The Church of Christ Is Calling." In [1941E] *Official Zion's League Handbook*, Herald House, 1941. In poem form.

1941G. Hymn, "Rise, O Youth," in [1941E] *Official Zion's League Handbook*, Herald House, 285 p. Written by a class in Religious Education under the direction of Roy A. Cheville, edited for publication by Floyd M. McDowell and C. B. Woodstock, 1941.

1941H. Hymn, "Forward," in [1941E] *Official Zion's League Handbook*, Herald House, 285 p. Written by a class in Religious Education under the direction of Roy A. Cheville, edited for publication by Floyd M. McDowell and C. B. Woodstock, 1941.

1941I. Hymn, "Come Up Higher," in [1941E] *Official Zion's League Handbook*, Herald House, 285 p.

1941J. Hymn, "Open My Eyes," in [1941E] *Official Zion's League Handbook*, Herald House, 1941. In poem form. First time published. Republished 1941J, 1950J, 1953L (in German), 1955F, 1956S, 1960AC, 1968L, 1974G, 1975B (in Spanish), 1981N. For a description of its writing see 1955F.

1950J. Hymn, "Open My Eyes, O Lord," Number 365 in *The Hymnal For Youth*. Herald House, 1950. First time set in print with music.

1953L. Hymn, "Open My Eyes, O Lord," translated into German by P. E. Radelow, with the title, "Offne Die Augen Mir," In *Lieder Der Heiligen*, Herald House, 1953.

1955F. Hymn, "Open My Eyes," in Cheville 1955A, *They Sang of the Restoration*. Herald House, 1955. In poem form.

1956S. Hymn, "Open My Eyes, O Lord," Number 355 in *The Hymnal*, Herald House, 1956. Text and tune set in print.

1960AC. Hymn, "Open my eyes, O Lord," Number 355 in *The Little Hymnal*, Herald House 1960, in poem form.

1968L. Hymn, "Open My Eyes, O Lord," No. 355 in *World Conference Hymnal* 1968. Text and tune reprinted from *The Hymnal*, 1956S.

1974G. Hymn, "Open My Eyes, O Lord," No 355 in *World Conference Hymnal* 1974. Text and tune reprinted from *The Hymnal*, 1956S.

1975B. "Open My Eyes" (Abre, Emanuel), translated into Spanish in *Hinario*, Herald House, 1975, 90.

1981N. Hymn, "Open My Eyes, O Lord," no. 454 in *Hymns of the Saints*, Herald House, 1981. Text and tune.

1941K. Hymn, "Prayer of Dedication," in [1941E] *Official Zion's League Handbook*, Herald House, 285 p. Written by a class in Religious Education under the direction of Roy A. Cheville, edited for publication by Floyd M. McDowell and C. B. Woodstock, 1941.

1944I. Hymn, "Forward Thro' the ages," In article in *Saints' Herald*, "Materials for anniversary on June 27." Vol. 91, #25:p. 790, June 17, 1944. In poem form. [for centennial of Joseph Smith's death]

1944J. Hymn, "We read Thy Word of Promise," in article in *Saints' Herald*, "Materials for anniversary on June 27." Vol. 91, #25:p. 790, June 17, 1944. In poem form. [for centennial of Joseph Smith's death]. Republished 1950T.

1950T. Hymn, "We read Thy word of Promise, Lord." p. 378 in *The Hymnal For Youth*, Herald House, 1950.

1944K. Hymn, "For All Those Saints," in article in *Saints' Herald*, "Materials for anniversary on June 27." Vol. 91, #25:p. 790, June 17, 1944. In poem form. [for centennial of Joseph Smith's death]

1950H. Third Stanza of Hymn, "O Jesus the Giver," Number 338 in *The Hymnal For Youth*. Herald House, 1950. Text set to music. Original text by W. W. Phelps. Republished 1950H, 1956I, 1968J, 1974D, 1981E.

1950I. Hymn, "Hast Thou Heard It," Number 354 in *The Hymnal For Youth*, Herald House, 1950. Text set to music. The text in poem form also appears on pp. 365f within an order of worship. The words are somewhat different. Republished 1950I, 1953M (in German), 1955D (altered), 1956U, 1960AD, 1975D (in Spanish), 1981K (altered).

1953M. Hymn, "Hast Thou Heard It, O My Brother," translated into German by P. E. Radelow, with the title, "Hast Du Es Gehort, Mein Bruder," In *Lieder Der Heiligen*, Herald House, 1953. Text set to music.

1955D. Hymn, Hast Thou Heard It, O My Brother, in Cheville 1955A *They Sang of the Restoration*. Book: Herald House, 1955. In poem form.

1956U. Hymn, "Hast Thou Heard It," Number 411 in *The Hymnal*, Herald House, 1956. Text set to music.

Cheville 1960AD. Hymn, "Hast thou heard it?" Number 411 in *The Little Hymnal*, Herald House 1960, in poem form.

1975D. "Hast Thou Heard It?" (Meu Irmao, Tu Ja Ouviste), translated into Spanish in *Hinario*, Herald House, 1975, 131.

1981K. Hymn, "Hast Thou Heard It, O My Brother," no. 390 in *Hymns of the Saints*, Herald House, 1981. Text set to music.

1950K. Hymn, "All Things Are Thine," No. 369 in *The Hymnal For Youth*. Herald House, 1950. Republished 1950K, 1953K (in German), 1955E, 1956V, 1960AE, 1968M, 1974H, 1975C (in Spanish), 1981L (altered).

1953K. Hymn, "All Things Are Thine," translated into German by P. E. Radelow, with the title, "Die Guter Welt Sind Dein." In *Lieder Der Heiligen*, Herald House, 1953.

1955E. Hymn, "All Things Are Thine, O Lord of Life," in Cheville 1955A, *They Sang of the Restoration*, Herald House, 1955. Text in poem form.

1956V. Hymn, "All Things Are Thine," Number 417 in *The Hymnal*, Herald House, 1956. Text set to music.

1960AE. Hymn, "All things are thine." Number 417 in *The Little Hymnal*, Herald House 1960, in poem form.

1968M. Hymn, All Things Are Thine, No. 417 in World Conference Hymnal 1968. Reprinted from *The Hymnal*, 1956V. Text set to music.

1974H. Hymn, All Things Are Thine, No. 417 in *World Conference Hymnal 1974*. Reprinted from The Hymnal, 1956V. Text set to music.

1975C. "All Things Are Thine" (Tudo E De Ti), translated into Spanish in *Hinario*, Herald House, 1975, 126.

1981L. Hymn, "All Things Are Thine," no. 397 in *Hymns of the Saints*, Herald House, 1981. Text set to music.

1950L. Hymn, "Master, Speak! Thy Servant Heareth," no. 370 in *The Hymnal For Youth*. Herald House, 1950. Text set to music. Republished 1950L, 1953J (in German), 1956T, 1981M.

1953J. Hymn, "Master Speak! Thy Servant Heareth," translated into German by P. E. Radelow, with the title, "Meister, Sprich, Dein Diener Horet." In *Lieder Der Heiligen*, Herald House, 1953.

1956T. Hymn, "Master, Speak, Thy Servant Heareth!," Number 367 in *The Hymnal*, Herald House, 1956. Text set to music.

1981M. Hymn, "Master, Speak! Thy Servant Heareth," no. 410 in *Hymns of the Saints*, Herald House, 1981. Text set to music.

1950N. Hymn, "Heaven can be where'er the Lord lifts us from lowly sphere." P. 367 in *The Hymnal For Youth*, Herald House 1950, reprinted 1951, 1955.

1950P. Hymn, "Commitment Hymn." P. 369 in *The Hymnal For Youth*, published by Herald House in 1950 reprinted 1951, 1955.

1950Q. Hymn, "We honor those, our Father, Whose service honored Thee." P. 370 in *The Hymnal For Youth*, Herald House 1950, reprinted 1951, 1955.

1950R. Hymn adapted from W. G. Tarrant, "Glory to the heroes," P. 373 in *The Hymnal For Youth*, Herald House, 1950, reprinted 1951, 1955.

1950S. Hymn, "Lo, the time is now fulfilled!." P. 374 in *The Hymnal For Youth*, Herald House, 1950, reprinted 1951, 1955.

1950V. Hymn, "Walk Thou with me, O Lord of love." P. 380 in *The Hymnal For Youth*, Herald House, 1950, reprinted 1951, 1955.

1950W. Hymn adapted from Adelaide Proctor, "Softly the shadows fall," P. 380 in *The Hymnal For Youth*, Herald House, 1950, reprinted 1951, 1955.

1950Y. Hymn, "Truth has no single voice." P. 382 in *The Hymnal For Youth*, Herald House, 1950, reprinted 1951, 1955.

1950AA. Hymn. "Sacred books, the Church's treasure." P. 385 in *The Hymnal For Youth*, Herald House, 1950. Reprinted 1950AA, 1956J, 1960B(partial), 1960X.

1956J. Hymn, "Sacred Books, the Church's Treasure," Number 235 in *The Hymnal*, Herald House, 1956.

1960B. Hymn, "Thanks to those who sought as prophets." In Cheville 1960A, *Meet Them in the Scriptures*, Herald House, 1960. Library of Congress Listing BS 571.C485. In poem form. Revised from 1950AA, 1956J, 1960B (partial), 1960X.

1960X. Hymn, "Sacred books, the Church's treasure," Number 235 in *The Little Hymnal*, Herald House 1960, test set to music (St. Asaph). Reprinted 1950AA, 1956J, 1960B(partial), 1960X.

1950AB. Hymn. "Thou, who through all the ages spoke." P. 387 in *The Hymnal For Youth*, Herald House, 1950, reprinted 1951, 1955.

1950AC. Hymn. "O send Thy Spirit, Lord." P. 387 in *The Hymnal For Youth*, Herald House, 1950, reprinted 1951, 1955.

1953D. Hymn, "Conviction." In Article in *Saints' Herald*, "These things I offer you." Vol. 100, #16:p. 372, April 20, 1953. In poem form. Republished 1953D, 1955C, 1962B.

1955C. Hymn, "Conviction," in Cheville 1955A, *They Sang of the Restoration*, Herald House,

1955. In poem form.
1962B. Hymn, "It May Be I Shall Never Trace" (CONVICTION). P. 26 in, *Did the Light Go Out?* Herald House, 1962. In poem form.

1955G. Hymn, "The Christ of Every Age" (Afar in Old Judea), in Cheville 1955A, *They Sang of the Restoration*, Herald House, 1955. In poem form. Republished 1955G, 1956P (altered), 1960P, 1960AB, 1964I (in Spanish), 1974E (altered), 1981F (altered).
1956P. Hymn, "Afar in Old Judea" , No. 287 in *The Hymnal*, Herald House, 1956. Altered text set to music.
1960P. Hymn, "Afar in old Judea," in "Hawaiian Saints Were Singing," *Saints Herald* 5 September 1960, p. 15. In poem form.
1960AB. Hymn, "Afar in old Judea," Number 287 in *The Little Hymnal*, Herald House 1960, in poem form.
1964I. Hymn, "Alla En Judea Antigua," ("Afar in Old Judea"), translated into Spanish by Clair E. Weldon, No. 89 in *Hinario*, Herald House, 1964.
1974E. Hymn, "Afar in Old Judea," No 287 in *World Conference Hymnal 1974*. Altered text set in music.
1981F. Hymn, "Afar in Old Judea" , No. 296 in *Hymns of the Saints*, Herald House. Text set to music.

1956H. Hymn, "My Soul, Praise the Lord," Altered by Roy A. Cheville, original by William Kethe, Number 12 in *The Hymnal*, Herald House, 1956. (Altered in 1952) Republished 1956H, 1960W, 1981D.

1956K. Hymn, "O Lord, Thy People Gathered Here," No. 240 in *The Hymnal*, Herald House, 1956. Text set to music. Tune: Truro. Republished 1956K, 1960Y, 1981J.

1960Y. Hymn, "O Lord, thy people gathered here," Number 240 in *The Little Hymnal*, Herald House 1960, in poem form.

1981J. Hymn, "O Lord, Thy People Gathered Here," No. 352 in *Hymns of the Saints*, Herald House, 1981. Text set to music.

1956L. Hymn, "Stand, Soldier of the Cross," altered by R. A. Cheville, Number 246 in *The Hymnal*, Herald House, 1956. Original words by Edward H. Bickersteth. Republished 1960Z.

1956M. Hymn, "O Master to All Children Dear," No. 249 in The Hymnal, *Herald House*, 1956. Text set to music. Republished 1956M, 1981I (altered).

1981I. Hymn, "O Master to All Children Dear," No. 347 in *Hymns of the Saints*, Herald House, 1981. Text set to music.

1956N. Hymn, "Friend of the Home," altered by R. A. Cheville, Number 251 in *The Hymnal*, Herald House, 1956. Original words by Howell Elvet Lewis.

1956O. Hymn, For Bread Before Us Broken," No. 268 in *The Hymnal*, Herald House, 1956. Text set to music. Tune: Ewing. Republished 1956O, 1960AA, 1978C, 1981H.

1960AA. Hymn, "For bread before us broken," Number 268 in *The Little Hymnal*, Herald House 1960, in poem form.

1978C. Hymn, "For Bread Before Us Broken," Printed in the proceedings of the 1978 World Conference Communion Service April 2, 1978. Reprinted from *The Hymnal*, 1956Q. Text set to music.

1981H. Hymn, "For Bread Before Us Broken," No. 340 in *Hymns of the Saints*, Herald House,

1981. Text set to music.

1956Q. Hymn, "Forth in Thy Name," altered by R. A. Cheville, Number 314 in *The Hymnal*, Herald House, 1956. Original words by Charles Wesley. Text set to music. Republished 1956Q, 1968K, 1974K, 1981P.

1956R. Hymn, "Oh, Sometimes the Shadows," altered by R. A. Cheville, Number 354 in *The Hymnal*, Herald House, 1956. Original words by E. Johnson.

1956W. Hymn, "Send Forth Thy Light, O Zion," No. 431 in *The Hymnal*, Herald House, 1956. Text set to music. Republished 1956W, 1960AF, 1968N, 1974I, 1976B, 1978B, 1980A, 1981G, 1992.

1960AF. Hymn, "Send forth thy light, O Zion!" Number 431 in *The Little Hymnal*, Herald House 1960, in poem form.

1968N. Hymn, "Send Forth Thy Light, O Zion," No. 431 in *World Conference Hymnal 1968*. Reprinted from *The Hymnal*, 1956W. Text set to music.

1974I. Hymn, "Send Forth Thy Light, O Zion," No. 431 in *World Conference Hymnal 1974*. Reprinted from *The Hymnal*, 1956W. Text set to music.

1976B. Hymn, "Send Forth Thy Light, O Zion," No. 431 in *World Conference 1976 Business Meeting Hymns*. Reprinted from *The Hymnal*, 1956W. Text set to music.

1978B. Hymn, "Send Forth Thy Light, O Zion," No. 431 in *World Conference 1978 Business Meeting Hymns*. Reprinted from The Hymnal, 1956W. Text set to music.

1980A. Hymn, "Send Forth Thy Light, O Zion," No. 431 in *World Conference 1980 Business Meeting Hymns*. Reprinted from The Hymnal,

1956W. Text set to music.

1981G. Hymn, "Send Forth Thy Light, O Zion," No. 317 in *Hymns of the Saints*, Herald House, 1981. Text set to music.

1992. Hymn, "Send Forth Thy Light, O Zion," No. 317 in *1992 World Conference Hymns*, Herald House, 1956. Text set to music.

1956X. Hymn, "Thou Hast Been Our Guide," altered by R. A. Cheville, Number 520 in *The Hymnal*, Herald House, 1956. Original author unknown.

1959O. Hymn, "Speak Thou Today, O Lord," in poem form. In article in *Saints' Herald*, "These are my people." Vol. 106, #52:p. 1235, December 28, 1959.

1968E. Hymn, "Hymn of Zion builders." in poem form. *Saints' Herald*, Vol. 115, p. 359 May 15, 1968.

1979A. Hymn, "Let Us Sing a Worldwide Anthem," No. A-27 in *Sesquicentennial Resource Booklet*, RLDS History Commission, 1979. [Cheville's choice of tune for this hymn was Nettleton.] Republished 1979A, 1980B, 1981O, 1982, 1984B, 1986.

1980B. Hymn, "Let Us Sing a Worldwide Anthem" No. B in *World Conference 1980 Business Meeting Hymns*.

1981O. Hymn, "Let Us Sing a Worldwide Anthem," No. 468 in *Hymns of the Saints*, Herald House, 1981.

1982. Hymn, "Let Us Sing a Worldwide Anthem" No. 468 in *World Conference 1982 Business Meeting Hymns*. Reprinted from *Hymns of the Saints*, 1981O.

1984B. Hymn, "Let Us Sing a Worldwide Anthem" No. 468 in *World Conference 1984 Business Meeting Hymns*. Reprinted from *Hymns of the Saints*, 1981O.

1986. Hymn, "Let Us Sing a Worldwide Anthem," No. 468 in *World Conference 1986 Business Meeting Hymns*. Reprinted from *Hymns of the Saints*, 1981O.

1995A. Hymn, "Here At This Altar," in Ritchie, M.L., *Roy Cheville: The Graceland College Years*, Graceland College, 1995.

1995B. Hymn, "What A Friend We Have in Jesus! He is Steadfast," in Ritchie, M.L., *Roy Cheville: The Graceland College Years*, Graceland College, 1995.

1995C. Hymn, "Home of the Open Heart," in Ritchie, M.L., *Roy Cheville: The Graceland College Years*, Graceland College, 1995.

1995D. Hymn, "This Is My Home," in Ritchie, M.L., *Roy Cheville: The Graceland College Years*, Graceland College, 1995.

Appendix C
Pamphlets by Roy A. Cheville

1923. Master's Thesis, "The function of music in Religious Education." University of Chicago, Dept. of Practical Theology, University of Chicago Library call number ML 3999.C54.

1925. D.B. Thesis, "The Junior Church." University of Chicago, Dept. of Practical Theology. University of Chicago Library call number BV 9999.C485.

1929E. Booklet, "Lamoni, The Story of a Town Established Fifty Years Ago, 1879-1929." 40 p. Published September 13, 1929 by the Lamoni Semi-Centennial Committee. The five members of the Booklet committee were, G. N. Briggs, Chairman, Lucy Lysinger, Emma Chasey, Lyda Elefson, and Roy Cheville.

1930J. (Editor) Quarterly, "Education" Gospel Quarterly, Adult April-June 1930, v5 #3, 58 p. (Church History Series). The history and place of education among Latter Day Saints.

1932A. Quarterly, "The Relation of Our Church to Other Churches, Herald House. Gospel Quarterly Senior High," 1932, v41 #1, 56 p. Revised in 1938 as Volume 47, in 1941 as Volume 50, in 1944, 1946, 1947, 1948, 1949, 1952, 1954 and 1955 as Volume 53, and in 1958-1959 as Course A.

1933D. Quarterly, "Beliefs Of Our Church," Herald House. Gospel Quarterly Senior High. 1933, v41, #2, 72 p. Revised in 1939 as Volume 47, in 1942 as Volume 50, in 1945, 1947, 1948, 1949, 1950, 1953, and 1956 as Volume 53, and in 1958-1959 as Course A.

1933E. Quarterly, "Membership Qualifications," Herald House. Gospel Quarterly Senior High. 1933, v41 #3, 71 p. Revised in 1939 as Volume 47, in 1942 as Volume 50, in 1945, 1947, 1948, 1949, 1950, 1953, and 1956 as Volume 53, and in 1958-1959 as Course A.

1933H. Quarterly, "The Program of the Church," Herald House. Gospel Quarterly Senior High, 1933, v41, #4, 61 p. Revised in 1939 as Volume 47, in 1942 as Volume 50, in 1945, 1947, 1948, 1949, 1950, 1953, and 1956 as Volume 53, and in 1959 as Course A.

1934A. Quarterly, "How the Bible Came to Be," Herald House. Gospel Quarterly Older Young People, 1934, v42 #1, 64 p.

1935B. Quarterly, "How to Read the Bible," Herald House. Gospel Quarterly Older Young People, 1935, v42 #2, 64 p.

1935C. Quarterly, "How the Bible Reveals God," Herald House. Gospel Quarterly Older Young People, 1935, v42 #3, 64 p.

1935D. Quarterly, "How Shall We Use the Bible?" Herald House. Gospel Quarterly Older Young People, 1935, v42 #4, 64p.

1936I. Quarterly, "A Journey Into Ancient Times and Places," Gospel Quarterly, Intermediate Grade, Vol. 25, #1, 64 p. Herald House, 1936. Revised in 1942 as vol. 31. Republished as 1936I, 1942E, and 1945A.

1937A. Quarterly, "People Who Lived in Book of Mormon Times," Gospel Quarterly Intermediate. Herald House, 1937, v25 #2, 64 p. (Revised in 1943 as volume 31, 1943G). Republished as 1937A, 1943G.

1937B. Quarterly, "How the Book of Mormon Helps Us Today," Herald House. Gospel Quarterly Intermediate. 1937, v25 #3, 61 p. (Revised in 1943 as volume 31) Revised as 1943H.

1937C. Quarterly, "How the Book of Mormon Helps Us in Everyday Living," Herald House. Gospel Quarterly Intermediate. 1937, v25 #4, 64 p. (Revised in 1943 as volume 31, 1943I)

1939B. Quarterly, "History and Significance of the Family in the Work of the Church," Herald House. Gospel Quarterly Adult, Oct-Dec 1939, v15 #1, 64 p.

1939F. Pamphlet, "Youth Shares, A Manual of Review, The Youth Conference, June 10-18, 1939 at Graceland College, edited by Roy Cheville, Herald House, 92 p.

1940A. Pamphlet, "Youth Shares in Evangelism," Herald House, 1940.

1941J. Quarterly, "The Branch of Today and Tomorrow," Herald House, 1941, 98 p. plus Study Guide, total 119 pages. First published in 1941 as the "Official Report of the Youth Conference of 1941." Revised as 1945J.

1942B. Pamphlet, "The Latter Day Saints and Their Changing Relationship to the Social Order," Herald House in Church School Leadership Series 75p. Library of Congress listing BX 8671.C45. (University of Chicago Library call number BX 8671.C52.)

1943E. Quarterly, "Torchbearers of the Bible," Herald House, 1943. Vol. 51, #2, Senior Young People, 72 p.

1943F. Quarterly, "Torchbearers of the Book of Mormon," Herald House, 1943, Vol. 51, # 3. Senior Young People, 77 p.

1944B. Quarterly, "Overviews of the Book of Mormon," Herald House, 1944, 75p. Gospel Quarterly, Young Adult, v52, 1944 #2. Republished as

1944B, 1945O, 1948R, 1957A.

1944C. Quarterly, "A Journey With the Church," edited by Roy Cheville, Herald House. Units by Georgia Metcalf, Lillian Maxwell, and Jane Ross. Gospel Quarterly, Junior High, 1944-45, v33, #1-4.

1944M. Quarterly, "We Build Loyalty to Christ," Herald House. Gospel Quarterly series, v52 #5, 32 p. 1944.

1945B. Pamphlet, "Does It Make Any Difference?" Herald House 108 p.

1945K. Quarterly, "A Journey Into Ancient America," by Roy Cheville and Charlotte Gould, Herald House. Gospel Quarterly, Junior, 1945 etc. v34 #1. 63 p. (The lessons were originally written by Roy Cheville for the junior high grade and adapted by Charlotte Gould for the junior grade.) Republished as 1945K, 1948K, 1955H.

1945L. Quarterly, "People Who Lived in Book of Mormon Times," by Roy Cheville and Charlotte Gould, Herald House. Gospel Quarterly Junior, 1945 etc. v34 #2. (The lessons were originally written by Roy Cheville for the junior high grade and adapted by Charlotte Gould for the junior grade.) Republished as 1945L, 1946E, 1948L, 1949N, 1954B.

1945M. Quarterly, "A Journey Into Old Testament Times," by Roy Cheville and Charlotte Gould, Herald House. Gospel Quarterly, Junior, 1945 etc. v34 #3. 63 p. (The lessons were originally written by Roy Cheville for the junior high grade and adapted by Charlotte Gould for the junior grade.) Second edition 1948M.

1945N. Quarterly, "People Who Lived in Old Testament Times," by Roy Cheville and Charlotte Gould, Herald House. Gospel Quarterly, Junior, 1945 etc. v34 #4. 63 p. Reissued as 1948N.

1947A. Quarterly, "How Shall We Look at Our World?" Herald House. Gospel Quarterly, Senior High, 1947 etc. v55 #1, 80 pages. First printing 1947, second printing 1950C.

1947B. Quarterly, "What Kind of World Shall We See?" Herald House in 1947, 75p. Gospel Quarterly, Senior High, 1947 etc. v55 #2. First printing 1947, second printing 1950D.

1948O. Quarterly, "What is our Church's Mission to the World?" Herald House, 1948. Gospel Quarterly, Senior High, 1948, v55 #3, 72 p. First printing 1948O, second printing 1951F.

1948P. Quarterly, "How Shall We Equip the Church For Her World Mission?" Herald House, 1948. Gospel Quarterly, Senior High, 1948, v55 #4, 79 p. Second printing 1951G.

1983. Pamphlet, "My Endowing Experiences in Kirtland Temple," Herald House 1983, 68 p.

Appendix D

Published Articles by Roy A. Cheville

1920. "Letter to the First Presidency," *Saints' Herald*, Vol. 67, #38, p. 918, September 22, 1920.

1921B. "Religious Education Department Editorial," *ACACIA, 1921*, Graceland College Yearbook, pp. 43, 44.

1922. "Pride and Porch Paint," *Autumn Leaves*, vol. 36, #3:p. 112-115, March 1922. (A Graceland College Contest Story)

1926A. "The Junior Church, I. Its Purpose and Meaning." *Saints' Herald*, vol. 73, #37:p. 872,873, Sept. 15, 1926. [Derived from Cheville 1925]

1926B. "The Junior Church, II. Its Administration." *Saints' Herald*, vol. 73, #38:p. 897, 898, Sept. 15, 1926. [Derived from Cheville 1925]

1926C. "The Junior Service, III. Activities and Program." *Saints' Herald*, vol. 73, #41: p. 976,977, October 13, 1926. [Derived from Cheville 1925]

1926D. "The Junior Church, IV. The Plan of the Service." *Saints' Herald*, vol. 73, #42: p. 1003, 1004, October 20, 1926. [Derived from Cheville 1925]

1927A. "She came to build," *Autumn Leaves*, vol. 40, #3:p. 135, March 1927. (Story about Mabel Carlile)

1927B. "Religious Life," in the *Report on Graceland College to the RLDS General Conference*, April 6, 1927, Pp. 50-51.

1927C. "Junior church services for the month of December," *RLDS Department's Journal*, vol. 1, #8, November 1927, p. 12.

1927D. "Junior Church services for LDS ordinances," *RLDS Department's Journal*, vol. 1, #9, December 1927, p. 10.

1927E. "The place of music in the church," *Saints' Herald, Conference Daily Edition*, April 16, 1927, pp. 84-86. Partly based on Cheville 1923.

1927F. "Graceland's answer to the College religious problem." *Saints' Herald*, vol. 74, P. 863, July 27, 1927.

1927G. "Loyalties of Life," *Graceland Record*, May 17, 1927.

1928A. "A service for juniors," *RLDS Department's Journal*, vol. 1, # 11, February 1928, p. 26.

1928B. "Lamoni Stake—a description," *Saints' Herald*, vol. 75, #3:p. 957, Aug. 15, 1928.

1928C. "Lamoni Stake—an interpretation," *Saints' Herald*, vol. 75, #34:p. 980, Aug. 22, 1928.

1928E. "Religious Education," in the report on Graceland College, in the *Conference Daily Edition of the Saints' Herald*. October 2, 1928, pp. 9-10.

1928F. "Our College Program in Operation," *Conference Daily Edition of the Saints' Herald*. October 4, 1928, pp. 39-40.

1928G. "Condition and Desires of the Church and Its Membership," Statement by Wilbur E. Prall and Roy A. Cheville in the *Conference Daily Edition of the Saints' Herald*. October 6, 1928, pp. 59-60.

1928H. "At a College Sanctuary." *Saints' Herald*, vol. 75, #41:p. 1171, 1172, October 10, 1928.

1929A. "The Old Man," *Vision*, vol. 42, #1:p. 7, Jan. 1929.

1929B. "Singing A Capella " *Vision*, vol. 42, #5:p. 216, May, 1929.

1929C. "New books in review," *Vision*, vol. 42, #8:p. 365, Aug. 1929. (Review of *Methods of Private Religious Living* by Henry Nelson Wieman, Macmillan).

1929D. "Good Sabbath," *Vision*, vol. 42, #9:p. 399, Sept. 1929.

1929F. "On discovering details," *Vision*, vol. 42, #10:p. 455, Oct. 1929.

1929G. "A Christmas vesper service," *RLDS Department's Journal*, vol. 3, #9, December 1929, p. 30.

1929H. "The Call of the Old West Door," *Saints' Herald*, vol. 76, # 47, p. 1428, November 20, 1929.

1930A. "What has the church done?" *Vision*, vol. 43, #4:p. 148-149, April, 1930.

1930B. "New books in review." *Vision*, vol. 43, #4:p. 204-205, Apr. 1930. Reviews *The Effective Christian College*, by Laird T. Hites.

1930C. "The intangible influence of a college." *Saints' Herald*, vol. 77, #28:pp. 762f, July 9, 1930.

1930D. "A cross section of Graceland life." *Saints' Herald*, vol. 77, #33:pp. 902-911, Aug. 13, 1930.

1930E. "Graceland makes men of the future." *Saints' Herald*, vol. 77, #37:p. 1011, Sept. 10, 1930.

1930F. "New books in review." *Vision*, vol. 43, #9:p. 491, Sept. 1930. Review of *The Reconstruction of Belief*, by Charles Gore.

1930G. "The graduate." *Vision*, Inside front cover of June 1930 issue.

1930H. "Growing up in religion." *Vision*, vol. 43, #8:pp. 397, 404, Aug. 1930.

1930I. "The positive life." *Vision*, vol. 43, #12:pp. 600f, Dec. 1930.

1931A. "New books in review." *Vision*, vol. 44, #1:p. 27, January 1931. Review of *Religion in the American College*, by Edward Sterling Boyer.

1931B. "The Teacher." *Vision*, vol. 44, #3, inside front cover, March 1931.

1931C. "New books in review." *Vision*, vol. 44, #3:p. 124, Mar. 1931. Review of *The College Student Thinking It Through*, by Jessie A. Charters.

1931D. "Does Graceland offer real preparation?" *Saints' Herald*, vol. 78, #30:pp. 706f, July 29, 1931.

1931E. "Friendly Queries about Revelation." *Zion's Ensign*, vol. 43, No. 34, August 20, 1932, pp. 538, 539. [Similar, but not identical to 1939D]

1931F. "The Function of Theology." *Zion's Ensign*, vol. 43, No. 39, September 24, 1931, pp. 612-614.

1931G. "Acting Your Age in Religion," reported in the *Graceland Tower*, February 17, 1931, under the headline, "Students Discuss Religious Life."

1931H. "The Greatness of Washington And Lincoln." Reported in the *Graceland Tower*, February 24, 1931.

1931I. "Sensing Our Needs," Reported in the *Graceland Tower*, February 24, 1931.

1931J. "Am I Religious?" Reported in the *Graceland Tower*, March 3, 1931.

1933A. "Worship in the young people's program." *Saints' Herald*, vol. 80, #23:p. 714, June. 6, 1933.

1933B. "High Priests in History," *High Priests Bulletin*, vol. 2, #1, October 1933, pp. 4, 5, 20-22.

1933K. "Worship in the young people's program, Reported in the *Graceland Tower* June 24, 1933, under the title, "Young People's Program Given."

1934C. "Report of Graceland College, Religious Life." *Saints' Herald, Conference Daily Edition*, April 7, 1934, pp. 59, 62.

1934D. "Themes of Worship." *Priesthood Journal*, vol. 1, #2:p. 37-41, October 1934.

1934E. "Religious Life," *Saints' Herald, Conference Daily Edition*, of April 7, 1934, p. 59, 62, within the Report of Graceland College.

1935A. "A worship service for young people." *Saints' Herald*, vol. 82, #45:pp. 1548, 1567, Dec. 3, 1935.

1936A. "Re-interpretation of religion for youth." *Saints' Herald*, vol. 83, #2:p. 40, Jan. 14, 1936.

1936B. "The setting for the sermon." *Priesthood Journal*, vol. 2, #3:pp. 28-33, January 1936.

1936C. "The preacher and his bible." *Priesthood Journal*, vol. 2, #3:pp. 68-71, January 1936.

1936D. "The use of songs for prayer meeting." *Priesthood Journal*, vol. 2, #4:pp. 29-33, April 1936.

1936E. "Religious Education," *Saints' Herald, Conference Daily Edition*, April 5-6, 1936, p. 39, in the Report of Graceland College to the RLDS General Conference.

1936F. "The priesthood in the local church school." *Priesthood Journal*, vol. 2, #5:pp. 41-43, July 1936.

1936G. "We start our educational year." *Saints' Herald*, vol. 83, #37:pp. 1159-1160, 1162, Sept. 19, 1936.

1936H. "The place of religion in Graceland." *Saints' Herald*, vol. 83, #47:p. 1482, Nov. 28, 1936.

1937D. "What the religious educator expects of a church building." *Priesthood Journal*, vol. 3, #2:p. 26-31, Apr. 1937.

1937E. "Foundations of worship." *Priesthood Journal*, vol. 3, #4:pp. 4-10, Oct. 1937.

1938A. "A tempered community," *Saints' Herald*, vol. 85, #13:p. 393-396, Mar. 26, 1938.

1938B. "From the book of experience." *Saints' Herald*, vol. 85, #25:p. 779, 789, June. 18, 1938.

1938C. "Guidance in religious thinking." *Priesthood Journal*, vol. 4, #3:p. 5-16, July 1938.

1938D. "The Christian philosophy of the home." *Priesthood Journal*, vol. 4, #4:pp. 7-12, October 1938.

1938E. "Teaching Values in Church History—Monday Class Study With Roy A. Cheville." (Reported by G. Wyatt) From *Saints' Herald Conference Daily Edition*, April 6, 1938, p. 67-68.

1938F. "Teaching Values in Church History," Reported in *Saints' Herald Conference Daily Edition*, April 7, 1938, p. 80.

1938G. "Teaching Values in Church History." Reported in *Saints' Herald Conference Daily Edition*, April 7, 1938, p. 88.

1938H. "Teaching Values in Church History." Reported in *Saints' Herald Conference Daily Edition*, April 10, 1938, p. 100.

1938I. "Teaching Values in Church History." Reported in *Saints' Herald Conference Daily Edition*, April 10, 1938, p. 104.

1938J. "Teaching Values in Church History." Reported in *Saints' Herald Conference Daily Edition*, April 11, 1938, p. 120.

1938M. "Survey of Reasons Why Families Come to Lamoni to Make Their Home." *Lamoni Chronicle*, August 11, 1938, p. 5.

1939C. "God's purpose for his chosen people." *Saints' Herald*, vol. 86, #4: pp. 107f, January 28, 1939.

1939D. "Friendly queries about revelation." *Priesthood Journal*, vol. 5, #2:pp. 30, 31, April 1939. [similar, but not identical to 1931E.]

1939E. "I met Nauvoo." *Saints' Herald*, vol. 86, #18:pp. 549, 542, May 6, 1939.

1939J. "Our branch plans." *Saints' Herald*, vol. 86, #44:pp. 1383f, November 4, 1939.

1940B. "The three delegates," *Saints' Herald*, vol. 87, #9:p. 267, March 2, 1940.

1940C. "Selection according to the circumstances and conditions," *Priesthood Journal*, vol. 6: #4:pp. 15-19, October 1940.

1940D. "Salvation of the people, the church and society," *Priesthood Journal*, vol. 6: #4:p. 61-62, October 1940.

1940E. "Guest Editorial," *Graceland Tower*, vol 20: #13, p. 2, May 31, 1940.

1941B. "These things are planned," *Saints' Herald*, vol. 88, #34:p. 1068, August 23, 1941.

1941C. "Religious education and life," *Saints' Herald*, vol. 88, #42:p. 1323-1324, 1333, October 18, 1941.

1941D. "A test in church loyalties," *Saints' Herald*, vol. 88, #42:p. 1326, October 18, 1941.

1942F. "From the book of experience—The Three Delegates," *Saints' Herald*, vol. 89, #5:p. 141, January 31, 1942.

1942G. "Latter Day Saint policy and procedure," *Saints' Herald*, vol. 89, #9:pp. 270-271, 278, February 28, 1942. [Continued in 1942H]

1942H. "Latter Day Saint policy and procedure," *Saints' Herald*, vol. 89, #11:pp. 331, 332, March 14, 1942. [Continued from 1942G]

1942I. "Religious Life," *Saints' Herald, Conference Daily Edition*, April 7, 1942, in Graceland College report to the Conference, p. 50-51.

1942J. "Freedom and vision," *Saints' Herald*, vol. 89, #28:p. 871-873, 888, July 11, 1942.

1942K. "From the book of experience," *Saints' Herald*, vol. 89, #20:p. 1238, September 26, 1942.

1942L. "This church school has an assembly period," *Guidelines to Leadership*, vol. 1, #1, pp. 10, 11, Oct. Nov. Dec. 1942.

1942R. "How is it at Graceland?," *Graceland Tower* (Supplement) December 4, 1942, p. 7.

1943A. "What of the church as a hobby?" *Saints' Herald*, vol. 90, #4:p. 109, January 23, 1943.

1943B. "The church's wartime ministry to family life," *Priesthood Journal*, vol. 9, #1:p. 24-29, January 1943.

1943C. "What of special days?" *Guidelines to Leadership*, vol. 1, #3, pp. 5-8, Apr.–June. 1943.

1943D. "We make covenant," *Saints' Herald*, vol. 90, #42:p. 1317, October 16, 1943.

1943J. "Democracy's place in a lasting peace," *Graceland Tower*, March 26, 1943, under the title,

"Doctor Cheville Speaks On Peace for G.F.T.A."

1944D. "Is Latter Day Saint Education Christian?" *Guidelines to Leadership*, vol. 2, #2, pp. 4-6, Jan.–Mar. 1944.

1944E. "Shall we utilize these days?" *Guidelines to Leadership*, vol. 2, #2, pp. 20-21, Jan.–Mar. 1944.

1944F. "What kind of church home do children need?" *Guidelines to Leadership*, vol. 2, #3, pp. 3-4, Apr.–June. 1944.

1944G. "Junior highs, are they intermediates?" *Guidelines to Leadership*, vol. 2, #3, pp. 22-23, Apr.–June. 1944.

1944H. "Materials for anniversary on June 27." *Saints' Herald*, vol. 91, #25:p. 790, June 17, 1944.

1944L. "We are victorious through praying." *Guidelines to Leadership*, vol. 2, #4, pp. 3-4, 32, July.–September. 1944.

1945C. "How to build a better vocabulary." *Saints' Herald*, vol. 92, #14:p. 315, 335, April 7, 1945.

1945D [probably written by Roy Cheville]. "Music, the Church, and Graceland College," *Saints' Herald*, vol. 92, #16:p. 367, April 21, 1945.

1945E "Camping objectives," *Guidelines to Leadership*, vol. 3, #4, pp. 3-4, July.–September. 1945.

1945P. "New Words come with new experiences says Dr. Cheville," *Graceland Tower*, 12 Jan 45, p. 2.

1946B. "How much education?" *Saints' Herald*, vol. 93, #1:p. 7, 15, January 5, 1946.

1946C. "Shall holidays be holy days?" *Guidelines to Leadership*, vol. 5, #1, pp. 12,20-21, Oct.–Dec. 1946.

1946D. "This year the league plans a balanced program," *Guidelines to Leadership*, vol. 5, #1, p. 17, Oct.–Dec. 1946.

1947E. "Over the Isthmus, thoughts on immortality," *Saints' Herald*, vol. 94, #6:p. 101, 102, 110, February 8, 1947.

1947F. "One world and the church," *Saints' Herald*, vol. 94, #26:p. 597, 598, June 28, 1947.

1947G. "How can I help my friend?" *Saints' Herald*, vol. 94, #34:p. 791, August 23, 1947.

1947H. "Dads are parents, too," *Saints' Herald*, vol. 94, #38:p. 845, 846, 870, September 20, 1947.

1948B. "Our college and missions abroad," *Saints' Herald*, vol. 95, #5:p. 111, January 31, 1948.

1948C. "What about pacifism?" *Saints' Herald*, vol. 95, #11:p, 261, March 13, 1948.

1948D. "Shall there be prayer meetings?" *Saints' Herald*, vol. 95, #21:p. 485, 486, 502, May 22, 1948.

1948E. "Suggestions in planning young people's worship services at reunion," *Guidelines to Leadership*, vol. 6, #4, p. 7, July.–September. 1948.

1948F. "Graceland Futuramic," *Graceland College Bulletin (Alumni Magazine)* September 1948.

1948G. "What is a woman's place?" *Saints' Herald*, vol. 95, #48:p. 1148, November 27, 1948.

1948Q. "Religious education at Graceland College," *Guidelines to Leadership*, vol. 7, #1, pp. 51-54, Oct.–Dec. 1948.

1949A. "Conducting discussion in the adult church school," *Guidelines to Leadership*, vol. 7, #2, pp. 29-30, Jan.–Mar. 1949.

1949B. "An authorized church," *Saints' Herald*, vol. 96, #17:pp. 392,f, April 23, 1949.

1949C. "We shall still sing together," *Saints' Herald*, vol. 96, #23:p. 538, June 6, 1949.

1949D. "I wanted to go to Europe," *Saints' Herald*, vol. 96, #44:p. 1039, 1054, October 31, 1949.

1949E. "I visited the Rotterdam branch," *Saints' Herald*, vol. 96, #46:p. 1090, November 14, 1949.

1949F. "I lived with saints in Germany," *Saints' Herald*, vol. 96, #47:p. 1114, 1115, 1118, 1119, November 21, 1949.

1949G. "I was at home in the British mission," *Saints' Herald*, vol. 96, #49:p. 1161-1163, December 5, 1949.

1950A. "Letters worth sharing," *Saints' Herald*, vol. 97, #18:pp. 424,f, May 1, 1950.

1950B. "The church on the move," *Saints' Herald*, vol. 97, #33:pp. 784,f, August 14, 1950.

1950AR. "The Financial Law and social responsibility, in *The Report of the Conference of High Priests*, held at Kirtland Temple, October 5-8, 1950, pp. 48-50.

1951C. "Religion on trial," *Saints' Herald*, vol. 98, #19:pp. 452-454, May 7, 1951.

1951D. "They come from many lands," *Saints' Herald*, vol. 98, #32:pp. 751, 758, August 6, 1951.

1951E. "The Graceland spirit," *Saints' Herald*, vol. 98, #42:p. 993, October 15, 1951. [From 1946A "Through the West Door"]

1951H. "The Book of Mormon in the life of the church." In *Book of Mormon Institute Outlines*, Independence, Herald Publishing House, 1951, pp. 29-32.

1952A. "Graceland inaugurates agriculture curricula," *Saints' Herald*, vol. 99, #23:p. 548, June 9, 1952.

1952B. "And gladly teach," *Saints' Herald*, vol. 99, #23:pp. 944-946, 950, June 9, 1952.

1952C. "Campus ministry calls us," *Saints' Herald*, vol. 99, #44:pp. 1039,f, November 3, 1952.

1952D. "How shall I make ready for a Patriarchal Blessing?" *Saints' Herald*, vol. 99, #50:pp. 1196-1198, December 15, 1952.

1953B. "An enduring heritage," *Saints' Herald*, vol. 100, #4:pp. 79-81, January 26, 1953.

1953C. "These things I offer you," *Saints' Herald*, vol. 100, #16:p. 372, April 20, 1953.

1953E. "Be not afraid," *Saints' Herald*, vol. 100, #25:pp. 584,f, June 22, 1953.

1953F. "In church life after Graceland," *Guidelines to Leadership*, vol. 11, #6, pp. 20-24, Summer, 1953.

1953G. "We make things come true," *Saints' Herald*, vol. 100, #42:p. 1000, October 19, 1953.

1953H. "Our curriculum research moves on," *Guidelines to Leadership*, vol. 11, #9, pp. 1-5, Nov., 1953.

1953I. "The kind of Christmas we need this year," *Saints' Herald*, vol. 100, #51:pp. 1205-1207, 1220, December 21, 1953.

1954C. "Young ministers at Graceland," *Guidelines to Leadership*, vol. 12, #1, pp. 21-22, Jan. 1954.

1954D. "Just population or persons," *Guidelines to Leadership*, vol. 12, #2, p. 40, Feb. 1954.

1954E. "When they seek counsel," *Guidelines to Leadership*, vol. 12, #4, pp. 16-18, April 1954.

1954F. "Faith for modern life." *Saints' Herald*, vol. 101, #8:pp. 174-176, February 22, 1954.

1954G. "She exalted common things," *Saints' Herald*, vol. 101, #10:pp. 224, 225, March 8, 1954.

1954H. Review of the book, "Face your life with confidence," by William E. Hulme, in *Saints' Herald*, vol. 101, #14:p. 329, April 5, 1954.

1954I. "My father's world," *Saints' Herald*, vol. 101, #27:p. 641, July 5, 1954.

1954J. "These things shall happen in us," *Saints' Herald*, vol. 101, #44:pp. 1049-1052, November 1, 1954.

1954K. "Remembering," *Saints' Herald*, vol. 101, #50:p. 1205, December 13, 1954.

1955I. "Youth and problem-solving," *Saints' Herald*, vol. 102, #2:pp. 38, 39, 45, January 10, 1955.

1955J. "That we be revived," *Reminder*, vol. 7, #2, pp. 1, 4, June 1955.

1955K. "Our people are singing," *Saints' Herald*, vol. 102, #42:p. 996, October 17, 1955.

1955L. "Let it be a rising sun," *Saints' Herald*, vol. 102,

#44:pp. 1041-1043, 1052-1053, October 31, 1955.

1956C. "Stand up! Speak out!" *Saints' Herald*, vol. 103, #2:pp. 29-31, 45, January 9, 1956.

1956D. "Benedictory prayer of blessing," *Saints' Herald*, vol. 103, #16:p. 373, April 16, 1956.

1956E. "Radiant impression in great teaching," *Saints' Herald*, vol. 103, #34:pp. 809-812, August 20, 1956.

1956F. "Conference summary (Science conference at Graceland)," *University Bulletin*, vol. 9, #1:pp. 28-32, September 1956.

1956G. "Third in four," *Stride*, vol. 1, #1:pp. 21-24, October 1956.

1957B. "Interpreting morals," *Guidelines to Leadership*, vol. 15, #2, p. 7, Feb. 1957. (paragraph filler)

1957C. "Under scrutiny," *Guidelines to Leadership*, vol. 15, #2, p. 17, Feb. 1957. (paragraph filler)

1957D. "The highest good," *Guidelines to Leadership*, vol. 15, #3, p. 18, Feb. 1957. (paragraph filler)

1957E. "How are we looking at Japan and Korea?" *Saints' Herald*, vol. 104, #10:pp. 221-223, March 11, 1957.

1957F. "A greeting to Australia," *Saints' Herald*, vol. 104, #41:p. 974, October 14, 1957.

1957G. "An exploration on social planning," *University Bulletin*, vol. 10, #1:pp. 8-13, Fall 1957.

1957H. "Lesson I've learned," *Stride*, vol. 1, #14: pp. 38-41, November 1957.

1958B. "Women testify through active membership," *Saints' Herald*, vol. 105, #1:p. 12, 13, 16, January 6, 1958.

1958C. "What kind of a date?" *Stride*, vol. 2, #10:p. 30, October 1958.

1959C. "In high expectancy," *Reminder*, vol. 11: #1, pp. 1, 2, March 1959.

1959D. "Ten considerations for family living," *Guidelines to Leadership*, vol. 17, #5, p. 29-32, May 1959.

1959E. "These are my people," *Saints' Herald*, vol. 106, #33:p. 780,781, August 17, 1959. [first in series?] "I single out the company of the Saints, and I say as I walk with them, "These are my people!""

1959F. "These are my people," *Saints' Herald*, vol. 106, #35:p. 828, August 31, 1959.

1959G. "Don't Wait—Serve Now!" *Stride*, vol. 3, #9, p. 2-5, September.

1959H. "These are my people," *Saints' Herald*, vol. 106, #41:p. 967,978, October 12, 1959.

1959I. "An inspired message given through the Presiding Patriarch at the 1959 Kirtland Conference of High Priests." *Saints' Herald*, vol. 106, #43: October 26, 1959.

1959J. "The branch as our laboratory." *Guidelines to Leadership*, vol. 17, #9, p. 1, Nov. 1959.

1959K. "These are my people." *Saints' Herald*, vol. 106, #48:pp. 1136-7, November 30, 1959.

1959L. "Bethlehem Potential." *Stride*, vol. 3, #12, p. 2, December.

1959M. "These are my people." *Saints' Herald*, vol. 106, #50:p. 1185, 1199, December 14, 1959.

1959N. "These are my people." *Saints' Herald*, vol. 106, #52:p. 1235, December 28, 1959.

1959T. "Inspired Message Through the Presiding Evangelist," pp. 73-74 in *The Report of the Conference of High Priests, Kirtland Temple, October 8-11, 1959*.

1959U. Action in Lamoni." In *Iowa Community Life*, Iowa Council for Community Improvement. (Cited in Lamoni Chronicle 30 Apr 59)

1960C. "Funeral Sermon for Steven V. Carter," pp. 47-51 *Congressional Record, 86TH Congress, Second Session*.

1960D. "These are my people." *Saints' Herald*, vol. 107, #7:p. 160, February 15, 1960.

1960E. "These are my people." *Saints' Herald*, vol. 107, #8:p. 185, February 22, 1960.

1960F. "These are my people." *Saints' Herald*, vol. 107, #10:pp. 211, 222, February 29, 1960.

1960G. "These are my people." *Saints' Herald*, vol. 107, #10:p. 233, March 7, 1960.

1960H. "It shall be Bethel." *Saints' Herald*, vol. 107, #12:p. 279, 290, 291, March 21, 1960.

1960I. "These are my people." *Saints' Herald*, vol. 107, #20:p. 474, May 16, 1960. 5 weeks in Hawaii. Describes.

1960J. "These are my people." *Saints' Herald*, vol. 107, #22:p. 524, 525, May 30, 1960. More about Hawaii, then Berkeley Provo, St. Louis.

1960K. "These are my people." *Saints' Herald*, vol. 107, #24:p. 567, June 19, 1960. Indiana.

1960L. "Letter to Orman Salisbury." In, Salisbury, Orman. "Memoirs of Patriarch Orman Salisbury, Part IX." *Saints' Herald*, vol. 107, #12, June 27, Pp. 620, 621.

1960M. "Winds and Tides on God's Ocean." *Saints' Herald*, vol. 107, #30:p. 709-712, July 25, 1960.

1960N. "These are my people." *Saints' Herald*, vol. 107, #31:p. 743, August 1, 1960.

1960O. "These are my people." *Saints' Herald*, vol. 107, #33:p. 784, August 15, 1960.

1960P. "Hawaiian saints were singing." *Saints' Herald*, vol. 107, #36:p. 863, 864, September 5, 1960.

1960Q. "Universals of the gospel in 1960." *Saints' Herald*, vol. 107, #38:p. 900-902, September 19, 1960.

1960R. "These are my people." *Saints' Herald*, vol. 107, #41:p. 984-985, October 10, 1960.

1960S. "These are my people." *Saints' Herald*, vol. 107, #42:p. 1006, October 17, 1960. [Source of title

"These are my People."]

1960T. "These are my people." *Saints' Herald*, vol. 107, #48:p. 1154, November 28, 1960.

1960V. "Report of the Order of Patriarchs," *General Conference Bulletin*, April 3, 1960, pp. 6-7.

1961B. "These are my people." *Saints' Herald*,108, #1:p. 9. Joe Baldwin. Belleville, IL. Liahona in Iowa City. Walnut Park. St. Louis.

1961C. "The common man is a philosopher." *Priesthood and Leader's Journal*, vol. 1, #1, pp. 2-4, January 1961. Subtitle: "Men and life's meaning: A study of philosophy."

1961D. "These are my people." *Saints' Herald*, vol. 108, #7:p. 155, February 13, 1961.

1961E. "Socrates: He turned to man himself." *Priesthood and Leader's Journal*, vol. 1, #2:pp. 64-67, February 1961.

1961F. "Plato: He sought the enduring." *Priesthood and Leader's Journal*, vol. 1, #3:pp. 112-115, March 1961.

1961G. "Four scenes out of the story of inspiration." *Saints' Herald*, vol. 108, #12:p. 268-270, March 20, 1961.

1961H. Article in Reminder, "Sharing the good news with our neighbors," vol. 13: #1, , p. 1, March 1961.

1961I. "These are my people." *Saints' Herald*, vol. 108, #17:p. 395, April 24, 1961.

1961J. "Augustine: He sought for the unchanging amid change." *Priesthood and Leader's Journal*, vol. 1, #4:pp. 141-145, April 1961.

1961K. "Aquinas: He sought to bring reason and faith together." *Priesthood and Leader's Journal*, vol. 1, #5:pp. 174-177, May 1961.

1961L. "Descartes: He dared to think and thought a dualism." *Priesthood and Leader's Journal*, vol. 1, #6:pp. 223-226, Summer 1961.

1961M. "These are my people." *Saints' Herald*, vol. 108, #25:p. 584-585, 591, June 19, 1961.

1961N. "These are my people." *Saints' Herald*, vol. 108, #26:p. 611, 618, June 26, 1961.

1961O. "These are my people." *Saints' Herald*, vol. 108, #36:p. 853-854, September 4, 1961.

1961P. "Kant: He stayed at home and saw a world view." *Priesthood and Leader's Journal*, vol. 1, #7:pp. 302-305, September 1961.

1961Q. "Nietzsche: He took apart and did not put together." *Priesthood and Leader's Journal*, vol. 1, #8:pp. 326-330, October 1961.

1961R. "The thrill of theology." *Saints' Herald*, vol. 108, #41:p. 964-965, 973, 978, October 9, 1961.

1961S. "14 questions people ask about Patriarchal Blessings." *Saints' Herald*, vol. 108, #42:p. 990, October 16, 1961.

1961T. "These are my people." *Saints' Herald*, vol. 108, #47:p. 1116, 1120, November 20, 1961.

1961U. "William James: He affirmed the right to believe." *Priesthood and Leader's Journal*, vol. 1, #9, pp. 373-377, November 1961.

1961V. "Here's your answer to administrative procedures." *Priesthood and Leader's Journal*, vol. 1, #9:p. 377, November 1961.

1961W. "Henry Bergson: He perceived something vital in the Universe." *Priesthood and Leader's Journal*, vol. 1, #10:pp. 405-407, 411, December 1961.

1962D. "Is the Restoration relevant in 1962?" *Stride*, v.6-#1:p.2-5, 13, January.

1962E. "Alfred North Whitehead: He perceived a Universe of process." *Priesthood and Leader's Journal*, vol. 2, #1:pp. 36-38, January.

1962F. "Karl Jaspers: He asks whether man will continue." *Priesthood and Leader's Journal*, vol. 2,

#2:pp. 63-65, February.

1962G. "A time for philosophy." *Priesthood and Leader's Journal*, vol. 2, #3:pp. 106-109, 112, March.

1962H. "The way of Graceland." *Saints' Herald*, vol. 109, #10:p. 352-354, May 15.

1962I. "Are they intermediates?" *Priesthood and Leader's Journal*, vol. 2, #6:pp. 239, 240, 244 Summer.

1962J. "Sons of the saints." *Saints' Herald*, vol. 109, #18:p. 644, 645, September 15.

1962K. "The witness came to me." *Saints' Herald*, vol. 109, #20:, p. 714, 715, October 15. [The story of Rhodes and his coming into the church]

1962L. Article in *Reminder*, "Four people in four places." v.14:#4, p. 2, December.

1962M. "The Order of Evangelists," *1962 World Conference Reports*, pp. 19-21.

1963A. "Theology—believing that makes a difference." *Stride*, 7-1:2-5, January.

1963B. "God—sustaining the universe." *Stride*, 7-2:24-28, February.

1963C. "The Restoration is a Message of Good Cheer." *Restoration Witness*, v.2, pp. 6, 7, 10, February 1963.

1963D. "Man relating himself to God." *Stride*, 7-3:6-10, March.

1963E. "Jesus Christ revealing and redeeming." *Stride*, 7-4:16-19, April.

1963F. "The Holy Spirit, enlightening, enlivening, harmonizing." *Stride*, 7-5:8-13, 15, May.

1963G. "Introducing the Work of the Patriarch." *Restoration Witness*, May, 1963, p. 16.

1963H. Abstract, "Basic Considerations in Theology for Today," in Saints' Herald article "Older Youth Conference." *Saints' Herald*, vol. 110, #9:p. 306, May 1.

1963I. "The church functioning as fellowship." *Stride*, 7-6:16-19, June.

1963J. "Scriptures guiding in purposive living." *Stride*, 7-7:14-17, July.

1963K. "Priesthood ministering with authority." *Stride*, 7-8:7-11, August.

1963L. "Basic considerations in theology for today." *Stride*, 7-9:12-14, September. (Reported by Bob Gunderson and Margaret McKevit.)

1963M. "Stewardship, expressing responsible relationships." *Stride*, 7-9:40-43, September.

1963N. "Zion-Providing Spiritual Nucleus." *Stride*, 7-10:16-19, October.

1963O. Article in *Christian Century* for October 30, 1963, "Mormonism on the Move," pp. 1328-30. Reprinted in Saints' Herald, *Saints' Herald*, January 1964.

1963P. "Needed saintly sharing not superselling." *Saints' Herald*, vol. 110, #22:p. 770, November 15. Editorial.

1963Q. "History, Disclosing God's purpose and plan." *Stride*, 7-11:12-15, November.

1963R. "Eschatology—indicating the outcome." *Stride*, 7-12:18-21,35, December.

1964B. "Mormonism on the move." *Saints' Herald*, vol. 111, #1:p. 10-12, January 1. Reprinted from *Christian Century* of October 31, 1963.

1964C. "Our times and our theology." *Saints' Herald*, vol. 111, #2:p. 44, 45, 51, January 15.

1964D. "Lights along the way—Book lists." *Priesthood and Leader's Journal*, vol. 4, #1:p. 31, January.

1964E. "The patriarch needs to see and sense the program." *Priesthood and Leader's Journal*, vol. 4, #1:p. 52, 53, February.

1964F. "Prayer for guidance." (offered at World Conference) *Saints' Herald*, vol. 111, #8:p. 254, 274, April 15.

1964G. "Our spiritual brotherhood in Christ." *Saints' Herald*, vol. 111, #23:p. 796-798, 806, 807, December 1.

1964H. [An article entitled "One Hundred and Forty Years of the Latter Day Saint Movement" was given to and printed in the conference report of the American Theological Library Association in Kansas City. On November 20, 1964 Cheville gave reprint permission to Calvin L. Porter, Associate Editor of *Encounter*, Christian Theological Seminary, Box 88267, Indianapolis, Indiana, 46208.]

1964J. "The Order of Evangelists," in *1964 World Conference Reports*, pp. 81-84.

1965A. "How did you get into this church?" *Restoration Witness*, January 1965, pp. 8-9, 11-12.

1965B. "What's your concept of God?" *Restoration Witness*, February 1965, pp. 8-9, 13-14.

1965C. "On narrating experiences." *Saints' Herald*, vol. 112, #3:p. 80, February 1, 1965.

1965D. "Are Latter Day Saints Christian?" *Restoration Witness*, March 1965, pp. 8-9, 14-15.

1965E. "Was another church needed?" *Restoration Witness*, April 1965, pp. 8-9, 11-12.

1965F. "The revelation in the crucifixion." *Stride*, vol. 9, p. 126-128, 130, April 1965.

1965G. "Was the Book of Mormon a public stunt?" *Restoration Witness*, May 1965, pp. 8-9,14-15.

1965H. "What's that other book of yours?" *Restoration Witness*, June 1965, pp. 8-9, 11, 13.

1965I. "Do you feel the spirit?" *Restoration Witness*, July 1965, pp. 8-11, 13.

1965J. "Words of adventuring faith." *Saints' Herald*, vol. 112, #14:p. 475, July 15.

1965K. "Words of expanding faith." *Saints' Herald*, vol. 112, #15:p. 511, August 1.

1965L. "Words of foundationing faith." *Saints' Herald*, vol. 112, #16:p. 547, August 15.

1965M. "Did you have your baby baptized?" *Restoration Witness*, August 1965, pp. 8-9, 14-15.

1965N. "How did you become a minister?" *Restoration Witness*, September 1965, pp. 8-9, 11, 13-14.

1965O. "Do you pay income tax to your church?" *Restoration Witness*, October 1965, pp. 8-9, 14-15.

1965P. "Do you think you're ready for baptism?" *Restoration Witness*, November 1965, pp. 8-9,11-13.

1965Q. "These are my people." *Saints' Herald*, vol. 112, #21:p. 734, November 1.

1965R. "These are my people." *Saints' Herald*, vol. 112, #24:p. 841, December 15.

1965S. "Has God had anything to do with my finding the church?" *Restoration Witness*, December 1965, pp. 8-10.

1965T. "The High Priest As Servant," in *The Report of the Conference of High Priests*, Kirtland Temple, October 7-10, 1965, pp. 25-27.

1966B. "How detailed in direction." *Saints' Herald*, vol. 113, p. 10, January 1, 1966.

1966C. "Our church polity in conference operation." *Saints' Herald*, vol. 113, p. 114, 115, February 15, 1966.

1966D. "1966—Conference Year." *Saints' Herald*, vol 113, p. 149, March 1, 1966.

1966E. "Are they let out?" *Saints' Herald*, vol. 113, p. 221, April 1, 1966.

1966F. "These are my people." *Saints' Herald*, vol. 113, p. 447, July 1, 1966.

1966G. "Glorying in martyrdom." *Saints' Herald*, vol. 113, p. 582, September 1, 1966.

1966H. "These are my people." *Saints' Herald*, vol. 113,

p. 742, November 1, 1966.

1966I. "What about Wednesday evening?" *Priesthood and Leader's Journal*, vol. 6, #10:pp. 406-408, December, 1966.

1966J. "The Order of Evangelists," *1966 World Conference Reports*, pp. 73-75.

1967A. "In our church by 1977." *Saints' Herald*, vol. 114, pp. 78-80, 95. February 1, 1967.

1967B. "Patriarchs in the congregational program." *Priesthood and Leader's Journal*, vol. 7, pp. 89-92, March 1967.

1967C. "A youth meets God in a grove." *Restoration Witness*, vol. 4, pp. 2, 11, 12 April, 1967.

1967D. "These are my people." *Saints' Herald*, vol, 114, p. 269, April 15, 1967.

1967E. "Why have patriarchs—Roy A. Cheville." *Saints' Herald*, vol. 114, pp. 402-404, June 15, 1967.

1967F. "In a north country." *Saints' Herald*, vol. 114, pp. 590-592, September 1, 1967.

1967G. "These are my people." *Saints' Herald*, vol. 114, pp. 700-710, October 15, 1967.

1968B. "What distinctives count today." *Saints' Herald*, vol. 115, pp. 8-10, 25 January 1, 1968.

1968C. "Living evangelism! Reaching out wisely and caringly." *Saints' Herald*, 115:119 February 15.

1968D. "These are my people." *Saints' Herald*, vol. 115, pp. 237-239, April 1, 1968.

1968E. "Hymn of Zion builders." (poem) *Saints' Herald*, vol. 115, p. 359 May 15, 1968.

1968F. "Beyond scriptural monopoly." *Saints' Herald*, vol. 115, pp. 440-441 July 1, 1968.

1968G. "These are my people." *Saints' Herald*, vol. 115, pp, 562-563 August 15, 1968.

1968H. "Twelve pointers for pastors when requesting ministry from patriarchs." *Priesthood and Leader's Journal*, vol. 8, p. 265 August 1968.

1968I. "The Patriarchs," *1968 World Conference Reports*, pp. 73-75.

1969A. "These are my people." *Saints' Herald*, vol. 116, pp. 13,21 February 1969.

1969B. "The temple in today's church life, part 1." *Saints' Herald*, vol. 116, pp. 5-7 March, 1969.

1969C. "The temple in today's church life, part 2." *Saints' Herald*, vol. 116, pp. 20, 21, 22, 29 April 1969.

1969D. "My favorite scripture." *Restoration Witness*, vol. 4, pp. 12-13 April 1969.

1969E. "Prophetic ministry at institute on Zion." *Saints' Herald*, vol. 116, pp. 4, 5, 14 November 1969.

1969F. "These are my people." *Saints' Herald*, vol. 116, pp. 33, 34 December 1969.

1970B. "Helpers in healing." *Saints' Herald*, vol. 117 #1 pp. 28, 29 January.

1970C. "In Palmyra grove today (Excerpts from 1970 conference sermon." *Saints' Herald*, vol. 117, pp. 10, 11, 12, 16 August 1970.

1970D. "These are my people." *Saints' Herald*, vol. 117, pp. 17, 18 September 1970.

1970F. "The Patriarchs," *World Conference Reports 1970*, pp. 36-37.

1971B. "These are my people." *Saints' Herald*, vol. 118, pp. 21, 34 February 1971.

1971C. "These are my people." *Saints' Herald*, vol. 118, pp. 25-36 June 1971.

1971D. "20 questions people are asking about patriarchal blessings, part 1." *Saints' Herald*, vol. 118, pp. 10-12, 62 October, 1971.

1971E. "20 questions people are asking about patriarchal blessings, part 2." *Saints' Herald*, vol. 118, pp. 16, 17, 34 November.

1971F. "These are my people." *Saints' Herald*, vol. 118, pp. 27, 28 December 1971.

1972B. "Out of inquiring and investing." *Restoration Witness*, 3/72:4 March.

1972C. "These are my people." *Saints' Herald*, vol. 119, pp. 35, 36 May 1972.

1972D. "Endowment for witnessing (Excerpts from conference sermon)" *Saints' Herald*, vol. 119, pp. 10-13, 38 September.

1972E. "These are my people." *Saints' Herald*, vol. 119, pp. 25, 26 October 1972.

1972G. "Patriarchs," in *World Conference 1972 Report*, pp. 40-41.

1972H. "A Conference Calls for Conferring," In *Courage: A Journal of History, Thought and Action*, Winter 1972, pp. 387-389.

1973A. "What kind of a God should the preacher play?" *Saints' Herald*, vol. 120, pp. 10-12, 49 February 1973.

1973B. "These are my people." *Saints' Herald*, vol. 120, pp. 30, 53 March 1973.

1973C. "Living distinctives, part 1." *Saints' Herald*, vol. 120, pp. 10, 11, 17 September 1973.

1973D. "Living distinctives, part 2." *Saints' Herald*, vol. 120, pp. 19, 20, 36 October 1973.

1973E. "These are my people." *Saints' Herald*, vol. 120, pp. 19, 52 December.

1974A. "Enthusiasm in living Zionically today, part 1." *Saints' Herald*, vol. 121, pp. 418-420, 425 July.

1974B. "Enthusiasm in living Zionically today, part 2." *Saints' Herald*, vol. 121, pp. 494, 495, 513, 514 August.

1974C. "Order of Patriarchs," *World Conference 1974 Reports*.

1976A. "The book of Revelation can speak to us today." *Saints' Herald*, vol. 123, pp. 238f(44f) April 1976.

1977B. "Priorities in Patriarchal Ministry-Part 1." *Saints' Herald*, vol. 124, pp. 46f January 1977.

1977C. "Priorities in Patriarchal Ministry-Part 2." *Saints' Herald*, vol. 124, pp. 112f February 1977.

1978D. "On Patriarchal Ministry," in Reed M. Holmes, *The Patriarchs*, Independence, MO: Herald House, 1978, 110-113 .

1981A. "A trilogy of memories." *Saints' Herald*, vol. 128, pp. 114-116 March 1981. Villy Lundin, George Ventura, Mariko Saito.

1981B. "A letter and a prayer." *Restoration Witness*, vol. 3, pp. 23-25 March 1981.

1981C. "Insight and foresight: Experiences in discernment." *Restoration Witness*, vol. 10, pp. 14-25 October 1981.

1984A. "God provides for continuing enlightenment." *Saints' Herald*, vol. 131, p. 410(26) September.

Appendix E
Travels of Roy Cheville

At the time of his ordination to Presiding Patriarch in October 1958 Cheville was teaching full time at Graceland College. He did not travel much while arranging the transition from Lamoni to Independence. He did participate in the High Priests' Conference in Kirtland Temple October 8-11, 1959.

From January to September of 1960 Cheville was free from teaching duties at Graceland. He preached a series of six sermons in the newly remodeled Davis City, IA church, then participated in Religious Emphasis Week at Central Missouri State College in Warrensburg. Starting in February he spent five weeks in ministry in Hawaii. There he ministered in several priesthood, women's, and Zion's League meetings; then participated in dedicating the new Makiki Church in Honolulu. He spent a weekend on the University of Illinois campus with church youth. He was also in Hot Springs, AR and East St. Louis, IL.

Free from all Graceland duties in 1961, he ministered in Houston, TX, Taylorville, IL, Main and Offenbach Germany, Zwaagwesteinde and Rotterdam in the Netherlands; Lannelly, Wales; Nuneaton, Birmingham, Lippenham, Sutton-in-Caskfield, and Hazel Grove, England; and Columbia, MO.

In 1962 he was in Iowa City and Knoxville, Iowa, Regina, SK, the New Mallery Monastery (where he did research for his book *Did The Light Go Out?*) in Dubuque, IA, Osceola, MO, Hot Springs, Ark, Bandera, TX, Lexington, MO, Wichita, KS, and Galien, MI.

In 1963 he was in Cedar Rapids, IA, Aurora, IL, Lewis River, WA, Camp Erdman, Hilo, and Honolulu, Hawaii,

Santa Cruz, CA, Canter's Cave, OH, Saskatoon, SK, and Warrensburg, MO.

In 1964 he was in Rockford, Mt. Pleasant, and Coleman, MI, East St. Louis, IL, Temple Grove, Philadelphia and Transfer, PA, Gaylord, MI, Muscatine, Ames and Cedar Rapids, IA.

In 1965 he was in Sandusky, MI, Miami, FL, Edmonton, Alberta, Peoria and Norton, IL, Louisville, KY, Osceola and Kirkwood, MO, and Bay Port, Harbor Beach, Owendale, Shabonna, Mayville, Juniata, Cooswell, Sandusky, and Deckerville, MI.

In 1966 he was in State Center, IA, Chicago, IL, Tulsa, OK, Flint, MI, Salt Lake City, UT, Excelsior Springs, MO, Painesville and Kirtland, OH, and Des Moines, IA.

In 1967 he was in Houston, TX, Fairbanks and Anchorage, Alaska, Ontario, Rancho Mirage, Riverside, and Redlands, CA, Billings, MT, Calgary and Red Deer, Alberta, Grand Junction, CO, Saltillo, Mexico, Odessa, MO, Pittsburgh, KS, Washington, D.C., and Lancaster, WI.

In 1968 he was in Taylors, Charleston, and Kingstree, SC, Raleigh, NC, Fort Worth, TX, Sweet Home, OR, Happy Valley Camp, CA, Weyburn, SK, Guthrie Grove, IA, Columbus, Cincinnati and Dayton, OH, and Ames, IA.

In 1969 he was in Madison, WI, Pittsburgh and New Castle, PA, Joplin, MO, Dayton and Middletown, OH, Tulsa, OK, St. Louis, MO, Camp Bountiful, OH, Wheeling, WV, Columbia, MD, Williamsburg, VA Dayton, OH, St. Louis, MO, and Ft. Lauderdale, FL.

In 1970 he was in Cedar Rapids, IA, Orem and Salt Lake City, UT, New Hope, PA, Camp Ramoca, CO, Park Pines, MI, Brookville, Maine, Ft. Collins, CO, Buffalo and Snyder, NY, New Hershey, PA, Derby, IN, Louisville, KY, Victoria, IL, Wichita, KS and Springfield, MO. From December 4 to 16 he was chaplain aboard a cruise ship, teaching classes on family living. He flew to Baltimore for three nights with his daughter, then back to his office for two days. On

Christmas day Cheville, Roger Bendorf, and Wayne Zion drove to a youth encampment at Prescott, AZ, then on to San Jose and Santa Cruz, CA. There they were with Ivan Vallier to begin the new year.

In 1971 Cheville was at Santa Cruz, CA, Orem, UT, Colorado Springs, CO, Creston, IA, Kanoehe, Kalihi and Honolulu, Hawaii, Papeete, Tahiti, Edmonton, Alberta, West Cleveland, OH, Phoenix, AZ, Happy Valley and Berkeley, CA, Racine, MO, Camp Romoca and Colorado Springs, CO, Stewartsville, MO, Honolulu, Hawaii, Ginowan, Okinawa, Tokyo, Japan, and Seoul, Korea.

Cheville left Kansas City again October 27, 1971. He spent two days in Honolulu, two days on Guam, four days on Okinawa, ten days in Japan, two weeks in Korea. He came back November 28 by way of Tokyo and San Francisco.

In 1972 he was in Lancaster, WI, Bethany, OK, Grand Rapids and Muskegon, MI, Madison, WI, Parsippany, Ridgewood, and Pompton Plains, NJ, Camp Doniphan, MO, Panama City, Panama, Lima, Peru, Atlanta, GA, Greenville, SC, Lancaster, WI, Lexington, MI, Colorado Springs and Greeley, CO, Columbia and Vandalia, MO, London, England, Nairobi, Kisumu and Nakuru, Kenya, Hannover, Germany, Baltimore, MD, and Dayton, OH.

In 1973 Cheville was in New Liskeard, Ontario, Camp Bountiful, Lima, and Columbus, Ohio, Philadelphia and Spring House, PA, Foundry Hill, TN, Brainerd, MN, Joplin, MO, Port Colborne, Niagara Falls, and Brantford, Ontario, North Hills, PA, and Ridgewood, NJ.

In 1974 Cheville was in Chicago, IL, Soldier's Grove and Lancaster, WI, Camp Manitou, MI, Topeka, KS, Washington, DC, Colorado Springs, CO, Orem and Salt Lake City, UT, Greeley, CO, Mississauga and Willowdale, Ontario, and Honolulu, Hawaii.

In 1975 Cheville was in Seoul, Korea, Goodland, KS, Madison, WI, Temple Grove, PA, Hannibal, MO, Buchanan, MI, Bluff Springs, FL, Fairfield, IL, Bridgeport, Moses Lake and Wenatchee, WA, Monrovia, Liberia, Abak and Orlu, Nigeria, Nairobi and Kisumu, Kenya, Barcelona, Spain, and London and Birmingham, England.

In 1976 Cheville was in Atlanta, GA, Milton, FL, North Platte, NE, Osceola, MO, Olathe, KS, Leavenworth, KS, Davis City, IA, Jefferson City and Columbia, MO, Washington, IN, and Topeka, KS.

In 1977 Cheville was in Topeka, KS, Evergreen, AL, Milton, FL, Atlanta, GA, Oak Ridge, TN, Fairfield, IL, Warsaw, MO, Brush Creek, IL, Ridgewood, NJ, Orem, Salt Lake City, and Hunter, UT.

In 1978 Cheville was in Seoul, Korea, Taipei, Taiwan, Binalonan, Philippines, Bandera and Austin, TX, Topeka, KS, Hannibal, MO, Boone, IA, and Eldorado, IL. On the Asian trip he did not do public ministry. He gave one patriarchal blessing in Seoul, eight in Taipei and five in Binalonan.

In 1979 Cheville was in Sao Paulo, Brazil, Panama City, Panama, Warner Robbins, GA, Camp Chihowa, Dayton, OH, Osceola, MO, Lancaster, WI, Dayton, MD, and Eldorado, IL.

In January of 1980 Cheville moved from Wayne Zion's home to Resthaven, an institution of the Church which had provisions for assisted living. In October 1980 he flew to Dayton, MD for a few days visiting his daughter and family, then he went on to May's Landing, NJ for a week of visiting with Malcolm Ritchie, who was consulting there. On Sunday they attended a meeting with saints in the area, followed by visiting in the home of George Griffith in Ocean City, NJ. During the week Cheville dictated several oral history tapes with Ritchie asking questions and managing the recorder.

In 1981 Cheville gave one blessing in Topeka, KS. This was his last ministerial trip outside the Independence area. He gave his last blessing July 10, 1985 in Independence.

Appendix F

Message to the 1959 High Priests' Conference

Article in SAINTS' HERALD, "An inspired message given through the Presiding Patriarch at the 1959 Kirtland Conference of High Priests." [D:1959I]

Even as I, your Master, walked in Galilee and called men to follow me, and to go out and minister for me, so I have called you to be my ministers and have sent you out to serve my people and to witness for me. In various times and places you have been called and ordained. Today, as if hands were placed upon you, sense anew your calling. This day your calling is reaffirmed by me. Let it be as if you were reordained to my service. I bring you counsel that you may minister more completely, more effectively.

The material things of this world are intended for the comfort of my people. You live in times when satisfaction in possessing things prevails. Success is often measured in terms of worldly goods, and social status is gained through possession of these materials and by the comfort and ease they afford. Let not these material things become a pressure upon you and decide your course in living.

Know you not that one day I walked the earth without place to lay my head? Are you willing to walk in strange places as I did, with no purse and scrip? Do not deny yourselves these needful things. I ask you only to keep them in secondary place. When you make accounting to your bishop, consider well what is essential. Let your needs be met for the effectiveness of your ministry, but let not desire for material things become a hindrance to your ministry.

You are pastors of my people. You are teachers and leaders of my ordained men. Return to them, not so much as officers and directors, but as brothers and coworkers. There is need that you reach out to undershepherds to extend cheering encouragement to them through the brotherly hand and helpful word.

You are fathers among my people. You are fathers in your homes. I send you to these homes to bear testimony of me. Speak of great things taking place in the church on earth. Inspire your sons and daughters to give their lives to my work and to live among my people. Let your and their ambitions in professional and occupational fields be motivated with intent to contribute to my church. Turn none of them from desire to participate in ministry. I need the contributions of your sons and daughters.

Return to other ministers and to your congregations and bear testimony. Tell them the Spirit that leads to do good is functioning, that this Spirit has been with you in this gathering. Encourage the spirit and practice of witness now among you and arrange for adequate opportunity for my people to bear testimony.

I charge you to go forth with the spirit and message of evangelism. Wait not for appointed ministers to come among you and do evangelistic work for you. Let your congregations be witnessing fellowships that reach out evangelistically to others. Lead your people to speak to those about them and to live evangelistically among them.

I charge you to go forth with the spirit and message of Zion. Sometimes the concern about developing Zion becomes low and interest fades. Go make faith in Zion increase among my people. Wait not for some direction from the Center Place. Build among your congregation a community of brothers who live together in mutual support and saintly living. Look to those called to lead for direction and leadership, but wait not for their word that your people may live Zionically.

I send you forth to carry the message of repentance. This is a message of hope. Dwell not on terrors and disasters to come upon lands and peoples, but concern yourselves with tempests of men's souls. Tell how with repentance there is available redemptive power which can lift and heal. This is a message of hope.

I send you forth with the message of endowment. My endowing power is available. Wait not for some quick experience as a sudden gift from on high might come. Look to the gradual coming of endowing power as you and your people are qualified, and as there is need for empowerment. First of all, it is required that you understand the functioning of the Good Spirit, that you may interpret the working of the Spirit to your people. Go with the expectancy of endowment, for it is your rightful heritage.

My sons, I need you. I rely on you. I call you anew. You have come here at the invitation of my servants who are appointed to lead my people. This invitation was of me. Here you have felt my presence. Now I send you forth. My Spirit will go with you as you go in love and wisdom.

Soon two of my servants are going to the Orient. (At this point Brother Cheville placed his right hand on the shoulder of Apostle Jensen and pointed with the other hand to Apostle Neff.) Even as my servant Paul, long ago, went to peoples strange to him, so you will go. Even as my Spirit attended him, so you can be helped and strengthened. Let them not be discouraged as they discover the lack of understanding of the gospel among those baptized. These are my people, and they are to learn of my gospel. Let my servants go among them with apostolic witnessing. In this exploration and testimony they shall be blessed with discernment and love.

Go forth with confirmation of your calling. Go forth with the promise that I shall go with you and before you as you live among my people. Let the love that is in my heart for you this day dwell in you for and with my people. Amen.

Appendix G
Message to the Institute on Zion

Message through Presiding Evangelist Roy A. Cheville to the Conference on Zionic Community in the benedictory meeting at Park College, August 24, 1969.

My Sons and Daughters,

You assembled here with commendable intent to confer about the developing of Zionic community among my people. You came together with desire to perceive how you might join in bringing to pass the Zion of my purpose. You are commended for the integrity of motivation that prompted your coming. You are entitled to recognition and to direction ere you go your several ways. Now your Father speaks to you in confirmation and commission.

Ever has the way of Zionic community been in my eternal program. Ever is it designed to bring into realization the quality of person in my design for man. Ever is it intended to express my gospel in corporate living. Ever is it needed to provide testimonial ministry to the many millions of persons in all the world. I call you to see this motivation for Zionic community and to sense the urgency for Zionic expression.

Many of my people have not understood. Some have wanted Zion as escape from turmoil in their social world. Some have expected deliverance from the responsibilities in a world of strain and distress. Some have hoped for security and ease. Many of these have looked for benefits for themselves as they interpret benefit. I say unto you that such as these cannot have effective part in bringing to pass my Zion until they are reborn in evangelistic love, with inclusive mission to all people.

In former times I have advised my people that Zion should be an ensign. Some have not understood. They have presumed that one day a glorious city would be set up that could be exhibited to draw others to the church. I say again that Zion does not come by such observation, that it does not proceed with exhibition. It cannot be pointed to with designation, "Behold! Here is Zion!" The Zionic way of living can be appreciated as people dwell with those who live Zionically. Rather is the Zionic ensign to rise to gather my people together for their mission of evangelistic outreach and service.

I charge you to beware of setting to the fore the realizing of values that stand foremost in the contemporary social world in which you live. Materialism abounds. Its pressures are strong. Desire to rate high in terms of prevailing standards can divert Zion builders from achieving their mission. I call you to summon my people to rise above these pressures, these appeals. Those who dwell in Zionic community are to be industrious and creative that they may contribute to the common good and to my continuing purpose, not that they may be acclaimed for their material possessions and social standing therefrom. I call you to see the fullness of Zionic community, which includes competency in materialistic matters but which rises above mastery of man by material forces.

I charge you to return to the congregations of your residences and work to bring to realization Zionic living among my Saints. Encourage them to work together in happy, worthful community. Look to such gathering of my people where you dwell as will enable them to unite in Zionic congregational living. This is not to bring provincial apartness nor to retreat from responsibility. It is that my people may help one another in achieving saintly character and expression, that they may reveal the gospel in consociational living, that they may afford community into which others may come.

I plead with you to give concern to building up the core region of the center place. The designation to this place as the heartland of Zion still stands. If this region is unbuilded in appointments, in spiritual relationships, the cause of Zion will falter. Even now there is urgent need to build up this core land in the expression of Zionic community.

I call you to include in your picture of Zion the developing of satellite communities. Some will be in the regions round about, some in distant places. Look to expressing Zionic living in the culture patterns of the peoples in distant areas, giving indigenous expression of enduring Zionic values and processes. Let these communities serve as nuclei in the inclusive functioning of my church.

I call you to expect expanding vision and continuing expression. Remember that Zion is not a finalized achievement but a way of living that is ever in process. Remember that in the work of your God, who is Source for Zionic living, there is no end in creative expression. Start where you are, simply, soundly. Continue step by step.

Unto my son, Leslie DeLapp, I speak in recognition and encouragement. You have longed for Zion. Let not the dream and the desire diminish in you. Let these days be a time for counsel and creative testimony among my people. Speak forth helpfully and confidently.

And to all I speak this call. The way of Zion is the way of charity for one another, charity that expresses the truly lovable. There is need that you lead out in expressing this in outlook, in relationships.

There are strains and differences in circles of my church. There are those who complain and censure. Some weaken in hope. I am needing Saints who will focus upon what is wholesome and enduring. I call you to encourage my people to develop the art, the disposition of saintly association. I call you to draw them to see Zion in current functioning, in evangelistic mission, in saintly brotherliness. I want you to say in forthright terms that the purpose of God will not be frustrated, that Zion will come into realization not in accordance with whims of partial believers but in the fullness of my purposes and process.

I send you forth to express the joy, the satisfaction of Zionic community. And I shall be with you with increasing insight and functioning resources as you move forward in adventurous faith and saintly competence. Amen. [1969E]

Appendix H

We Are Called to Be Friends of God

This paper was written by Roy Cheville and presented to a gathering of 16 ministers in Korea in November 1971.

How you and I think we are related to God makes ever so much difference. The gospel of Jesus Christ is good news about this relationship. This gospel tells us that God loves, cares very much about us, calls us to live so we shall be God's sons and daughters. God wants us to go to all men and tell them how God is wanting them to come to him, to live his way with him, and thereby be *blessed*, that is be happy, with an enduring quality of happiness.

Some Gods Are Pictured As Not Liking Man

Go through the centuries, through the countries, and look at the long procession of gods that men have held up before them. How often these gods have looked upon man as a slave who was to be servile to these gods. Man was looked upon as a low-down creature who was to bring gifts and do service and bow in homage. And if man did not please the gods, these gods would take out their vengeance on man. Some gods were thought of as requiring fathers and mothers to sacrifice their own children, to offer their own farm animals to pacify the angry, displeased gods. And some gods have been pictured as really enjoying the sight of man's wiggling and shrinking as he suffered. Sometimes Christians have been inclined to picture our God this way. Let us affirm that this is a misinterpretation of the true God. Rather let our God be pictured as a Father who wants all to love him as he loves them.

During That Last Supper

One of the most inspiring pictures we have of Jesus Christ is that of him on that evening when he was with his twelve men in his farewell meal with them. He had called these men that they might be with him. He wanted them to get his message, his mission through living with him. Jesus Christ himself was the living expression of the gospel of God. Jesus spoke words; he lived words.

Now Jesus was going to be leaving his men. He wanted to prepare them for his going. He wanted them to get ready for carrying on his work after he should leave. As he talked with these men that evening, as they asked him questions he perceived that they did not yet understand why he was leaving, how he was leaving. He saw that they did not understand what he wanted them to be doing.

> What did Jesus do?
>
> (1) He could have looked at himself with self-pity, so alone with no one understanding him.
>
> (2) He could have complained at his men and denounced them because they did not get hold of his message.
>
> (3) He could have spoken out fiercely against the Jews who were going to kill him.
>
> (4) He could have railed against the Jews, his own people to whom he had come, who were going to turn against him.

He did none of these things. Rather did he speak with confidence and say to his men, "Let not your hearts be troubled!" and "Be of good cheer!" What a courageous faith! What a confident hope!

Jesus pointed out weakness of some of his men. Judas Iscariot would betray him. Thomas would doubt him. All of them would flee for their own safety. And Peter would deny that he knew Jesus. But Jesus never cast these men aside. Rather did he say, "I am relying on you men. I am turning over my work for you to carry on." Here is the supreme expression of God's high expectancy of man.

While Jesus was speaking to his men, he rose to new height of relationship. He told his men that he wanted them to love one another, as he was loving them. He said that the greatest expression of love that a man could have for his friends was to give his life for them. Then he said this, which is worthy to be engraved in gold and held before us all. It is more worthy of being lived by us. Hear his words,

> "You are my friends as you do as I have directed you.
>
> "Henceforth I am not going to call you servants; I am calling you friends.
>
> "A servant does not know what his master is doing.
>
> "I call you friends, because I have told you everything I have heard from my Father.
>
> "I have chosen you and ordained you that you might go out and bear forth the kind of fruit that endures.
>
> "Yes, I call you friends." John 15

Let these words of Jesus Christ that he spoke to his men in Jerusalem ring out strong and clear, "You are my friends." This is what he would be saying to us here today, in Korea, "You are my friends." He would express confidence in men of Japan and Korea as he did to men of Judea and Galilee.

That Diversity Among Jesus Men

What a picture it would make if we could see these twelve men here before us now, the twelve men whom Jesus chose and commissioned to be his apostles. What a diversity! I would like them to be standing before us now, talking to one another, in Japanese and Korean languages, dressed in the clothing we see on the streets of Tokyo or Seoul. What contrasts! What differences among these men!

Sometimes I wonder if Jesus Christ deliberately chose twelve apostles of such diversity that he might demonstrate how men of different temperaments and interests and backgrounds could be united in fellowship as they came to have common loyalty and common cause. And this was to be centered in Jesus Christ. In him they would be one. In his farewell prayer that last night Jesus prayed that his men might be one as he and his Father were one. The would have to catch the soul of this Jesus Christ, if they were going to be one in him.

Let us notice some of these contrasts.

(1) Peter and James

Often James is called "The Silent." It would seem that he did not speak up and speak out very often. It appears that Peter was an impulsive, forthright man who was the first to speak out. I can imagine James thinking and saying to Peter, "I wish you would think about what you are going to say before you speak up." And I can imagine Peter saying to James, "Why don't you say something so we can know what you are thinking." Two such men could irritate each other. I would presume that today we can find such a contrast in Korea.

(2) Matthew and Simon the Zealot

How these men could have suspected and hated each other! Matthew was a tax collector working with and for the Roman government. Simon the Zealot said, "Down with the Romans!" They are invaders of our Jewish homeland. Get them out. Such a zealot as Simon would say, "Kill off the Romans!" Some would say, "Take up the sword and God will strengthen your right arm!" We can get contrasts in political views today that resembled these. Think of a Marxist Communist and a Democratic Capitalist. How would two men of these modern differences get along. In Korea? In America? In Britain? In the council of twelve apostles.

(3) Nathaniel and Judas Iscariot

I have always wanted to have a clearer understanding of Judas. I believe that in him there was a struggle between two sets of loyalties. In one he had affection for Jesus of Nazareth. In the other he was enamored by the money bag. Money or Messiah. There was the struggle between insuring his own welfare, as by selling his Christ for "thirty pieces of silver" and establishing for himself a high place in Jesus' kingdom. It is to his credit that his remorse for what he had done eventuated in his taking his own life. Here was Judas who was unsure of his loyalties.

Over against Judas stands Nathaniel. He was the opposite. Of him Jesus said, "An Israelite in whom is no guile." Here was saintly Nathaniel and unsaintly Judas.

And Jesus selected both men.

As the circle of Jesus' apostles in those days included such diversity, so would his circle of saints today include people of all temperaments, of all backgrounds, of all races, of all lands. And as then, they would be one, as they would be one in Christ Jesus.

Abraham, a Friend of God

In the Book of James is a significant phrase about a good man of ancient times—Abraham. Here is the statement, "Abraham was called the friend of God." (2:23) Then the writing goes on to say that Abraham was so considered because of what he did—with God—for God. This statement follows, "You see that a man is right with God by what he does." There is pointed out that faith and works are never separable. A man who truly believes in something goes into action for it. A man who truly believes in God will work for God, with God.

Friends do not sit and look at each other, and nothing more. Friends do not merely smile at each other, and do nothing more. Friends do not merely eat rice together; they will give attention together in producing some rice, in providing means for purchasing some rice. And eating rice together will express the fellowship they have in doing worthful things together.

Abraham was God's friend because he and God were working together.

When Abraham was past seventy years of age, God called him to move out on a new adventure. At this age many a man wants to settle down and take things easy. At such an age, Abraham was spoken to by God with a call to leave his homeland and go to a country where he had never been. Abraham might have said, "Surely you are not expecting me to leave my home and go to a far-away country. God, don't you know I'm past seventy years of age? No, Abraham said nothing like this. He made ready to go. Here was the healthy combination of faith and works! Here was adventuring faith! Here was courageous faith!

God was saying to Abraham, "What you do is part of my long, long program for all men. I want you to develop a people who will reveal me to the world. I will bless you that through you others will be blessed." Abraham responded and started for what was to be the land of Canaan. He has been called "the prince of pioneers." He has been called "the father of the Hebrew people." He has been called "the friend of God." Let us say again that Abraham could be "the friend of God" because he ventured with God, worked with God.

Would you like to be a friend of God here in Korea? God needs a people to reveal him, to represent him here in Korea as he needed a pioneer to develop a people in ancient Canaan. Are we ready to move out in adventurous, courageous faith as was Abraham? Here, as there, now as then, God is wanting us to be his friends.

A Friend Shares with Friends

One of the marks of friendship is the giving out of one's very self to others. Something good is given with joy. Jesus Christ did not come to the earth and live among men because this was decreed, because this was his duty. He came because he loved men, because he wanted to help them. He came because his Father cared so much for mankind. This is a climactic sentence in John's writing, "God so loved that he gave..." And Christ the Son so loved that he came.

And a friend always shares himself and what he has with others. He does not give because social customs say he must. He does not give that he may receive a gift in return. He does not give so he can receive publicity so people will know how generous he is. He does not give because the person to whom he is giving has given him a present. No, he gives to his friend because he loves him, because he believes that the friend will be benefited by what he gives. He gives in happy, humble spirit.

Jesus was the outstanding friend because he had so much to share with his associates. He did not give to them; he shared with them what his Father had shared with him. He called his men to develop such a wealth of love, of understanding love, of outreaching love, of God-inspired love. They would share lovingly the good news of their Christ, the good love of their Christ.

Today it is urgent that we develop a wealth of what we can share with others. And we have to become friends with these others, in order to share the good things of God.

Faith and Works in Friendship

In some religions there is argument about *faith* and *works*. Some insist that we are "saved" by faith and that what we do does not make any difference. There has been a song that ran like this, "Only Believe, Only Believe." This kind of thinking says that all we have to do is to say we believe in Jesus Christ and this belief takes care of everything. There are those who say all that is required is that we say the name of "Jesus" and that this is the one thing, the only thing to do. Many like this doctrine for it is easy in its requirements. It means that we do not have to do very much. This leaves everything to God.

Yes, Paul did say that we are not saved by "works." He was using this term as the Jewish legalists used it. By "works" they meant carrying out the proscriptions of the Jewish law of Moses, of carrying this out in details, with many regulations. Jesus told these legalists that they got so taken up with rules and regulations that they never caught hold of the love, of the purpose of God. And if by "works" we mean these prescriptions and legalistic rules, we shall say that we are not saved by "works."

But Paul had another use, another meaning for "works." This referred to the living we do, in which good "works" are expressed. In this meaning faith and works are not separable. If a person believes something; he works at it; he gives himself to what he believes in. Paul was aware that when he believed in Jesus Christ he worked with Jesus Christ with his full powers.

James, in his writings, now included in the New Testament gave some helpful counsel. He said that a faith that is not expressed in doing something is pretty poor, pretty worthless faith. He put it this way,

> "My brothers, what use is it for a man to say that he has faith, when he does nothing to show it?... Suppose a brother or a sister is in rags with not enough food for the day, and one of you says, 'Peace to you, keep yourself warm, and have plenty to eat' but does nothing to supply the needs of his brother or sister, what is the good of that? He really does not have faith. Faith leads to action, and if it does not lead to doing something, it is a lifeless thing; it is dead." (James 2:17)

And this applies to true, vital friendship. My brother and I, as friends have to be doing something worthful together with God. If we do not our so-called friendship will dry up and die.

Friends do things together that are worthful. So does the friendship thrive and continue in vital living.

In the Church of Jesus Christ brothers and sisters do things together. So we live as friends. Joining in a great and marvelous work can produce great friendships that will continue and expand.

Friendship in Christ Bridges Cultural Differences

The Day of Pentecost in Jerusalem brought to pass something miraculous. Luke tells how in the gathering there were people from many places, from many languages, from many cultures. Ordinarily these would look at each other with some uncertainty, possibly with hostility. The Jews tended to look upon themselves as the chosen people of God. They tended to think of themselves as the favorites of God. They thought of God as looking as they did, as speaking the Hebrew language. They believed that they were to be the favorites in the Messiah's kingdom. Later on, many Jewish Christians thought that a Gentile would have to become a Jew if he was to become a member of Christ's cause.

That Day of Pentecost something happened that was truly miraculous. These people of many languages, of many cultures were together. There came a remarkable outpouring of the Holy Spirit. Men spoke out in different tongues. These Jews saw that God was not limiting his work to those who were speaking the Hebrew language. The story of Luke says that these men understood each other. They were doing more than speak in strange sounds that did not carry meaning. And these men of different tongues had spiritual fellowship. Here was the foundation of the universal, the worldwide church of Jesus Christ. Here believers in Christ had oneness that rose above their differences of nationality, of language.

We are needing such a day of Pentecost. We are needing such a gift of tongues. We are needing this oneness in friendship that came out of this common mission, this common loyalty to Jesus Christ.

Those Christians, after the Day of Pentecost lived together in friendship. They helped one another. They studied together. They prayed together. They ate together in fellowship meals. God was with them. The outcome of this is told by Luke in this significant statement, "And every day the Lord added to their numbers those who were seeking salvation." Those about them saw the gospel expressed in their gospel living.

We are needing this to happen today.

My Brother and I Became Friends in Faith

In late spring 1961 I went to Europe. I was there fourteen weeks. It was arranged that I should spend some time in our German Mission. A few days were to be in East Germany. With the apostle to Europe and the president of the German mission who resided in West Germany and the appointee to Germany, I crossed over the border lines and went into East Germany. We were in West Berlin in the section that was connected with the United States. Into this West Berlin came Alfred Urban to be with us during a three days church institute. So we had a circle of five ministers of the Church of Jesus Christ.

Alfred Urban had been an appointee of the Church when Germany was divided after World War II. He had chosen to remain in the East section because he believed that he was needed there. I had never met him before. When we greeted each other, we could not converse. He spoke no English and my German was very limited. But we smiled and we clasped hands. We were brothers. We were one in spirit. And God was with us by his Good Spirit.

> It is worth noting that before World War II there were more members of our church in the Eastern part of Germany than in the West. After the war, several made their way to the West, some by flight.

A few others came in from the East zone of Germany to this meeting in West Berlin. At that time there were no restrictions on travel between the two parts of Germany. At that time we hoped that those from East Germany would be able to come to meetings in the West, as they could afford time and money.

During this gathering of the Saints, the leaders of the mission asked me to lead the Saints in singing. They had a new hymn book in German. One hymn we sang, a new hymn to these German Saints, was "Work, for the Night is Coming." In German it reads, "Auf, denn die Nacht Wird kommen!" I felt impelled to sing this. During our closing meeting, I stood before the Saints and spoke in counsel and encouragement to them as God directed. Again, there came the direction to encourage them and to strengthen them for days ahead. I did not see what it all was meaning.

The next day we three brothers met in an upper room. At God's direction I stood before Alfred Urban and spoke to him. I spoke in English. Joe Bayless translated this into the German. A little later I stood at his side and spoke in benedictory prayer. Again Joe Bayless translated. That day I really talked to God for the helping of this good brother as he would be moving among his people. When I had finished there was silence for a while. And then Alfred Urban spoke. He said that this ministry had come at a time in his life when he needed it ever so much. He had felt so alone. He had wondered what he should do. This is what he said to me, "When I came to this meeting, I was feeling so forgotten. Now I can return to my people and tell them that God is in his Church. I can say that the Spirit of God is in the Church today, for I have felt this Spirit here. I can say that prophetic ministry is in the Church today, for I have received this ministry here." As Alfred Urban said this, I knew that my mission was accomplished for then. This man would stand alone, courageously, if this would be necessary.

When I bade Alfred Urban farewell the next night, there was little I could say. And he had no English words. Our hands met. And the hand of God was there, too. We saluted each other as "Brother." We were friends in a friendship of eternal quality.

I left Europe, from England, on the last day of July. Two weeks later, on August 13, the wall went up between East Germany and West Germany. No more could there be travel between the two sections. The Saints in East Germany would now be separated from those in West Germany.

That Sunday when the wall went up, Alfred Urban and his wife were in West Berlin, for the marriage service of his niece. He might have stayed on the West side and been assured of protection and financial support. This he did not do. He felt that the Saints in East Germany needed him and his ministry. So while the wall was being constructed and the police were being stationed, Alfred Urban and his wife Gertrude walked through the rubble, through the disturbance, through the dividing gate and went back to their people in East Germany. Here was spiritual courage. Here was devotion to duty. I do not look to the past for men of spiritual valor. I can look to Alfred Urban today. What was ahead Brother and Sister Urban did not know, but they would not shrink back in fear. They believed God wanted them to return.

Almost two months later I received from Louis Zonker, the president of the German Mission a brief letter that Alfred urban had sent to him. This is what this brother wrote from East Germany, "We had to return to the people who needed us. We are not afraid. God's purpose, God's work will not be frustrated by man. They may be delayed by man, but man cannot block them forever. One day the gospel will be preached here in this country. We shall be true to God's call." Yes, I read this and I reread this. My brother stood before me in my mind's eye as a spiritual giant. he is my friend, my chosen friend in Jesus Christ. We speak the language of Jesus Christ together.

A Friend Who Speaks in Spanish

Three years ago I went to Saltillo Mexico for the reunion, the one general gathering for the Saints in the Mexico mission. We had two young men ministering as "native" ministers. When I went there, Apostle Earl Higdon advised me to consider giving patriarchal blessings to these two men, if I felt this the thing to do. One day four of us were in the upper room of the church house. Here was the apostle to the Mexico mission. Here was Clair Weldon, who is gifted, capable in the use of the Spanish language. He was to translate. This native minister, Humberto Salas was not at home with English-speaking individuals. He was somewhat distant from those who came from the United States. I wanted so much that his barrier would be overcome. I wanted so much that Humberto and I would find friendship together.

I gave the blessing in English. Clair Weldon recorded it on a small recording machine. Then he translated it into Spanish. When he had completed the translation, I stood before Humberto with extended hand. He received it readily. He could not say anything in English, but he did something in his own cultural pattern that spoke and said ever so much. He moved toward me and surrounded me in a manly embrace. Here was a day of Pentecost. Differences in language and in culture were dispelled. Humberto and I were brothers. God by his Spirit was uniting us. I said in Spanish "Mi hermano en Cristo Jesus"—"My brother in Christ Jesus." Humberto and I had had a uniting Pentecostal experience.

Let us also include in this circle *you* of your land in the Orient, with your own language. I want to be in this circle. And Christ will be with us. We would not be strangers and foreigners. We would be brothers in Christ Jesus. And he would say to us what he said to his men in the upper room in Jerusalem, "I am calling you friends."

Our Prayer Together

In many languages I have joined with brothers and sisters in faith in common prayer. We have used the prayer that Jesus taught to his men in Judea and Galilee. It begins with these two words, "Our Father." When we say this we have to be brothers. With Spanish-speaking brothers I say, *Padre nuestro*. With German-speaking Saints I say, *Unser Vater*. With Tahitian Saints I say, either *Notre Pere* in French or *E to matou Metua* in Tahitian. We can say this together, "each in his own tongue." When we say "Our Father" we are linking ourselves with our brother who is at our side.

Recently a man said this prayer, "Forgive me, God, when I say 'Our Father' and do not really mean it, when I leave some out of your inclusive family. Help me to remember that all persons are to be my brothers and sisters." It will be good for all of us to say this prayer.

The Other Sheep

When Jesus was completing his ministry in Judea and Galilee, he told his disciples that he had some *other sheep* to whom he was to go. Then he visited his people on the western hemisphere. To me this great message stands out in the Book of Mormon; the witness of the universal Christ. He went to the western land. There he said again, "There are other sheep to whom I must go." And he added that there was to be "one fold and one shepherd." This is what we are to help bring to pass.

Sometimes when I listen to some Christians talk about "one fold and one shepherd" I get the impression that these believe that in this one fold, there will be separate "pens" that will maintain a certain kind of isolation, so that different peoples will not be mingling freely. Not at all. There is to be one fold.

When I conversed with a man of Africa about the Book of Mormon, I told him what Christ Jesus had said about the "other sheep" when he came to the western lands. Then I said, "You of the African continent are some of Christ's other sheep." This man of Africa responded.

When patriarch Eugene Connell went to South India he told them of the visit of Christ to ancient America and of what he had said about going to his "other sheep." He told them that the many people of India are some of Christ's other sheep. And they responded. I wrote and sent to them a simple song about "the other sheep."

Today the call comes strong to let all people, all peoples, hear the call and extend ministry to all other sheep.

Harmony with Diversity

Jesus never tried to make his chosen men become identities. Each man maintained his individuality. Peter was Peter and Nathaniel was Nathaniel. He never tried to make all "other" people into Jews. He wanted each to become a son of God in his own way, finding brotherly relations with fellow disciples, coming to be friends in Christ Jesus.

In a great symphony orchestra each instrument maintains its individuality and contributes to the whole. But the players follow the conductor who leads them together. They play on the same key. They play the same message. So let us be in the church of Jesus Christ. We get together as we get with Jesus Christ. Then all of us are friends with him, with each other.

Let the words sound out today, the words of Christ, "I call you friends."

Would I Be Without Genuine Friends?

I did not grow up in this Church of Jesus Christ. My parents were not affiliated with any church group. I came in contact with the church when I was a teenage youth. I was baptized when I was a youth of sixteen and a half years of age. A few faithful Saints invited me to come to their meetings. God drew me. The Spirit of God ministered to me. Just before I made my decision to affiliate with the Church of Jesus Christ a friend advised me against it. She said something like this, "It looks to me as if you are becoming very interested in this little church. I hope you do not get connected with it. If you do this will change the total course of your life. You get along with others very well. You are what might be called a popular fellow. If you are baptized by these Latter Day Saints, you will lose all your friends, you will not have the friends you are capable of having. And you have the ability to make something out of your life."

One winter day I was baptized. There was no church building in the village that had a baptismal font. So the ministers cut a hole in the ice that covered a small lake. Those baptized had to walk a way on the ice and then get down a step ladder to get into the water to be baptized. The townspeople came out in numbers. They had never seen anything like this. On the upper bank stood many of the townspeople. Down on the edge of the ice stood a small group, the Latter Day Saints. Yes, it was clear that I was making a choice that would affect all my life.

"But my friend's warning and prediction did not prove true.

First, my friends, my neighbors did not turn against me. At the time of my baptism I was participating in the Methodist Church. A foremost member of that church said to me, "We regret that you are leaving us, but we want you to be happy where you are going." A few months after my baptism I received my patriarchal blessing. This word was spoken to me, "Be consistent and even in your life...and you will make friends among those who oppose the church and they will respect it because of your integrity." This has happened in my life. I have met those of many faiths. I have been friends with three presidents of the Mormon church. I have known priests of the Roman Catholic church and rabbis of the Jewish faith. In my fifty and more years of life in this church, I do not recall one statement of a disparaging nature that has ever been made to me about my faith, about my church. And I have met Hindus and Moslems.

"Second, there has come to me in this Church of Jesus Christ a company of friends of precious quality. This circle reaches around the world. It includes those of every continent, of every race, of many languages. What a wealth of spiritual friendship has come to me. Once in a prophetic message I was told that an outstanding blessing of my life would be the friendship of the Saints, a friendship that would carry the love of brothers and sisters in Christ. I never expect to be rich in material goods, although I expect to have the things that will be essential for adequate living. But I shall be rich in spiritual friendship."

In This Circle of Friends

I would like each one of you to join me in this circle of friends. Here is the circle. Christ Jesus has the center chair. Here is *Anthony Onumajuru* of East Nigeria, Africa. His skin is black and his hair is kinky. As by miracle, he and his family came through the ravages of civil war. Here is *Jean Tapu*, of French Polynesia, of Papeete, Tahiti. His skin is brown. he speaks French and Tahitian and English. Here is *Georg Sofke*, now our native-born mission president of our German mission. He and his mother escaped from East Germany and found refuge in West Germany. He is my brother, my German speaking brother, from Europe. Here is *Humberto Salas*, from Jojutla Mexico, a blend of Spanish blood and native American Indian blood. He speaks in the Spanish language. Here is *James Clardy*, considered a Negro, who lives in Chicago. In him are strains of Irish, of Negro, of American Indian. Here is *W. S. Chawla* of East India, of Berhampur. He is a native son of that area of the world. He read about the church and the gospel and on his own initiative explored. Then one year two apostles came to his country and he was baptized.

Appendix I
The Thrill of Theology

Cheville D:1961R. Article in SAINTS HERALD, "The Thrill of Theology."

Poets tell us of the thrill Columbus felt when he first saw islands of the West Indies.... The field of theology brings this kind of excitement to me.... I believe God intends us to be spiritual adventurers in the realm of insights and to enjoy the excitement of discovery.

We see in part.

We build our concepts and conclusions out of our experience. We apprehend reality in terms of what has happened in our lives.... This total working capital includes our thinking, our feeling, our doing in one single fund of life experience.... Paul reminded the Corinthian Saints.... "We know in part, and we prophesy in part." He was reminding them to be humble and restrained in drawing their conclusions.... He applied this to prophesying—to speaking forth for God. Since we see God "in part" we shall speak forth for him with partial vision. No one of us dares claim fullness of comprehension of God.... Some years ago I stood on the shore of an ocean for the first time. I watched; I smelled; I listened to the ocean. I took some of the Atlantic ocean in my hand. I could say with sureness that the ocean was there. yet I had no right to set limits on what the ocean was.... Such also is my approach to God. I have made personal contact. I shall not hem him in by my partial experience.

Theology is concerned with the nature of God and with God's relation to the universe and man. It seeks to achieve a systematic, consistent interpretation of God... It is significant that the great panoramic visions of God, the mountain-top ones such as Moses related in Section 22 of the

Doctrine and Covenants, glimpse God's total, ongoing, creative process. There is a largeness in them. Such seeing always involves interpreting and understanding. This is the heart of theology. Saints are theological in spirit; we endeavor to see God, to see with God.

Some years ago when I began to turn toward theology, I sensed the need of reaching out into ever so many fields for exploration. I could understand God as I came to perceive in some small way his operations in astronomical, biological, chemical, geological, sociological, and other fields. I sensed how knowing the works is not enough; one has to live with the person himself. Everything that would throw light upon God at work in any field would enable me to enrich my theology.

In this continuing quest to understand God I came to see the Scriptures as selected writings of those who had lived before me, of those who in their times had sought to understand God. These writings were worthy to be selected because these prophetic pioneers saw beyond the average of their day. There was an unusual quality in them. At my best I caught the spirit of prophetic searching in these spiritual adventures. I sensed how they phrased their insights in the thought world and the language patterns of their times. They phrased what they saw of the eternal and the universal in the most advanced forms they knew. I caught something of their spiritual genius as I lived with them. This genius always has impelled me to go on in the quest they were advancing.

The Restoration movement has contributed something invaluable to my theological explorations. The Book of Mormon and the Doctrine and Covenants have delivered me from reliance on some one scriptural source. Without diminishing in any way the contribution of the Bible, these Scriptures picture God at work on another continent in ancient times and in our modern age, enlightening exploring souls who tried to see him at work through history.

They widen the witness and extend the inspiration of God. They break down the limitations that men have imposed on God....

There is a commendable restlessness well expressed in Kipling's "The Explorer." While others said, "There's no sense of going further," an inner voice kept saying to the pioneer, "Go and look behind the ranges."

For me there is a thrill in this continuing exploration. There is adventure in living with God and loving with God to achieve experience for expanding interpretation of him. One cannot interpret God by standing on the sidelines any more than one can diagnose friendship by never experiencing friendly association. Such a man cannot identify what he is setting out to explain. Likewise, one cannot interpret God without living with God creatively, lovingly in God's way. Theology, as interpretation of religious experience, should guide us in achieving ever-deepening experience with which to build expanding concepts. The process continues on and on.

So now I say of a given conception, "It is the noblest, most harmonious, clearest idea of God that I have to date." For it, I am using the best framework of thinking that I know. Ten years from now I expect to have pushed forward beyond present insights....

Sometimes we do need to discard whatever gets in the way of constructing a sound theology. Sometimes we need to toss aside disintegrating stones and ill-formed rocks in our foundation. This tossing aside is preliminary to the main business. Some never get their foundation built; they keep on denouncing and stating what they do not believe... We cannot build a life on what we do not believe....

An oft-spoken criticism of religion is that it frequently uses an archaic terminology and an outgrown thought pattern. Theologians and preachers are credited with tossing about in parrot-like repetition phrases that do not carry meaning to moderns. Words so listed are *"atonement," "re-*

demption," "sin," "salvation," "grace," "justification." When originally used these words spoke to their times. Men of today are telling theologians to drop them and find fresh, meaningful words or interpret them in terms that carry clear, functional meaning for now. These comments invite the exploring theologian to exacting study.

Today we have and use concepts such as "process," "person," "evolution," "natural law," and "relativity," Scarcely glimpsed—if at all-by early Christian thinkers and by those of the era of the Protestant Reformation. They are indispensable in describing God at work in our space universe and our social relationships. This holds for many disciplines of learning. Members of a wide-awake movement will endeavor to see the enduring fundamentals of the Christian gospel in universal terms and phrase these in the most expandable, most meaningful concepts of the living now. It is a great day for a movement that affirms contemporary revelation!

Every so often I am asked to what brand of theology I ascribe. Often I am classified. I ally myself with no school. There is something of soundness in all. There are weaknesses and inadequacies in all. I am not an authoritarian. To me this is expressed in Roman Catholicism and Utah Mormonism. Here the propositions are given and members are to assent. To me this is assent, not consent. Authority by virtue of office, *ex opere operato*, generally leads to entrenchment rather than to investigation.

I am not a fundamentalist....

I am not a liberal, although I consider myself liberal. Liberalism, in its technical and historical meaning, left God too general, too removed from personal communion...

I am not a modernist, although I use data and methods of the modern era....

I am not neo-orthodox. I do not adhere to its conception of man. It relies on "grace" which I do not find it meaningfully indicates....

If I were to select a name for my own school I think I would use "explorationist." It is not adequate, but it speaks of a quality of spirit....

It is essential that we listen and learn of fundamental questions set forth by those who are thinking in modern patterns. The theologian will seek to see and speak in enduring insight and universal perspective. Here are fields pressing for exploration:

(1) the functioning of God in space-size universe;

(2) the working of natural law in personal spiritual phenomena;

(3) the process of history in relation to dialectic Marxism and other materialistic interpretations of human experience;

(4) the functioning of revelation in terms of the kind of universe we live in and the kind of creatures we are;

(5) the nature of man as a spiritual being in the light of biochemical processes, depth psychology, etc.;

(6) the role of the community, Zion, in the total socioeconomic world order;

(7) eschatology in the light of a process universe;

(8) the functioning of the Holy Spirit as inherent in a dynamic cosmos;

(9) the basis for ethics in the universe itself; and

(10) human relations expressed in harmony with racial and cultural diversity.

Such questions point up the necessity for speaking the Restoration evangel meaningfully to our world. What an agendum for explorers!...

I see two extremes that are to be avoided. On one hand is confining legalism that sets itself to finalize doctrine. On the other hand is open-mindedness that reaches empty-headedness and becomes so critical that it spends its time negating. I have faith in a core of searching Saints who want to see God more clearly and speak for him more convincingly.

Just now I am grateful for the finest of our theological heritage in the Restoration movement. I am not thinking of the provincial, the superstitious, the self-centered, the doomful. I am thinking of the heritage of questing, of expecting to be enlightened through divine empowerment, of the multiple scriptural and other resources, of sharing for common consent.

I shall go as far as I can. I shall enjoy the questing. One day I expect to take courses in theology in the graduate school of the University of Eternity. Today I feel the thrill of theological exploration.

Appendix J
A Trilogy of Memories

Cheville D:1981A. Article in SAINTS HERALD, "A Trilogy of Memories."

Villy Lundin

The story of the Reorganized Church in Denmark dates back to where the first two missionaries from the United States arrived in Copenhagen on May 16, 1875. The attitude of many Danes seemed to be, "We are satisfied with what we have." They were polite but unresponsive. By 1876 there had been only two baptisms—in Aalborg, North Denmark. Even the translation of the Book of Mormon into Danish by Peter Andersen and Peter Muceus in 1903 brought little response. Gradually the appointees turned their attention to Norway.

In April 1961 I went to Europe for a weekend institute at Rotterdam, The Netherlands. Also present were Richard Andersen and Fred Banta, appointees to Scandinavia. After the institute I traveled north with them. During the journey they reported an unusual happening. A young man of Denmark—a Mormon—had sailed to Australia a few weeks before our meeting. After arriving there he set out to locate his church. Instead he found the Reorganized Church. The Australian Saints were friendly and considerate. They invited Villy Lundin into their homes, even when he became ill.

After his return to Denmark, a brother in Australia wrote to Richard Andersen, explained what had happened, and sent him Villy's home address in Odense. The two appointees tried to contact the young man but were unable to find him. Now they were perplexed. They did not know how to continue their search.

The three of us traveled to Aalborg, North Denmark, for a meeting at the home of a Danish brother. The next day, as we drove to Copenhagen, Dick and Fred continued to express their concern about Villy. That evening when we met in Tivoli Park, Dick enthusiastically announced that he had just met Villy. Soon the four of us were together in a brotherly circle. Villy told us how he had been investigating our church's history and message. His interest was genuine.

The next evening our foursome traveled to the rural home of Brother Blume. In his "Danishized" English Villy made further inquiry concerning the church, and at the house meeting that night he experienced again the warm fellowship he had known in Australia.

On the way back to Copenhagen Villy indicated his desire to become affiliated with the Reorganized Church. This was not possible, however, for the next morning the three of us crossed over into Sweden. As we bade Villy farewell, in my heart I was singing, "God be with you till we meet again."

After I returned to Independence, I wrote to Villy, and he attempted to answer, but he was sensitive about expressing himself in "blundering" English. After a time the correspondence ceased.

Then in the spring of 1970, I received a letter from him. He apologized for his long delay and then asked, "Can you come back to Denmark and baptize me?" I was thrilled! Since I could not make the journey at that time I wrote to Appointee Kasper Anholt in Oslo, Norway, asking if he could contact Villy. Kasper went into action right away. It was arranged for him and his wife Ann, and Olav Kristiansen of Oslo, to cross over into Denmark. There in the ocean waters near Odense on June 13, 1970, Villy Lundin was baptized. The confirmation prayer was given by Brother Kristiansen. The next year Villy and his family attended the church reunion in Norway.

In the spring of 1980 I wrote to Villy. He answered in English, concluding with this request, "Can you come to Denmark once again and visit me awhile? I need some brotherly visiting."

Villy, a postman, appreciates his employment but regrets that he does not have adequate financial means to come to World Conference. He must give priority to caring for his family which now includes three children. Villy is eager for gospel news and fellowship with Saints. He signs his letters, "Your brother in faith," and I respond by addressing him as "Brother Villy, my brother with Jesus Christ."

George Ventura

George Ventura and I first met in Salt Lake City, Utah. Through Houston Hobart, appointee assigned to that field, I learned of this young man who had come from Barcelona, Spain, as a member of the Mormon church. Later we were introduced and spent four hours together before my train left for California. During that time he told me his life story, including why he was withdrawing from the Mormon church.

Born in Barcelona on August 7, 1932, Jordi [Spanish for George] had grown up in the Roman Catholic Church. He was fervently loyal to his native province, Catalonia, which did not always line up with Franconian Spain. As a youth he had spoken out for freedom of speech and religion.

On a visit to Southern France he was contacted by Mormon missionaries and later baptized by them. When he returned to Barcelona, filled with zeal for his newly embraced religion, his enthusiasm led to strained relations. He also began having difficulties with government leaders. As the opposition intensified, Mormon church administrators helped him to migrate to the United States. Because of his linguistic ability he was assigned to work on translating liturgies for use in the Swiss Temple. For him this was a distressing experience. He said that he had chosen baptism on the foundation of the basics of the gospel, and that now he was being introduced to "the mysteries of the kingdom." With his usual frankness he reported to church leaders his intention to withdraw from the Mormon church. They endeavored to save him from "the sin of apostasy," but he stuck to his decision.

Before he and I parted in Utah, he gave he his address in Spain. There he was to enter military service, in accordance with national requirements. I wrote three letters to him but received no reply. Two years later I read a letter that had come to Charles Hield. When I came to the closing paragraph, I "stood on the clouds."

Jordi began by saying he wondered why no one had ever written to him. He reported that he had been searching for a satisfying church life, but had found none. Then he wrote that he had found two things in the Latter Day Saint movement that he would not give up: the restoration of the gospel and the Book of Mormon. He closed with, "If you would receive me, I would like to become a member of the Reorganized Church."

The question was twofold: where and how? Our elders would not be permitted to go into Spain to baptize him. The solution seemed to be for Arthur Oakman, apostle to Europe at that time, to arrange for him to come to Hannover, Germany. On November 15, 1959, Jordi Ventura made his covenant there. He was baptized by Vern Webb, an American appointee in Germany, and confirmed by Arthur Oakman, a native of England. Then he was ordained a priest by Anton Compier of The Netherlands. It was truly an international milestone for the church.

Jordi was working for living expenses and studying at the University of Barcelona in the field of economics (eventually he received his doctoral degree). As soon as he could accumulate enough money, he paid passage for the return of his mother to Spain. While Jordi was in military service, his brother and sister-in-law who were in Utah had effected her migration and baptism into the Mormon church. Jordi was determined to "rescue" his mother.

The next face-to-face contact I had with Jordi was in England. Church administrators had assisted him in coming to the British Isles reunion in the summer of 1961. We shared a room. After the reunion we went to the home of Roscoe and Mabel Davey in Nuneaton. Here he received his patriarchal blessing.

I next saw Jordi in Independence. He had come to the States to teach a course on "Contemporary Spain" at Graceland. Before he left Independence for Lamoni, eight of us met in the Clara Morrell home. Here Jordi received the Lord's Supper for the first time in months. Jordi gave the Communion prayers in Spanish. I had made copies of the first stanza of "Redeemer of Israel" in Spanish, and the eight of us sang it. At the close of the service we joined hands and sang, "God Be with You Till We Meet Again."

When he finished his work in the States he returned to Spain, where he continued to speak out for freedom. For a time it was not safe for him to walk the streets alone. Some church members in other countries did not understand his reticence in responding to them.

In early December 1975 I was again with Jordi in Barcelona. We met in a room at the Colon Hotel after he finished teaching an evening class. I had procured a can of orange juice and a bread roll; these were the sacramental emblems for our communion in Spain.

That evening, Jordi spoke in testimonial spirit. He said he had hungered for such spiritual fellowship. After his departure I relived our experiences in Utah, in England, in Lamoni, and now in Barcelona. My prayer was that we might always be "brothers in Christ."

Mariko Saito

"Meet Sister Mariko Saito." The introduction was made by Pastor Hiroshi Yamada at our church in Tokyo in the autumn of 1971. I extended my hand, understanding that she would not extend hers first, as that might be interpreted as pushing herself forward in social relations. I smiled, and she responded.

At that time Mariko was fifty-five. She had been baptized in 1965, and the depth of her commitment was reflected in a single statement she made to me: "Now Christ gives me my life work."

She had been married twenty-five years to Hiroshi Saito, a man who had become very successful in the business world. Although he never became a member, he treated her with kindness and consideration with respect to her church affiliation. Their home was always available to church members and for church activities.

During this first visit of mine to Japan, Pastor Yamada spoke to me about conferring a patriarchal blessing on Mariko. After he told her about the ministry of a patriarch, she responded with quiet approval. Although I pronounced the blessing in English it was translated into Japanese for her. Of the experience she said, "I did not understand all the words as they were spoken in English, but I sensed the wonderful spirit." She cherished this blessing as "God's word" to her.

The Japan mission was officially opened in 1960 and the Seijo church was constructed shortly thereafter. This building also became the meeting place for the "language school" sponsored by the church. There were classes for children, youth, and adults who wanted to learn English. Mariko gave of her time, energy, and material means for this project.

She came to Independence and participated in two world conferences (On the years she did not attend it was because Conference took place during the busy season of the

Seijo school.) At the first of these two conferences she had an experience that she cherished. I invited her to come to a meeting of the patriarchs, in which their wives would be joining them. With her came Mrs. Howard Andersen, her hostess, and Mrs. Dayle Bethel, a native of Japan who served as translator. This group included patriarchs from Scandinavia, the British Isles, Germany, Australia, and many states (including Hawaii). During the service we joined in singing from especially prepared song sheets the first stanza of "In Christ There Is No East or West" in Japanese. She was deeply moved. When I asked if she had something she would like to say, she stood and took a step forward. Then she hesitated, because her Japanese background would not permit her to display the deep emotion she was feeling. After a few moments she spoke one English word, "Hello." This moved the entire congregation. Some responded with tears. Then we sang "In this old, old path are my friends most dear." Later she spoke of this as her outstanding experience in the conference.

When the Seijo church became inadequate, a new building committee was appointed; Mariko was one of the four members asked to serve on it. When she told residents of the neighborhood about the needs for funds, many responded with contributions. Some members of the church in other lands also sent gifts of money to her. After the building was consecrated Mariko wrote to me. "We are so gratified our new church building has been constructed. We shall use it in God's work. That is why we built it."

The World Conference of 1980 gave the International Youth Service Award to Mariko for her outstanding ministry to youth. In the citation she was listed as one of the first women in Japan to obtain a college education. She had participated in the "Women's International Council," had served administratively in the language school (focusing on developing the children's section), and had an inclusive concept of the Restoration Church. Unfortunately she was not present to receive the award. Early in 1980 she had become ill; the diagnosis was terminal cancer. Three months before her death on June 3 she wrote to me. Her letter contained no hint of complaint or self-pity. Instead she wrote of the joy that had come into her life quite recently. "I am happy to tell you one good news. A friend, Mrs. Toki Sakai, an older sister of Mrs. Taira, is baptized. It took a long time for her to decide. Now she expresses belief in the Restoration gospel. We hope that she will have a good tomorrow." Mariko was not thinking of her own illness but rejoicing over the good happenings in the life of her friend. Her final paragraph included these words: "I think of you and others who have helped me so much. You have brought great purpose, great satisfaction, great joy in my life. You have helped me to live with God."

For a decade I experienced spiritual friendship with Mariko though miles separated us. Truly my life has been enriched because she was a part of it.

Appendix K
The Church of Jesus Christ

An Interpretation and Testimony in response to a letter from Washington Bot Otiene of Nairobi, Kenya. January 1977.

(*A summarization and presentation of beliefs and practices of Our Restoration Church of Jesus Christ, in functional ways, in the thinking, operating world of today.*)

The church is a company of people covenanted together with Jesus Christ to live with God in God's way and to carry forward the mission of Jesus Christ. This mission is to share in saintly living the gospel of eternal life. This means life of *eternal quality*, here on earth.

The church can be pictured as a living organism that expresses this good life. Paul, the apostle referred to the church as "the body of Christ, in which every member affects every other member, in which all members are designed to function together in mutual support" (Romans 12). Like the human body, the church draws on resources that God provides for the health, for the vigor, for the functioning of the church in action.

The following are set forth as basics in the beliefs and the practices of our Restoration Church in Jesus Christ. They are to be considered together as a unified and unifying theology.

1. *God.* God is designated as the eternal and universal Father of all mankind, as the continuing Creator and Sustainer of the universe. God has been, is now, and ever shall be creating, carrying on his work of bringing into realization people of eternal quality. God responds to every person to the degree that this person will respond to him. God is present-tense in nature, in operating in his ongoing work.

2. *Christ*. Jesus Christ is designated "the Son of God." He chose to come to earth to live here as a man, that he might reveal to man God's nature and purpose, in terms that humans could understand and appreciate. He came to reconcile man to God. In love, he gave his life that man might be saved from forces that pull man away from God. This plan to come to earth to man was in the program of God.

3. *Universe*. God designs, created, maintains the inclusive universe. This includes the range from galaxies to atoms, from people to particles. God provides this universe for man's habitation, for man's worthy enjoyment. Especially on our planet *Earth* does God provide resources for man's good, for man's spiritual good. Man is to use these resources to good purpose. The elements are eternal. What we call spiritual and what we call material are aspects of this unified universe. They are not to be seen as being in opposition. God provides both material and spiritual.

4. *Man*. God designs man to become a person who manages his or her life in accordance with God. God designs man to be more than robot or automaton or slave. God wants all people to learn to live cooperatively with God, each one as a son or daughter. God designs every man to be a steward, managing resources available to him or her with accountability to God. Man is intended to live with his fellow human beings in mutual helpfulness, in wholesome relationships, with God as Eternal Father.

5. *Baptism*. This is provided by God and required by God to help the person get right with God, to link with God. Preparation for baptism involves repentance. This means voluntary turning from ways and forces that pull away from living with God. In baptism God and man make covenant. Man does this of his own choosing. In baptism by immersion man pledges to God to live God's way. Immersion symbolizes how the whole of man gets into this

relationship with God. In *confirmation* priesthood men chosen by God, place their hands on the person recently baptized and present this person to God for the ministering of the Holy Spirit. In this way God makes covenant; God promises to endow with the Holy Spirit to foster spiritual living, as the person will ready and respond.

6. *Holy Spirit*. The Holy Spirit is the personal spiritual power that emanates from God, for enabling the person to live the saintly life. Jesus promised to his disciples that this Spirit would minister to them, after he would be away from them in bodily presence. As the sunlight enables plants and trees to grow, this Spirit enables people to live, to grow spiritually. This spirit is designed to develop spiritual *fruits* in people (Galatians 5:22). God endows certain people with additional expressions that are called spiritual *gifts* (I Corinthians 12). Jesus advised that this Holy Spirit is to comfort (strengthen) his disciples for good works, to enlighten, to achieve harmony and peace in the person, with God, with the saints.

7. *Prophecy*. Prophecy is designated as a *gift* experienced through the enlightening ministering of the Holy Spirit. The prophetic person lives with God, so he or she becomes able to see with God. Then this person is qualified to speak forth for God. This is more than future telling. The prophet looks into the past, into the present, into the future, to give meaning and direction for the present. A living church experiences present-tense prophetic ministry. Members are called to qualify for reception and for application of this prophecy.

8. *Priesthood*. Through the ministering of the Holy Spirit God calls those who are to be his representatives, his spokesmen in his church. Those who are so called by God are to receive the sanction of the church, through the consensus of the members in conference assembled. There are several priesthood offices. Each office has specialization of function and there is place for specializations within

a given office. The Church of Jesus Christ has those priesthood offices designated in the scriptures: the prophet; the apostle; the patriarch; the bishop; the high priest; the seventy; the elder; the priest; the teacher; the deacon.

9. *Scriptures*. The Church adopts and uses the scriptural writings that God has prompted and inspired, for guidance, for inspiration. These are seen as expressed in the thought world, the language expression of the times of their several writings. The canon of scripture is open. God keeps speaking as humans will respond and will see aright. A spiritually competent church will have continuing scriptures. Today the Church of Jesus Christ has three major scriptures: (a) the Bible, from out of the Near East, (b) the Book of Mormon, out of Ancient America, with Hebrew heritage, (c) the Doctrine and Covenants, a compilation of God's counsels to the Church in contemporary times.

10. *Sacraments*. God provides sacrament rites in the Church for the spiritual good of his sons and daughters. These are administered by God's designated, ordained ministers. These are the major sacraments: (a) baptism and confirmation; (b) ordination to priesthood; (c) marriage, for the mutual pledging of man and woman to live together as husband and wife, in family relationship; (d) blessing of children, speaking God's role in helping parents and others in the upgrowth of the child; (e) the Lord's Supper, for the renewing of the covenant made in baptism; (f) administration to those who are ill in body, or in mind, or in soul, for God's helping ministry; (g) patriarchal blessing.

11. *Zion*. Zion is the coming together of saints for mutual helpfulness, for divine endowment through living "together with God." Zionic living expresses gospel living in testimonial witness. Zionic centers develop witnesses and witnessing resources for witnessing to others. The Center Place of the Church is designated to be in a central "city" in the United States of America. The church is commissioned to develop Zionic centers of spiritual living in

places around the world. Basic is the affirmation that Zion is to be developed here, now, on earth. The living church does not wait for Zion to be postponed until arrival in heaven.

12 *Conference.* The church is directed to proceed with enlightened insight, with mutual concern in directing the ongoing life of the church. Administrators are those who are called of God, who will lead with prophetic insight, with brotherly love, with efficiency. The church is a God-directed democracy. God wants an enlightened company of saints on mission who work together with "common consent." Members qualify to confer together. Saints are expected to develop in understanding, in saintly relationships, so they will be qualified, inclined to confer together, to move on together with God.

13. *Life Hereafter.* Inclusive living with God develops life that has eternal quality. This is life that is worthy to continue. Life on earth is viewed as a segment of ongoing life. This ongoing life expresses the dynamic, creative, harmonious nature of God. His provisions for life hereafter expresses the fairness, the justice, of God, with his appreciation of diversity in human nature. Each person is assigned to the quality of "glory" that his or her spiritual condition merits. The conventional division that provides only heaven and hell as dwelling place for "the spirits" does not accord with God's sense of justice and with God's appreciation of diversity in people. God does not lump off people en masse. The gospel of Jesus Christ focuses on saintly living here on earth as foundational for living in the hereafter.

14. *Health.* The gospel of Jesus Christ looks to the inclusive healthiness of all covenanting sons and daughters of God. The gospel looks to the covenanting of every person that this health may be realized. Jesus said that he came that all people might have "abundant" life. This inclusive health includes biological health, mental health,

social health, and spiritual health. There is to be a unified program of healthiness. This looks to the effective contribution of every person, of every group in the life of the church. The Zionic community is a colony of saints that live together healthfully, that radiate healthfulness. This healthiness involves the hopefulness, the happiness, the harmony of saints who live together with God. The influence of the healthy living of saints is to be outreaching.

15. *Prayer*. Praying is two-way communing with God. This involves reaching to God and responding to God. Such conversation involves the entire personhood. Praying involves living with God, working with God, so the person has something to converse about with God. Praying is much more than bargaining with God, more than asking for favors. Saints are expected to mature in the life of praying. The growing-up saint seeks from God more than things for favors, more than signs and miracles that can be narrated. The growing saint wants to increase competency for conversing with God. The more such a person grows up, the more he or she sees need for effectiveness in living with God, in praying in relationship with God. This applies to the family, to the congregation, to the church general.

16. *Centrality of Jesus Christ*. Jesus Christ is at the heart of the Church. This Christ is more than a name, more than a doctrine, more than a symbol. This Christ is the living, responding, loving Son of God. This is phrased with directness in the foreword of the Book of Mormon. The core mission and message of this Book is stated as affirming, as witnessing that Jesus is the Eternal God, "manifesting himself unto all nations." Peter affirmed this on the Day of Pentecost. This was basic in the experience of Joseph Smith in the spring of 1820. The youth sensed the spiritual presence of the living, responding Jesus Christ. The word spoken that day was the word spoken to

seeking people in diverse situations, "This is my beloved Son: Hear him." In this Christ the Church is to experience enlightenment, restoring life, spiritual harmony, spiritual fellowship.

Theology interprets God to man. This theology is expressed in words and concepts meaningful to learners, to communicants. Saints are called to develop for, to seek for more adequate theological experience. Man will see what he has as means for searching for more. Man does not go on recess while he searches.

A vital theology speaks in functioning terms and applications. Such a theology cannot be memorized and transmitted. The laboratory work is ever in process. Such is the way of revelation.

This Church in History

Jesus of Nazareth called men to his side and initiated his church as a company of chosen disciples. He carried on a laboratory school in evangelistic ministry, in Zionic living. The church began as a fellowship in action.

When Jesus Christ was making ready to leave earth, he commissioned his men to carry on his work, to minister for him, to witness for him. He told these men that in his stead there would be the ministering of the Holy Spirit. What he had been giving them, the Holy Spirit would afford them.

The fulfillment of this promise came to pass on the Day of Pentecost. On this day of endowment, the Holy Spirit came. That day these disciples sensed the ongoing, universal quality of the Church on mission. (1) They sensed that Christ was not limited to a place, to a people. This endowing Holy Spirit would have universal outreach. (2) They sensed *the universal fellowship* of the church. For instance, their speaking in tongues transcended linguistic, cultural fences. (3) They sensed *the universal Mission*.

After some decades those who were leading the Church became concerned about maintaining correct theology and correct operations in the Church. Institutionalism developed. Doctrines, sacraments, priesthood organization became finalized.

In the Reformation era there came movements to release from this definitized institutionalism. In many cases a new definitization took place.

In the early years of the nineteenth century God moved to bring to pass restoration of the original gospel, the foundational, functional theology, with the church organization that would enable this restoring experience. The Holy Spirit was sought and experienced in functional ministering.

Today this restoring spiritual experience in theology is to carry on.

Appendix L

Consociating Comrades

Wilson Ritchie wrote Roy Cheville in October of 1984 asking for guidance on putting together a meeting on evangelism. Cheville wrote an eight page response in long hand on October 27:

Your letter came yesterday. I am replying today, for I sense that you want to get plans on the way for the project you have in mind. It sounds promising. You are not wanting to have a debating or a denouncing or a delaying project. You are wanting to bring together people with competence, conversation, cooperation in "a grand and glorious work," in which evangelistic Saints line up with God for the good of the world today.

I have appreciated the observation of a man of a century ago who observed that the early Christians did not spend time and energy lamenting about the evils of a dying world. Rather did they rejoice in sharing the good news about who has come into this world. The view is needed today. So many are looking for "the end to come."

The size of the group you have in mind looks promising. We need to "get together in our evangelistic endeavor." It is possible to convene in a "general conference" of three hundred people and never sense spiritual fellowship, with fellow saints and sister saints, with our Eternal Father, with our Eternal Friend. We need to feel at home with these two, our Father, our Friend. This involves "working with" and "rejoicing with."

The time unit calls for concentration in your considerations, with identifiable specificity, with designation of expression after the gathering.

I have sought for a designating title. Not for publicity terms but for phrasing that speaks meaningfully. I refrain from the much-used term "retreat." To some this does not imply getting into action. Here is a "try." You may use it or drop it. If you use it, give it vital meaning. Your project can be termed, *A Consociation of Gospel Comrades*. The prefix *con-* and the prefix *com-* signify *together*. The word *conference* is fitting in general meaning but usually in our Church it connotes "business meetings," etc. Usually strains and differences come to the fore. Basically *confer* means "to carry together."

You are familiar with the word "association." The word "consociation" has a tone of "togethering." We are needing this in our Church today.

The word "gospel" needs to be used evangelistically. It signifies "good news." This applies to happenings *today*. As a church we need to apply gospel to good happenings in the living present. We are needing to "bring to pass" as we line up with our Eternal Father and our Eternal Friend some good happenings in the lives of people, as we help them and inspire them to be "spiritually reborn" through living with Christ Jesus.

We have been inclined to designate the "gospel" as "principles" listed in the scriptures, six of them. We are needing good newsers who are bringing to pass good happenings in the lives of people, of families, of peoples. We are needing the bring to pass good happenings that can be recorded in today's Book of Acts." What a challenge to your "Consociation of Gospel Comrades!" Such a gathering does not involve in argumentation, in denunciation, in expectation of "the end of the world."

We are needing to use the words "blessedness" and "blessing" rightly, vitally. Healthy religion requires this. Usually we hear the word "blessing" connoting a favor asked of God and received from God. In the Sermon on the Mount Jesus centered on this word "Blessed" with its true connotation. Here "blessedness" signifies happiness with genuine enduring quality. Saints as disciples of Jesus are to be a happy people with happy life centering on God, our Father, with Christ Jesus, our Eternal Friend. They are to radiate genuine happiness.

Praying is involved in the planning for your Consociation. So often praying denotes asking God for favors, for "blessings," and thanking God for favors received. What a self-centered notion! In your gathering praying can include planning with God, communing with God.

The word "consensus" should have basic consideration. Our church, our families need to perceive this and apply. It has foundations in the section of Doctrine and Covenants that sets forth counsel about settling the Hiram Page incident centered on the "stone for revelations" (D&C 27). This is a foremost happening with regard to the procedure for handling the matter. Oliver Cowdery was to go alone to Hiram Page and counsel him. The outcome makes a first-class story in our church history. This counsel was spoken, "All things must be done in order and by *common consent* in the church, but the prayer of faith." "Common consent requires more than taking a vote, more than agreeing to the edict of a presiding officer. Members of the Church need to confer and consider together and ask for divine direction. You can contribute something significant to the life of our church by setting this forth and practicing it in your area, the way of enlightening, uniting "common consent." Sometimes there has come dissent or assent.

In this light I set forth suggestions for a schedule. This can involve periods for people to experience individual meditation. Most people need to learn how to reflect. Reflection and Meditation requires something that calls for clarification, extensive appreciation. You might find it advisable to provide for twenty minutes of individual or dual reflection after the field for this reflection is made clear. Without this, many do not know how to proceed. Meditation and praying can go together very helpfully, very healthfully.

The following sets forth fields for consideration, with respect to gospel living,

Friday Evening

Opening meeting for expressing friendship in our Consociation of Gospel Comrades.

The introductory explanation of the gathering, singing of Gospel songs (perhaps 3). Not songs for praise and adoration.

Presentation of "Comrades" by name, by location.

Inquiries about Comrades. About _____, about family, about membership in the church, etc.

Inquiries, What in the Church affords evangelistic appeal?

Assigned testimony responses about the appeal of the Church, about foundationing experience.

Handclasp greetings.

Prayer season

The healthy practice of praying
Hymn of prayer
Silent prayer in response to stated concerns
Hymn
Prayer of dedication.

Saturday Morning

My concernees past and present

The evangelistic person has concernees
people outside the church,
people inside

Considerations involve, concerns, concernees
Testimonies are spoken
Concernees are pictured

Saturday Afternoon

Good News of Evangelistic Happenings in Our Church Today, Here, Elsewhere.

World Mission requisites

Members of the Consociation participate as good newsers

About our contemporary church life

e.g. Haiti, Taipei, Spain, Tahiti

Saturday Evening

Gospel news in the Los Angeles Area—an unusual field

Gospel possibilities in the Los Angeles area

Sunday Morning

Living with Jesus Christ, Our Eternal Evangelist

Portrayal of the living, friendly, reliable Jesus

(Some Mis-portrayals may be noted!)

Stories of Jesus Christ in the New Testament,

In the Book of Mormon,

That portray this Friend.

Rebirth through getting with Jesus Christ

Some misinterpretations of Christ

The Man of Sorrows

The Monarch wanting praise

The portrayal in a limiting culture.

Songs portraying the Evangelistic Christ.

Sunday Noon—Fellowship Meal

Sunday Afternoon

Testimonial affirmations

Our evangelist expressions

The coming three or four months

The chosen time unit and chosen times

e.g. Christmas time, New Years, Epiphany (Jan 6)

Fields—family, community, congregation, city, other lands.

Pledge to our national flag

Pledge to our church flag—Peace

I pledge allegiance to the flag of our church
the Church of Jesus Christ
An ensign of peace to the world
A signet of fellowship in Zion
A banner of Saints on mission with Jesus Christ

Testimonial, prayerful expressions
Resolutions for these times

Evangelistic circle
Song
Prayer

Appendix M
Belief in God

On October 11, 1971 Roy Cheville wrote a three page letter to _____, My Good Friend:

I start out with this salutation, "dear friend" for it brings this kind of sense of relationship when some one inquires and indicates personal condition and outlook as you have done. No pretense. Straightforward concern and honesty.

You get right to the problem of believing in God. This is basic and foremost today. With thinking, exploring people, the much-heard injunction, "Have faith in God!" often does not elicit an affirmative response. Nor would this get such a response from me. If some one asks me if I believe in God, I would need to ascertain what they mean by God. I could not and would not say "Yes" to some people until I should find out what this term "God" meant to them. I could not respond affirmatively to some notions of God. These notions would be opposite to the genuine nature of God. This is not being finicky: this is being honest. Today people of inquiring mind are wondering about the kind of God they can and do believe in, in the light of the universe and of the history of things as they see things. These people ask, What kind of God can I believe in?

There are those, however, who do not develop a sound, functioning approach and pattern. These want to get everything out in front and then make a decision. We do not do this in the great vitalizing processes of life. And I consider believing in God such a vital process. If I insisted on understanding the digestive processes and the breathing processes and the circulatory processes before I would breathe and eat and the like, I would die. Nor could I get anywhere in personal relationships of affection and trust, were I to insist that I comprehend the nature of personhood and personal relationships before I would consociate with any other person.

On the other hand there are those religionists who get hold of a meager and rather childish conception of God and relationship with God and get grooved in this pattern of thinking and relating. These become grooved in their concepts and getting with God. Often these people insist that others do this.

Rather is our living with God, our working with God, our interpreting of God to be a thrilling experience of continuing exploring in which our experiences with God ever move to higher levels of seeing and doing.

People use their worlds of experience to interpret God. I employ the world of personalism. The person is an emerging creation coming into reality out of the Universe. Here is an ongoing process. Here is a miracle. God does not provide ready-made people. Nor does God provide us with some ready-made, automatic process. We have to learn how. We have to learn how to draw on the person-producing forces inherent in and available in this universe. These resources, these person-producing resources are there, else no person would ever come to be. Here is where we come into the realities, the processes that we call "spiritual."

Through the centuries we have tended to try to identify what is real. We have developed in the material sciences. We have got to identifying this material reality. Then we have shoved the other part of the universe which I shall call "spiritual reality" into a chance operation, never truly describable. I think that today it is urgent that we have an inclusive picture of reality. And this includes spiritual reality. This gets into the God area. Most moderns have a limited conception of the universe. This spiritual reality is left out.

Our Restoration movement and message gives us something of tremendous significance for our believing, for our living. There is no dichotomy in this world of reality with "spirit" and "matter" opposing one another. They are aspects of a unified reality. "Spirit" and "element" are set forth as inseparable.

There is something more. Religionists have tended to live with this two-parts universe. We have said that natural phenomena are describable in terms of operation. We have called these descriptive statements "natural law." I believe that during coming decades, if we will, we shall come to appreciate that spiritual reality can be described in terms of operation and that these descriptive statements may be identified as natural law in the realm of spiritual reality. What a call! What a need! What an adventure!

I see the Holy Spirit as the spiritual, personal presence of the divine, functioning in the Universe. In the Doctrine and Covenants we are reminded that this spiritual presence, this power pervades the universe and affords life and light. A tremendous affirmation.

This Holy Spirit identifies God working in his Universe with people. Here God is wanting the people to accord with the fullness of reality, including the spiritual. So shall man become a "new creation" developing life of eternal quality.

This God has an ongoing program. In D. & C. 22 we are directed to see that God never ceased creating. To me, if he ever did, God would become a had-been, a God emeritus. The creative process goes on. This includes the creating of people, people who grow in fullness of relationship with the fullness of the life-affording powers of the Universe.

God is wanting the person to come into fullness of right relationships with his God, with his Universe, with his fellows (all men) and with himself. God has a worthy conception of man. Most religions make man a wreck who is diabolical and depraved. God wants every man to live as his son.

To do this God arranges for a nucleus group with special assignment. This is the functioning of the "chosen people." This for functioning, not for favoritism. God called the Hebrews to function to reveal him to the world. Often they became more concerned with their privileges and their favoritistic status and they lost out. Today God is needing ever so many nuclei to work with him. Competency never comes through opening up to anybody without requirements. The Restoration church has a call to mission. Many twist this and make it a call to favoritism. The "chosen people" conception is the way of competency and service. It can become the conception of secluded apartness and privilege. The church as a chosen people has to be working with God on his mission.

And getting with God and knowing God requires more than looking on from the bleachers or observation platform. We have to get in the game with God and adventure in the laboratory of living. This seeking is more than asking questions. This calls for searching and applying in the quest. God has never given me ready-made, finalized answers. I was directed to the counsel to Oliver Cowdery (D. & C. 9) and I have always had to explore. And the exploring continues. What a thrill!

Here is a start. If this quest of yours needs more, we shall try again.

Sincerely and Expectantly Yours, Roy A. Cheville

Appendix N

Thirty Predictions

For Development of the Church [From D:1967A]

1. God will be identified in terms of what he is doing, as ever creating, as ever loving, as ever understanding. Honest seekers will look for expanding revelations of him as he functions in process in all his universe. Many notions of him will have died. He will be very much alive.

2. Jesus Christ will be seen as the revelation of God in terms of human nature. His divinity will be seen in his total personhood and total ministry. Single "proofs" of his divinity, such as his virgin birth, will not be considered adequate or functional. He will be considered divine because he acts divinely.

3. Man will be considered a being designed to live in right relationship with God, intended to become increasingly personal. He will be seen as conditioned by his biological and social heritage, as living below his potential, but uncondemned by God in "original" guilt. Man will be seen as designed to live with others in mutual support with utilization of God's life-affording powers. The church will be utilizing the resources of man's explorations to further understanding of his nature and operations.

4. The gospel will be interpreted as "good news" about the way men can live together with God. It will be interpreted in terms of functioning in everyday living. It will be shared with others for their good. It will be proved in terms of lives transformed and lifted Godward. It is to be shared, not sold.

5. Atonement will be explained in terms of bringing man who is alienated from God into reconciling relationship with God who awaits him in loving concern. Jesus Christ will be seen in bridging the gap. Theories of paying a debt

or of assuaging divine wrath will be seen as doing violence to God's nature and to man's needs. In Jesus Christ will be revealed the way of atoning ministry.

6. The Holy Spirit will be understood and wanted for ministering in the lives of people, of congregations; for spiritual fruitage in creative, constructive living. The endowment will be seen in terms of expression of love in the total living of the church, of love understanding and constructive. There will be increased study of the nature and function of the Holy Spirit.

7. The church will be conceived and conducted as a fellowship of disciples of Jesus Christ who are covenanted to live his way, to reach out to all people. There will be less concern in "proving" by arguments that this is the "right church," more concern with the living the right way with God. More and more the sense of worldwide spiritual fellowship will be increasing.

8. The congregation will have high significance in the life of the church. It will be (a) a laboratory school in developing Saints, (b) a corporate witness of gospel living, and (c) an evangelistic fellowship for reaching to and receiving people into the living of the church. The congregational program will be expressed in multiple functions. The congregational plant will be the home base for inclusive activities. Incomers will explore the gospel in the congregational life.

9. Priesthood will be ministering with increasing specialization of function. These specializations will make possible varied and more competent services in accordance with the needs of people and groups and the capacities of ministers. There will be more learning and laboratory expression in congregational settings.

10. Health in the inclusive sense will be receiving continuing consideration. Concern for wholesome spirituality will replace interest in signs and wonders and narratable miracles. The church will look to studies and

services that develop wholeness and healthiness in people and in families.

11. Zionic living will be cultivated in single-congregation and several-congregation areas of the church. This Zionic living will be developed in terms of conditions of modern society without servility to values of this society. "Gathering" will be studied and practiced in areas other than the center region of the church, that Saints may live with mutual support and in congregational expression.

12. Center Stake will be developing in community building in material expression and in spiritual neighborliness. The area in a mile radius of the Auditorium will be expressing its role as the heartland of the church. It will be the core region with satellite communities in adjacent regions and with expectancy of communities in more distant places.

13. Missions in lands whose culture is non-Occidental will be exploring in indigenous expression in message, in meetings, in administration. There will be growing pains in the experimentations. Members will look for spiritual genius that will afford harmony with diversity. They will endeavor to identify the basic universals of the gospel and to express these in thought patterns and custom patterns of different cultures.

14. Communication methods will be explored. This will look to multiple-way conversation. More effective media will be sought. This will apply to members with administrators, age-group with age-group, center regions with distant regions, English-speaking with non-English-speaking areas. This communication will be directed toward achieving enlightened common understanding.

15. Standing in the church will be more conditioned by Jesus' criterion of service. Ministers and members will be appreciated for quality of character and for contribution of effective, brother-minded, God-inspired service. There will be diminished concern with ecclesiastical protocol and prerogatives.

16. The quorums and staff of the General Church will include people of many racial groups and many cultures. Personnel will include Polynesian, Oriental, Negro, American Indian, and white. The beginning will be small, but a start will have been made.

17. Ministry to families will be directed toward guiding families in doing things together. There will be "ministering to families" rather than "home ministry." The functioning of the family will be recognized in congregation, stake, district, and other church activities. Teachers and counselors will be developed to participate in this ministry to families.

18. The church educational program will be adapted to the lifelong developing of people and to the development of the person as a whole. There will be institutions with specialization of function from childhood through college years and on through senior years. The congregation will function as a laboratory church school. Services of nonchurch agencies will be utilized. The entire program will carry a spiritual motif of searching and serving with Jesus Christ, the master teacher.

19. Education of children for and in membership in the church will be broadening in scope and in length of time. There will be more training in self-managing and in problem-solving. There will be less busywork and child-sitting. Educational programs will be geared to recent discoveries of potentials of children. Every age will be respected in its own right. Education for church membership may take as long as four years and continue after baptism—for participation in church living.

20. Youth will participate in church life as youth; their education will be more than preadult. They will participate in deliberating and deciding what is to be done in the church. They will have increased opportunity to ask questions and make responses.

21. Senior adults will be encouraged to keep in the flow

of life of the church. Education and laboratory service will enable them to live in and contribute to the church functioning in the modern social order.

22. Counseling services will be available in several fields: finance, vocational guidance, education, recreation, family living, health, and theology. There will be counselors in specific fields and in general guidance. A vital spiritual quality will pervade the counseling. Clinical centers will be established.

23. Common consent will be seen as inherent in the healthy operation of the church. It will operate in educational and administrative procedures. It will be seen as the developing of common understanding through consociational consideration of matters that concern the church. It will be seen as essential to the soundness of the church and to the development of members. It will be directed toward enlightened deliberation rather than assent in voting.

24. Revelation will be seen and practiced as spiritual insight in problem solving. It will apply to all fields of searching for truth. It will be seen experientially possible by all people in relative ways, on differing levels, in various fields. In administrative matters revelation will be considered operative in the field of administrative involvement. The church will be concerned with developing increasing competency for expanding revelation.

25. Worship will have organic relationship to work. Members will strive to relate themselves to God through co-ministering with him. Erstwhile emphasis on adoration and praise will decline as the church is engaged in working worthfully with God. Worship will increase in spiritual vitality and vision for the creative, communicative relationship with God.

26. Meetings will have variety in objectives and operations in accordance with the needs, the resources of the people, and local conditions. There will be more express-

ing of members. Testimony will be pervasive. There will be more opportunity for God to break through to disclose himself in diverse kinds of meetings.

27. Scriptures will be used for their guidance potential in the business of saintly living. They will be seen in terms of their times. The Book of Mormon will be shared with members and nonmembers for its witness of the universal Christ. The Doctrine and Covenants will be a symbol of contemporary revealment. The Latter Day Saint version of the Bible will be interpreted for the functions originally intended. The church will consider qualifying for further scriptural counsel.

28. The church will cooperate with agencies and other churches in projects that further the welfare of man and afford a common spiritual witness. At the same time members will look to the identifying and developing of distinctives of the Restoration movement that prompt them to maintain identity for ministry to the world. They will develop the spiritual competency that will enable them to bring this distinctive and essential contribution.

29. Members will become more aware of the richness of their spiritual heritage and of the responsibility of their calling. They will see themselves as a creative, consecrated minority in the world, a little people with a big assignment. Self-pity and a sense of secondary position will decline.

30. The Saints will continue to be a singing people. They will sing on several levels, in many languages. They will sing a sound present-day theology. They will have more hymns that speak the Restoration message and mission and mood. Their singing will be evangelistic: it will share the good news. They will sing up to times. They will sing "songs of everlasting joy."

Members of the church will do well to cultivate a hopeful, pioneering spirit for the decade ahead. In these thirty items I prognosticate what can come to pass.

Once Robert Frost wrote of this nation, "The founding fathers didn't believe in the future. They believed it *in*. And he added, "The most creative thing in us is to believe a thing in."